THE
MODERN
SAVAGE

ALSO BY JAMES McWILLIAMS

Just Food: Where Locavores Get It Wrong and How We Can Truly Eat Responsibly

A Revolution in Eating: How the Quest for Food Shaped America

The Politics of Pasture: How Two Cattle Inspired a National Debate About Eating Animals

The Pecan: A History of America's Native Nut

THE MODERN SAVAGE

Our Unthinking Decision to Eat Animals

JAMES McWILLIAMS

THOMAS DUNNE BOOKS   ST. MARTIN'S PRESS   NEW YORK

THOMAS DUNNE BOOKS.
An imprint of St. Martin's Press.

THE MODERN SAVAGE. Copyright © 2015 by James McWilliams. All rights reserved. Printed in the United States of America. For information, address St. Martin's Press, 175 Fifth Avenue, New York, N.Y. 10010.

www.thomasdunnebooks.com
www.stmartins.com

Designed by Steven Seighman

Library of Congress Cataloging-in-Publication Data

McWilliams, James E.
   The modern savage : our unthinking decision to eat animals / James McWilliams. — First edition.
       pages cm
   ISBN 978-1-250-03119-8 (hardcover)
   ISBN 978-1-250-03120-4 (e-book)
   1. Food animals—Moral and ethical aspects.   2. Animal Industry—Moral and ethical aspects.   3. Animal welfare.   4. Vegetarianism—Moral and ethical aspects.   5. Human-animal relationships.
I. Title.
   HV4757.M39 2015
   179'.3—dc23

                                                              2014032364

Thomas Dunne books may be purchased for educational, business, or promotional use. For information on bulk purchases, please contact Macmillan Corporate and Premium Sales Department at 1-800-221-7945, extension 5442, or write specialmarkets@macmillan.com.

First Edition: January 2015

10   9   8   7   6   5   4   3   2   1

For Cecile

CONTENTS

INTRODUCTION: THE AGENDA   1

1. GETTING EMOTIONAL   13

2. THE OMNIVORE'S CONTRADICTION   40

3. HUMANE SLAUGHTER   70

4. BACKYARD BUTCHERY   100

5. HUMANE CHICKEN   132

6. UTOPIAN BEEF   166

7. PAINFUL PORK   195

CONCLUSION: OUR UNTHINKING DECISION   222

NOTES   229

INDEX   279

THE
MODERN
SAVAGE

THE AGENDA

These are animals!

This is a personal book so I'll start with a personal story: I stopped eating animals in 2007 after watching a video of a calf being born on a dairy farm. A worker dragged the calf from his mother immediately after he hit the ground. The calf strained his head backward to make contact while being yanked away. The mother exploded into a rage. She bolted after her baby and bucked madly when the gate slammed in her face. Seconds later, denied contact with her calf, she wailed the saddest noise I'd ever heard an animal make. The mother dug at the ground and buried her nose in the placenta. People always say that cows are stupid animals. Well, sitting in my office, I decided that this one wasn't.

I was in a trance. I had no idea what was happening respecting brain chemistry, animal instinct, or bovine behavior. I just knew that I was upset. Repulsed. I knew I wanted nothing to do with what I'd just seen. Absolutely nothing. No amount of milk, cheese, or meat—no matter how delicious it tasted or how central it was to my culinary tradition or how it connected me with a community—could justify this long-obscured form of cruelty, cruelty so hidden in plain sight that it somehow took me thirty-six years to recognize and identify it as wrong.

My thoughts went directly to the birth of my son. His delivery was problematic. His little body refused to push his big head into the world. A bleary-eyed team of medical people gathered around, looking less and less assured as they worked. Something about the umbilical cord and his neck. He finally emerged, but when he did, all hell broke loose. He wasn't nestled into his mother's arms the way you see in the movies. Instead, he was rushed to an examining table and surrounded by a scrum of doctors and nurses, who worked on him in a silent, terrifying frenzy. There's no describing how I felt at that moment, but I do know that the floor rocked beneath me and I thought, "If they take him out of this room, I'll go crazy." Then, in an act of mercy I'll never forget, a male nurse looked over his shoulder and assured me that I was the father of a healthy boy. Seconds later, I was holding him.

DARWIN

Over a decade later, with my son now almost as tall as I am, recalling these events still moves me. Many people, though, have a different reaction to this juxtaposition. They're disturbed by it. How, after all, can a human birth be compared to the birth of some wobbly calf? How can my emotional reaction, without indulging in childish anthropomorphism, be legitimately juxtaposed with that of a farm animal? How dare I even mention these experiences on the same page, in the same breath, with the same level of concern? As one skeptic commented to another in response to an article I wrote on animal emotions, "These are *animals!*"

To which I respond, *exactly*. These *are* animals. And the differences between us and them are, no doubt, inexplicably vast. But not as vast as we might like to think. No rational person would claim that the psychological nature of my reaction was equivalent to the mother cow's psychological reaction, or that a person is in any way inherently equal to a cow. That would be unfair to humans and to cows, and it would cheat the beauty of biological diversity. The emotions of fear, sadness, betrayal, and the primordial urge to connect with one's offspring are unique for bovines and humans alike. In so many ways, we'll never understand their emotions and they'll never understand ours. We are worlds apart.

But we're not in different universes. I have a perfectly legitimate reason for tapping my own experience to appreciate the cow's experience: we share an evolutionary heritage. Evolutionary biology connects my anxiety about my newborn child to that of a mother cow. It highlights an essential emotional bond that links us across time and space and ensures that, when I look into the eyes of a farm animal, I'm not looking into the eyes of an alien creature. I'm not looking at an object. I'm connecting with a sentient being who, like me, hates pain, craves pleasure, and, at the end of the day, doesn't want to be slaughtered or have her child raised in a crate to become someone's dinner.

Just as our physical eyes developed through biological evolution, so too did the emotions those eyes express. The

mother cow I witnessed erupted in anger for the simple reason that she wanted her baby. I nearly passed out with fear
because I wanted mine. In the heat of the moment, we both
experienced an amalgam of horror, rage, and a sense of loss.
That I'm able to write a book about it and the cow can't is,
when it comes to eating animals, irrelevant. What essentially matters for this comparison to be meaningful is that
we both suffered. Not the same suffering. But suffering nonetheless. To think that mother cows don't suffer when their
calves are taken is to willfully ignore the evolutionary bond
we share with them.

The idea that such a connection exists isn't as radical as
it might seem. Charles Darwin wholeheartedly endorsed it.
He insisted that humans shared not only physical but cognitive and emotional space with nonhumans. "We have seen,"
he wrote in *The Descent of Man* (1871), "that the senses and
intuitions, the various emotions and faculties, such as love,
memory, attention and curiosity, imitation, reason . . . may
be found in the lower animals."[1] Building on this observation,
he argued, "There is no fundamental difference between man
and the higher mammals in their mental faculties." The
"difference in mind between man and the higher animals,"
he added, "is one of degree and not of kind."[2]

My experience with the birth of my son confirmed this
point in a very personal way. At a time when concerned consumers of food have never discussed the details of food and
agricultural production with more interest and conviction,
I am motivated to write this book because this fundamental
claim—the claim that animals, like us, are living creatures
that have an immense capacity to suffer—has been left off

the table while the animals we claim to care so much about remain very much on it.

MORAL WORTH

To an extent, we've taken the necessary steps to treat animals with dignity. We're already intuitively aware of our emotional connection to them, as well as the nature of their inner lives. The anger currently directed at factory farming reflects this sentiment. It highlights the intensifying frustration we feel about how animals are treated in industrial agriculture. Decent people condemn the systematic confinement of animals in cages so tight they cannot turn around or spread their wings. We find it abhorrent that they live in squalor and die in slaughterhouses that collectively kill twenty thousand animals every minute in the United States. We think it's obscene that these animals are treated instrumentally, pumped with antibiotics, vaccines, and growth hormones to enhance their productivity. We lament the routine mutilation perpetrated on their confined bodies—the tail docking, dehorning, debeaking, ear notching, branding, nose-ringing, and castration—all without anesthesia. We feel disgust when we watch undercover videos of animal abuse on factory farms. We are genuinely moved, often powerfully so, by the ubiquitous reality of factory farming because we know intuitively that animals experience the harm that's being inflicted upon them.

Through this recognition we've come to acknowledge that animals should be treated as living beings instead of inanimate objects. In acknowledging this point, we're hardly advocating a radical "animal rights" agenda. Instead, we are participating in a productive shift in consciousness regarding the reality of animal lives. When we oppose factory farming because factory farms treat animals poorly, we're confirming our deep belief that animals matter. They matter because they're sentient beings with a sense of self and a desire to live as the embodiment of that self. While we may not explicitly recognize it, we are in fact admitting that they have intrinsic worth, worth that warrants our moral consideration and, by extension, a fair and decent set of standards to guide that consideration. Popular condemnations of factory farms aren't false rhetorical postures. We don't protest factory farming just because it feels good to do so. We do it because we know that it's the right thing to do. Our concerns for animals in factory farms are thus genuine expressions of a basic moral truth in the face of a tremendous injustice. Our honest expressions of concern have direct implications for our most basic behaviors. Such as eating.

As a population of conscientious consumers that has both vociferously condemned factory farming and implicitly recognized the intrinsic worth of animal lives, we've yet to behave according to the logic of these actions. For all its force, our expressed concern for the welfare of farm animals has yet to translate into a collective decision to stop intentionally breeding them, taking their lives, turning them into commodities, and consuming them—all unnecessarily. This failure to act according to our inclinations demands some kind of explanation. If we loathe the poor treatment of sentient animals, we are saying that they deserve moral consideration. And if we're saying that animals deserve moral consideration, we're suggesting that they deserve not to be killed and eaten. And if we're suggesting that animals deserve not to be killed and eaten, then, alas, we should, logically, stop killing and eating them.

Let me be clear: I'm no philosopher (although I sometimes play one in the classroom). But if we're as appalled as we claim to be by the suffering of sentient animals imprisoned in factory farms, doesn't it make sense to minimize that suffering as much as possible through intentional actions that are consistent with our moral beliefs about animals? The answer, in the abstract, would seem to be an overwhelming, resounding, uncontested yes.

ALTERNATIVES

But we're not prepared to take yes for an answer. Our intransigence stems from our having been distracted by the seductive alternatives to factory-farmed animal products. Please understand: The groundswell of opposition to factory-farming animals has assuredly been cause for considerable praise. The improvements it provides for animals fated to become commodities should never be downplayed. As we will see throughout this book, the alternatives that are currently being offered to consumers who oppose factory farming are in many ways real improvements for farm animals—at least until the animals are slaughtered. That said, our general response to the horrors we've discovered on factory farms has failed to adequately match our outrage. We have continued to support the production of goods—animal products—that remain central to industrial agriculture's existence. Our response to industrial agriculture has been, when you get right down to it, *to keep eating animals*.

This time around, though, the animals must come from "sustainable," "small-scale," "organic," "free-range," and "humane" farms. They have to be adorned with labels confirming that the animal was raised "responsibly," "on pasture," and "according to the highest welfare standards." Rather than have us directly question the deeper ethics of eating animals—something more and more people can afford to do—these options rely on optimistic agrarian narratives enhanced by bucolic imagery. Increasingly, we are choosing comparatively responsible nonindustrial alternatives produced by well-intentioned farmers who claim to be sensitive to an animal's experience. Note that our embrace of these alternatives is never presented as *a step* toward abolishing animal agriculture as a whole (something that, in my mind, would make these measures more acceptable). To the contrary, it's celebrated as an absolute and final alternative to industrial production, a righteous path to carnivorous enlightenment and consumer compassion undertaken by the good guys of sustainable agriculture—the locavores and the slow foodies and the small farmers. These improvements are worthy because they are making the lives of farm animals more tolerable. But here's the thing: As a long-term strategy of reform, they will do little—and possibly nothing—to challenge the dominance of factory farming. You cannot kill and eat animals and expect to help them, much less challenge the food system that profits from our choice to keep eating them.

It's important to remember that the small farms that consumers are increasingly choosing to support, just like the factory farms we abhor, exist to accomplish the same goal: to provide animal flesh and fluids for us to eat and drink. This is an easy fact to lose sight of, but it's the damning commonality between industrial and nonindustrial animal production. Filter out the rhetoric of sustainability, forget for a moment that your grass-fed beef farmer is a terrific guy you see every week at the market, and you'll find that things don't look so different between factory and family farms. You'll find that the cruelty of slaughter, using animals as a means to an end, and favoring consumer preference over a sentient animal's right to live are endemic to any method of providing animal products. This book explores these supposedly virtuous alternatives with a sober analysis stripped of agrarian myth, bucolic marketing, media hype, and self-interested rationalizations that sound wonderful but are, when it comes to the fate of animals and the future of food, meaningless alternatives to the serious problems we face as responsible consumers.

THE AGENDA

This book's agenda is to challenge this overwhelmingly popular but ultimately ineffective response to the industrial production of animals. I will go about this project in two primary ways. The first few chapters explore some of the more abstract moral problems with eating the animals we claim to care about, highlighting how the leading thinkers in the "food movement" routinely downplay or ignore the ethical implications of eating animals at great cost to animal welfare and the prospects of food reform. During the latter chapters I shift gears to explore the mundane but critical logistics of life on small, nonindustrial farms, illuminating the disturbing ways in which the rhetoric of nonindustrial alternatives departs from the empirical reality. The abstract and the concrete, the two sides of the same coin, work best when absorbed together. But I also realize, from a decade of writing about the ethics of eating, that many consumers will find one approach more appealing than the other. Either way, the unifying message is the same: if we want to improve the lives of farm animals and if we want to radically challenge our dysfunctional food system, the absolutely most effective act we can take is to stop eating animals raised (or hunted) for food we don't need.

The human-animal relationship is endlessly complicated, and I hardly have all the answers. The manner in which we currently go about simultaneously caring for and slaughtering animals is vexed and open to all sorts of rationalizations and debate. I'm humbled by the complex nature of this topic, and I'm not writing as a vegan zealot delivering a sermon from on high. To the contrary, by questioning the decision to eat animals raised on "alternative," nonindustrial farms, I hope to show that a diet free of domesticated animals is, despite its many imperfections, and despite the necessary imperfections of my arguments, the most ethically consistent and pragmatically effective response to the pervasive problems that plague the American way of eating. No matter how many feel-good rhetorical touches and pithy rationalizations we devise to justify eating animals from alternative farms—the meat is local, organic, pasture-raised, grass-fed, free-range, humane, whatever—the profound injustices of the industrial food system are so deeply entrenched that they can only be uprooted by stigmatizing and eventually ending the cultural habit of eating domesticated meat, cheese, and dairy. These products are the pillars upon which industrial animal agriculture stands. They should be eliminated by those who are in a position to do so.

If we want to end the industrial production of food as we know it, we can do one thing, right now, without hesitation: we can stop eating animals raised as food. Every word in this book seeks to promote this revolutionary response to our dysfunctional food system. Because what we've tried so far isn't working.

I

GETTING EMOTIONAL

The horror that stirs deep in man is an obscure aware-
ness that in him something lives so akin to the animal
that it might be recognized.

—WALTER BENJAMIN

Thinking about animals—especially when it comes to eating them—is essentially a matter of the heart. But when it
comes to opening our hearts to animals, we humans tend to
be emotionally arbitrary beings. We express genuine affection for some creatures but withhold it from others. We do
so, moreover, with scant regard for their comparative abilities to suffer or nurture a sense of self. Typically, we tap
deep emotional reserves when we've spent substantial time
with a particular animal (usually a dog or a cat), having
learned to recognize that this companion critter is not a ro-
bot moving through life as an automaton, without thought
or feeling. By contrast, we're reluctant to expand our circle
of compassion to include animals that we grill and eat. This
reluctance perhaps stems from our having spent so little time
with those animals we cook and our not having had the
chance to form an emotional connection with them. That

pigs can be as smart and as affectionate as dogs generally doesn't dissuade dog lovers from indulging in a plate of bacon.[1]

This disconnection should not imply that bacon-eating dog lovers are psychopathic. Rather, I would suggest they are unthinking of the deeper nature of the human-animal bond, a bond that all forms of domestic animal agriculture do an excellent job of obscuring. The goal of this chapter is to demonstrate the critical role our emotions must play in thinking about our relationship with animals in general, and farm animals in particular. Through an investigation of the psychological and historical nature of the human-animal bond, I hope to illuminate our shared emotional origins, thereby suggesting that, when it comes to our feelings about animals, what we see is often what we get. We just have to learn to see animals with greater clarity and better appreciate the essential qualities we share with them.

We must get emotional about animals if we are ever going to treat them with dignity and, in so doing, start to reform the standard American diet. From emotion comes empathy. We have to imagine animal suffering. Many of us—eaters of animals or not—already do this intuitively. Unfortunately, we're guarded, even at times embarrassed, about it. Getting explicitly emotional about animals is frequently frowned upon. People who actively interpret the feelings of animals through their own experiences are, in many circles, dismissed as weepy sentimentalists, suckers for a fuzzy face. We're censured for the sin of anthropomorphizing. To project human emotions onto animals is often characterized as an intellectually soft, if not childish, way to approach the animal world. Grow up and face reality, we are told, or, as one of my bolder students once said, "Get *real.*"

These claims, which constitute a major obstacle to a fuller consideration of the human-animal relationship, are almost always leveled unfairly. We should never assume that an animal's experience is a mirror reflection of our own; nor should we assume that the entirety of their emotional lives could be understood by direct analogy to the entirety of our own emotional lives. But to thoughtfully and humbly anthropomorphize—to draw upon our own experience to access how another animal might feel—is an altogether different task. Not only is it based on intuition and common sense, but it's absolutely essential to evaluating the mental and emotional lives of animals about whom we routinely claim to care about. Responsible anthropomorphizing is what we must do if we are to ever understand our place among animals on the evolutionary spectrum that defines modern biological life. How else are we to grasp their wants and needs, such as the wants and needs that justify our support for free-range and small-scale alternatives? These questions are critical to consider as we think about animals as a source of food.

Anthropomorphizing might be portrayed as sappy and sentimental. But at the center of evolutionary biology one finds a decidedly unsentimental continuum of emotional experience. This continuum requires us to anthropomorphize as the only way to assess how an animal might be feeling. How else could we possibly have an opinion that a sow kept in a crate might be unhappy? That a cow wants to nuzzle the calf she birthed? That a chicken is decidedly displeased about being yanked off the ground by one foot and jammed into an inverted cone to be "humanely" slaughtered? That a baby pig might not want to be castrated or have his tail chopped off without the medical benefit of anesthesia? These are not emotionally vacant, species-specific, instinct-driven scenarios. Suffering is suffering. When we assume that animals experience it, we are anthropomorphizing. There's nothing sentimental about it. Perhaps the only reason we'd ever avoid anthropomorphizing would be to protect ourselves from what we don't want to know—that is, that animals have authentic emotional lives that are surprisingly familiar and available to us.

Anthropomorphizing thereby remains an invaluable method of maintaining our emotional connection to non-human animals—which is to say much of the world around us. As a culture, we've been systematically educated to suppress this connection while worshipping at the altars of objectivity, scientific skepticism, and human exceptionalism. But when we drop these protective barriers to emotional awareness, we find that the idea of eating animals, however they are raised, seems a little less normal than it once seemed. We find that factory farming and the purported alternatives have surprising similarities as well as differences. We find, if we look especially hard, that these similarities can only be appreciated when we allow ourselves to become emotionally available to the animals we claim to care about so deeply. When we imagine their pain matters start to look very different. Fundamentally so.

WHY BOTHER?

If we fail to nurture the fine art of anthropomorphizing, agricultural reform will be little more than a marginal endeavor. Without responsibly anthropomorphizing, we'll never appreciate, much less penetrate and understand, the authenticity of animal emotion—a prerequisite for acting according to animals' basic interests and, in turn, radically changing the broken food system. We'll never even contemplate the possibility that the animals we slaughter and eat suffer precisely because of our choice to slaughter and eat them, no matter how they were raised.

That said, a perfectly reasonable question to ask at this point would be: *Why bother?* If there are no obvious consequences to our current actions, if the animals aren't going to rise up and kick our ass for the way we have treated them,[2] much less write manifestos exposing the nature of our cruelty, why should we lose sleep over their suffering? Why bother to be morally consistent in our thinking about how animals should be treated? We are Humans, after all, the undisputed Kings of the Hill, rulers of the food chain, dictators of all genetic fate. Given our power, what does it really matter if we neither acknowledge animal emotionalism nor respond emotively to animal suffering with a shift in behavior? Why not just enjoy animals' flesh and fluids and unfertilized eggs, source them from the right places to feel good about our choices, and get on with the business of living the good life? *Why bother?*

It's a tough question. It should be noted, for those seeking quantitative assurance, that it cannot be answered with hard data. The question requires an altogether more reflective and less measurable answer. We might start with Isaac Bashevis Singer's remark that "when a human kills an animal for food, he is neglecting his own hunger for justice." This strikes me as an apt observation. With Singer, I too am consumed by the very real, if not entirely obvious, possibility that if we persist in neglecting the authentic emotional lives of sentient animals, as well as our feelings for them, the depth of our collective moral failure will quietly corrupt those aspects of our society anchored in love, compassion, and a profound capacity for decency.[3]

Of course this all sounds a bit earnest and righteous. But any civilization that more or less renounces violence but tacitly excuses—or even celebrates—the depth of suffering that's at the (largely hidden) core of its existence is a civilization that's inflicting psychic wounds upon itself. Failing to acknowledge the ethical implications of killing, commodifying, and eating sentient beings erodes, with quiet banality, our sense of collective self-worth and, as Singer noted, our capacity for justice. Eating animals might make us happy as individuals. It might unite humans as communities breaking bread together. But—no matter how deeply we repress the inevitable violence required for that act—it could be compromising our capacity to tune in to life with the truest authenticity and honesty. Violence and injustice are insidious forces that surround us like air. Easily ignored, muted by the pleasures of the palate, they have the potential to undermine a society before society even realizes it's being undermined. This is part of the reason why I care so much about how we treat animals. It bears directly on how we treat each other and the cultures and communities we create. It's why I think we should bother to think seriously about animals.[4]

Until we actively acknowledge and embrace our shared evolutionary context, until we forthrightly recognize that the emotions of a human and the emotions of a cow are, in some mysterious but not totally mysterious way, meaningfully connected, we'll continue to deny the human potential for peace, compassion, and justice. We'll continue to live below our moral potential, denying ourselves one of the greatest opportunities to do what's right while plodding through life as decent and well-intentioned modern savages.

"AN AWKWARD IRRITATION"

If my appeal to emotion rings hollow, perhaps an appeal to a more scientific perspective will have greater resonance. While the meaningful emotional connections we forge with animals might seem vague and intuitive, they've been of tremendous interest for decades to experts in the fields of animal thought and behavior. Darwin's affirmation of the human-animal emotional connection is even more valid today than it was in 1871. Most animal experts avoid positively affirming the existence of animal consciousness, or attempting to ground it in empirical evidence. Still, prominent scientists and philosophers widely espouse the idea that animals experience feelings comparable to our own. Donald Griffin, a retired Harvard University biologist and the father of animal ethology (the study of animal minds and behavior), notes that the central nervous systems of complex animals "operate by the same basic processes regardless of the species."

This means, Griffin explains, that "conscious thinking" in humans reflects conscious thinking in other species. Anyone who believes otherwise should recall, as Griffin writes, that "when animals live in complex social groupings, where each one is critically dependent on cooperative interaction with others, they need to be 'natural psychologists.'"[5] They must, in essence, think and emote to protect themselves and to reproduce. These expressions, as with our physical features, are the direct result of an evolutionary process that includes you and me, humans and nonhumans, in the steady flow of biological time.

Griffin's pivotal book *Animal Minds* further delves into the idea that cognition "takes place in any animal with a reasonably well-organized nervous system."[6] Moreover, Griffin continues, animal cognition means that animal behavior is driven not by instinct alone, but by thoughts and feelings to which the human mind can and should attempt to engage. Griffin concludes that consciousness "confers an enormous advantage by allowing animals to select those actions which are most likely to get them what they want and to ward off what they fear." These acts both draw upon and hone emotional awareness. By making situational decisions to improve the quality of their lives, animals, in their exhibited behavior, are perfectly recognizable to humans, who also have something of a knack for acting on our feelings to get what we want.

Bernard Rollin, a pioneer in the field of veterinary ethics, further establishes the idea that animals experience emotions familiar to humans, relying on them to guide behavior. He writes, "If morphological and physiological traits are evolutionarily continuous, so, too, are psychological ones."

What this continuity suggests is that "the learning behavior of animals is based on the implicit assumption that human cognitive behavior bears significant analogies to animal intellectual processes."[7] For this reason—this analogous evolutionary continuity—animals remain emotionally receptive to our anthropomorphism. They may be even more emotionally open to us than our fellow humans, unburdened as animals are by the arts of denial and suppression. Their feelings, unlike ours, are expressed with rawness, unmediated by artifice. They can even make us uncomfortable. Any pet owner can attest to this quality. Animals might lack a formal language, but they are speaking. And they do this with the purest intentions. Rollin's work reminds us that we ignore their expressions at great peril to the noble project of improving the human condition while, at the same, reforming the agricultural system that currently downgrades it.

A final animal ethologist worth noting is Marian Stamp Dawkins. Dawkins, professor of zoology at Oxford University, is especially cautious about asserting with hard scientific confidence the precise nature of animal consciousness. She freely admits that we'll never fully grasp the mysterious nature of an animal's mind. This skepticism, however, makes her ultimate assessment of animal thought and feeling all the more worthy of attention. The bulk of the extant evidence regarding animal consciousness, she writes, provides "an awkward irritation to anyone who tries to maintain that only one species in the whole history of the earth has ever felt and experienced an inner, conscious life." Dawkins argues, "Consciousness can and should be studied by scientific methods and thought of as a biological phenomenon." She further acknowledges that humans and animals "share a common evolutionary heritage," thereby challenging the species barrier that we too often assume to be more divisive than unifying. More than that, she explores the prospect of a nonhuman consciousness just as open to interpretation as the consciousness of another human person. Weighing the implications of hundreds of documented cases whereby animals have demonstrated compelling evidence of conscious decision making, Dawkins writes, "If we accept the argument from analogy to infer consciousness in other people on the grounds that they are like in us in certain key ways, then it is going to be very difficult to maintain that consciousness should not be attributed to other species if they have at least some of those same key characteristics."[8]

Through these prominent scientists, of which I've only offered a small sample, Darwin's 1871 message lives strong, reminding those willing to listen that humans and animals share the same rich evolutionary heritage of consciousness and emotional awareness.[9]

THE ORIGINS OF BONDING

If the only way to make a meaningful emotional connection with a nonhuman animal is to responsibly anthropomorphize, and if that process has sound scientific grounding, then we should have some appreciation of where and how this connection originated. The bond is ancient and time-honored. Some evolutionary anthropologists posit that meaningful human-animal connections began to solidify at least forty thousand years ago, leading to a notable upsurge in human curiosity about the nonhuman world. When humans realized, in the words of one animal psychologist, "that a ball of fur could be a friend rather than a meal," they worked to grasp the mental status of that alien ball of fur. This self-interested quest for mutualism necessarily assumed some level of emotional similarity between humans and animals. It also sharpened the human mind while keeping humans increasingly inquisitive about the nature of animal thought. Humans observed. They probed animal behavior. They asked questions and entertained hypotheses. Animals, in their own ways, did much the same. Over thousands of years of collective investigation, human minds came to evolve in tandem with nonhuman minds. The "neurobiology of bonding" linked us to the animal world in ways we're only now starting to grasp. The roots of *biophilia*, to use E. O. Wilson's famous term, thus run to prehistoric depths. These roots, moreover, were watered in floods of emotion.[10]

The connections that resulted between humans and nonhumans established a foundation for animal domestication. With domestication came a delightful boost in oxytocin to the human brain. Oxytocin is pleasure-inducing endorphin that often accompanies affectionate and nonexploitative human-animal interactions. (It is also, do note, released during orgasms.) Meg Daley Olmert, author of *Made for Each Other*, writes, "The satisfaction that washes over us as we watch our pet sleep is the ancient reminder that when all is well in their world, all is well in ours."[11] James Serpell, a professor of ethics and animal welfare at the University of Pennsylvania, probes even deeper into the core of this "ancient reminder," suggesting that the human ability to consider animals the way we consider other humans was integral to "taming wild creatures and forming bonds with them."[12] Other scholars have elaborated on Serpell's work to argue that the emotional relationship that formed between domesticated animals and humans may have inspired humans to treat other humans with empathy. Although only a hypothesis, it's intriguing, and one that highlights the enormous social implications of the human-animal emotional connection, not to mention the social benefits that can derive from it.[13]

Further evidence of an authentic and historically grounded human-animal bond comes from the discovery that not only humans enjoy an oxytocin rush when connecting with animals emotionally. Animals get one from humans too. "It was," writes Olmert, "our oxytocin-inspired biophilia tendencies that ushered us ever closer to animals until they became ours—and we became theirs." One experiment that Olmert describes "found that women and their dogs experienced similar increases in oxytocin levels after ten minutes of friendly contact." Lab technicians who affectionately stroke stressed rats find not only calmed rats, but calmed rats in the throes of an oxytocin rush. One need not speculate too wildly to think that when cave-dwelling humans, armed with scraps of food, eventually lured wolves to hang around the caves to offer protection from predators, the lives of both species changed permanently. And, hormonal drip by hormonal drip, for the better.[14]

This connection reveals that without anthropomorphic behavior in humans, without the quest to seek out emotional similarities regarding basic desires and interests, domestication (for better or worse) wouldn't have been possible, nor would have the subsequent visceral pleasures we currently derive from our companion animals. Any oxytocin-producing interaction we have with animals today derives from our ability to place our emotional frameworks upon them. That animals respond accordingly says a lot about the nature of our bond with them, not to mention the depth of its evolutionary reach and the role played by our shared emotions.[15]

While humans were nearly always eating animals, we were also simultaneously working hard to understand them. As human societies were forming relational bonds with animals (first as hunters, then as domesticators), we were, throughout that long and arduous process, trying to discern what made those animals happy, bored, tired, angry, scared impatient, sad—in essence, what made them tick emotionally as sentient beings who were capable of communicating with us. We may not have thought about it in such terms, but that's what was happening. It's true that we worked to know animals *not* because we wanted to liberate them, or to treat them with moral consideration, or to make them loving members of our own families. To the contrary, we wanted to exploit them and, in many cases, kill and eat them. Still, we cannot overlook the critical point that we worked to understand them—especially during domestication—through a process of emotional engagement. This emotional assessment of animal interests was something humans simply assumed we could do. And we did. And it worked.

AMBIGUITY

Evidence of this long-nurtured bond surrounds us, but too often we seek excuses for not opening our eyes to what we fear might be an inconvenient reality. One reason many of us typically fail to appreciate the implications of the human-animal bond is the ambiguity of the science surrounding animal thought and feeling. Ambiguity can be a handy little foil, one that detracts from our otherwise compassionate intuitions. Reference to scientific ambiguity can effectively downplay essential connections between humans and animals. Many conventional scientists and philosophers—in contrast to the ones presented earlier in this chapter—are the most aggressive players of the ambiguity card. Bound by a narrow sense of what it means to be objective, they've entered the stormy waters of animal emotionalism and cognition with a caution so engrained that the possibility of their acknowledging animal emotions is automatically foreclosed.[16] The leading questions that guide their investigations are ostensibly judicious but ultimately unanswerable. They ask, Can we really know what an animal thinks and feels? Is it ever possible to *truly understand* the mind of another species? Could what looks like suffering and joy actually not be suffering and joy? These questions and doubts remain integral to the dutiful practice of science and scholarly skepticism. They advance careers, garner respect, warrant publication, and sustain high standards of proof. That's the problem.[17]

High burdens of proof are one thing. Impossible burdens another. Here's a fact: nobody will ever be able to verify animal emotions with any sort of empirical exactitude. Ever. (Here's another fact: nobody will ever be able to verify human emotions with any sort of empirical exactitude.) As a result, the quest to understand animal consciousness requires us to do something that academics—especially scientists—aren't rewarded for doing: we have to trust our guts, or at least our informed judgments. We need to accept a reasonable level of ambiguity. The inability to verify the *exact* nature of an animal's mind should not lead us to conclude that animals lack meaningful thoughts and feelings. It's hard enough, after all, to comprehend our own mind, our best friend's, our lover's, the minds of our children. How can we possibly expect to scientifically gauge an animal's internal emotional compass? This lack of empirical exactitude doesn't mean that we should completely reject animal consciousness and emotionalism. To the contrary, until it can be proven without a doubt that animals *do not* experience emotions and cannot suffer, the most responsible choice is to live our lives as if they do. We have to make reasonable inferences, assume similarity over difference, and learn to accept some ambiguity while conceding the strong likelihood that the animals we kill and eat are emotional beings that suffer when we kill and eat them.

Embracing ambiguity, moreover, can be enlightening. It allows us to seek a different kind of caution, one that's more humane, humble, and liberating to humans and nonhumans alike. As moral agents imbued with compassion, humans have a duty to assume—based on common sense and anthropomorphic observation (and not necessarily hard scientific evidence and "objective" analysis)—that animals experience a vibrant spectrum of emotional responses to the world around them.[18] We must act accordingly until we prove beyond a doubt that the situation is otherwise. This responsibility requires (whether we're convinced of animal emotionalism or not) that we radically rethink our relationship with the animal world. As Lorraine Daston and Gregg Mitman, who

have edited an excellent book on contemporary anthropomorphism, explain, if "humans [are] correct in their anthropomorphic assumption," then "humans would no longer be
justified in using animals as stage props to act out certain ways
of being human—no more than other humans may be used as
a means to serve the ends of others."[19] Granting to animals
the emotions that they show every indication of having—even
if we lack the hard evidence to prove it according to the demands of science—lays the foundation for a benevolent shift
in human-animal relationships and, in turn, a shift in the way
we eat. In this way, a dog wagging his tail or a pig nuzzling
your leg can provide the basis for an awakening that encom-
passes new depths of compassion, empathy, and freedom from
the hidden world of suffering obscured by slavish adherence
to standards of scientific rigor. To me, that's a thrilling way
to improve your perspective on life.

That we're one of the first generations with the means to
do so makes the prospect of taking animal emotions seriously all the more momentous. How many generations have
faced such a rare opportunity—a chance to tip the scales
toward justice in such a deeply humanitarian way? We'd be
foolish to allow scientific ambiguity to interfere with this
chance to dramatically reduce intentionally caused suffering. We'd be foolish to give up so easily on the prospect of
genuine compassion for animals.

THOUGHTFUL OBSERVATION

Taking off the shackles of ambiguity liberates us to pursue
the emotional rewards that come not from quantification

but from something much more accessible and meaningful: observational thought. When it comes to animals, we can all, irrespective of our training, become observational thinkers. We can all free ourselves from excessive academic skepticism or vague indifference to explore the benefits of empathy and common sense. As humans, we are unique in that we can practice abstract reason. Abstract reason can liberate us from logic, transfiguring the most obvious meaning of virtually anything into a self-serving version of reality.[20] If we want $2 + 2$ to equal 5, we'll find a way to make that happen. If we want to square the circle, we'll do it. Thoughtful observation, however, is different. It quietly resists disingenuous and self-serving distortions. It is an altogether less manipulative and ultimately more honest way to approach animals (not to mention life in general). Thoughtful observation strongly suggests that animals exhibit powerful and recognizable emotional responses to a range of experiences. It acknowledges that animals have been around the evolutionary block a few times and it concedes that their feelings run to depths that demand our consideration as decent people who care about the animal world.[21]

As any pet owner can attest, the purity of animal emotions, and the human ability to engage those emotions, is confirmed in inspiring ways. Popular media reports routinely tug at our heartstrings with stories of human-animal interaction. Even if we ignore the deeper implications of these stories (that is, even if we reduce them to entertainment), they remind us that, when it comes to animal emotions, what you see is often what you get—and what we often get from animals is compelling evidence that they have emotionally rich inner lives. So rich and present are these emotions that we are called upon to connect with and treat animals with compassion. This compassion raises the question of not killing animals for food when we can live healthy lives without eating it.[22]

Everyday stories routinely affirm the emotional complexity of the animals around us. I could dedicate the whole book to these stories, as they speak so powerfully for themselves, but a few examples should suffice. In 2005, when five deep-sea divers struggled to rescue a humpback whale tangled in crab-trap ropes off the coast of San Francisco, the whale became unnaturally calm as the divers sawed at the cords entangling her. She was probably in shock. When rescuers finally liberated the whale, she gently approached the divers and, in a gesture of apparent appreciation, nuzzled each one, bolting to the surface and performing a series of seemingly appreciative dramatic leaps.

Such an exhibition could be dismissed as the preprogrammed response of a lucky whale. Many people, perhaps uncomfortable about what such a story might mean for our vaunted place at "the top of the food chain," do precisely that—after all, how could we ever slaughter an animal who acted so consciously, so intentionally, so humanlike? This incident, however, demands a substantially more reflective response. Is it such a stretch, given what we know about the mechanics of evolution and emotion, to interpret this anecdote as reasonable confirmation of that ancient and powerful human-animal bond? The whale was in trouble, terrified, and wasn't ready to die. The divers empathized with her, saved her, and she thanked them in her whalelike way.[23] She literally jumped for joy. Nobody can prove any of this, of course. But even when there's ambiguity—and there always will be (she'll never tell us *why* she was jumping, and even if she did, why should we believe her?)—shouldn't we err on the side of emotion and grant this whale her due feelings, as well as the legitimacy of her expression of them? Thoughtful observation encourages us to answer yes.

Also consider elephants—a species that's been around for about 55 million years. Thoughtfully observing elephants reveals their acute capacity to grieve. These beautiful animals visibly mourn when members of their family die. They don't forget that tragic event. When elephants lumber past the exact place of death years later, they will often stop and pause in a gesture of respect. Cynthia Moss, who has spent decades studying elephants in the wild, discusses the elephant practice of "herd circling," an elephant ritual intended to honor a dying companion. She explains how members of the elephant clan "come to an uncertain halt" and surround the sick elephant while "fac[ing] outward, their trunks hanging limply to the ground." They then rotate the circle inward, poke the ailing elephant in an attempt to rouse her back to life, and when the elephant finally dies, they will sometimes "tear out branches and grass clumps from the surrounding vegetation and drop these on and around the carcass."[24] An elephant calf has been seen lingering after such a ceremony to gently touch the matriarch's foot with her own.[25] Elephants cry.

Standing in an open field and mourning the loss of a herd member hardly provides an animal an evolutionary advantage. Instead, elephants seem do it because, like us, they possess feelings. Emotion, in this case, is acute enough to transcend the instinct for physical self-preservation. It would take great feats of denial to ignore the tender spectacle of a

grieving elephant, to convince ourselves that these choreographed rituals and reactions were vacant jerks of instinct,
the mechanized movements of lower-order automatons.
When thoughtful observation delivers its message—and it
often does with powerful clarity—we should trust that message. The human tendency to avoid the obvious emotional
implications of animal behavior, according to the evolutionary biologist Marc Bekoff, explains why we "consistently
underestimate what animals know, do, think, and feel."[26]

Another poignant example of such observation comes
from Holly Cheever, a veterinarian working in upstate New
York. Cheever was called to a nearby dairy farm because a cow
who'd just given birth wouldn't produce milk. Every time the
mother was brought to the barn and milked, she was found to
be dry. Everyone was understandably frustrated (especially
the dairy farmer). "Despite the fact that she was glowing
with health," Cheever writes, "her udder remained empty."
Stumped, Cheever investigated. She eventually learned from
a neighboring farmer that the cow in question—who'd already
had five babies taken away by her owner (to become veal or, if
female, to be turned into an artificially inseminated milk-
producing machine)—had this time delivered twins out in the
pasture. Evidently sensing the fate of her previous five babies,
the cow chose to hide one of her twins in the nearby woods
before leading the other one into the barn, sacrificially yield-
ing her calf to the farmer, who she knew from experience
would be expecting only one offspring. Then she went into
the woods to feed her baby, who was drinking the milk her
owner had intended to sell to humans.

It's a remarkable story. And it warrants an emotional response. The mother appeared to be lacking milk for the

simplest of reasons: she'd been saving it for the baby she'd kept in the woods. Cheever spends her life around these animals, working with them at their most vulnerable moments. Notably, she never tried to overanalyze the situation, concluding, "All I know is this: there is a lot more going on behind those beautiful eyes than we humans have ever given them credit for, and as a mother who was able to nurse all four of my babies and did not have to suffer the agonies of losing my beloved offspring, I feel her pain."[27] If only all professionals who work with animals were so genuinely accepting of the obvious emotional similarities between humans and animals rather than duty-bound to the strictest standards of scientific proof.

As Cheever's reaction suggests, many scientists and medical experts, despite professional pressure to remain icily skeptical, choose to think and feel as well as record and analyze. They trust their emotions, value their observations for what they are, and explicitly acknowledge—despite everything we still don't know about animal cognition—the meaningful inner lives of our nonhuman companions.

One more story: Biologist Marcy Cottrell Houle spent considerable time thoughtfully observing two peregrine falcons and their five babies. When the female left to find food one morning (as she did every morning) but failed to return, the male falcon became visibly agitated, initiated a series of painfully plaintive calls, and waited patiently for her return. The panic in these calls intensified. After three days of incessant pleading he gave up the search and emitted, in Houle's description, "a cry like the screeching moan of a wounded animal, the cry of a creature in suffering." This response, although Houle had never before heard it,

was perfectly intelligible to her well-trained ears. "The sadness of the outcry was unmistakable," she wrote. It was a cry
of loss. "Having heard it, I will never doubt that an animal can
suffer emotions that we humans think belong to our species
alone."[28] Here we have yet another reminder of the powerful
effectiveness of thoughtful observation, an open heart, common sense, and the boldness to anthropomorphize in the face
of a scientific establishment that frowns on such a natural,
deeply human response to the nonhuman world.

Houle and Cheever reached their conclusions not as a result of their scientific training, but in spite of it. They decided
to trust their guts rather than outthink themselves on the
question of animal emotions. When animals "spoke," these
scientists listened. They erred on the side of emotion. In this
sense they confirm another observation of Marc Bekoff's:
"Personal experiences with animals are essential to coming
to terms with who they are."[29] How true. Only through these
experiences—these thoughtful observations—can we allow
ourselves to be amazed and emotionally moved by animals.
Only through them can we avoid reducing animals to objects,
or rationalizing their emotional lives out of existence to nurture skepticism and keep our palates guilt-free. Only through
thoughtful observation can we start getting emotional about
animals and, in turn, start treating them with the compassion
and moral dignity that they deserve.[30]

OPPORTUNITY

Which brings us back to our food choices. If animals have
authentic emotional lives—and there is every reason to

think that they do—then, as morally concerned humans, we are strongly encouraged to act according to that reality. The scope of our compassion—of our moral consideration—must, as a result, widen beyond just supporting animal products from alternative, small-scale, local, organic, and humane farms. We currently face profound but generally unrecognized truths about many species of animals (and certainly the ones we raise to eat). There is no clear reason to reject the premise that farm animals feel pain and pleasure. There is no clear reason to deny that they have authentic emotional lives. That they suffer. If an animal is emotionally sensitive enough to symbolically grieve, to undertake a burial ritual, to thank her rescuers, to sense her impending slaughter, and to hide a baby from her owner, then we have no choice, as humans who claim to care about animals, but to rethink our decision to eat them. We must acknowledge, forthrightly and without qualification, that they matter. As concerned consumers, as decent humans, we have to be honest that animals are not objects for the whimsical purposes of our exploitation.

Admitting these realities about animals is difficult. In a world where eating animals generally goes unquestioned, there's little encouragement of this mode of thought. Moreover, to acknowledge that an animal is sentient, and that an animal can suffer, is to acknowledge that we currently live in a world defined by systematic injustice. Worse, it is to acknowledge that we are actively complicit in that injustice. It can be a weighty reality to ponder. Rather than dwell upon it or become debilitated by these difficulties, however, it is important to see the problem of eating animals in more optimistic terms. To acknowledge that an animal is sentient is also to acknowledge that we face a historic opportunity. For the first time in human existence, we have a chance to end a long tradition of suffering that we've inherited. As agriculturally advanced societies, we are poised to stop the violence and abuse that's integral to animal agriculture and, based on our legacy of shared emotions, create a world marked by empathy and reduced suffering. We can seek genuinely radical agricultural alternatives rather than continuing to support systems that kill and commodify animals just as assuredly as factory farms kill and commodify animals.

I'm not naïve. I live in the world and am a pretty skeptical member of it. I'm a professionally trained historian, and I've had the mantra "proof, proof, proof" drilled into my head for decades. I'm also well aware how endemic animal exploitation is to modern material life. Our meat-infused culture overwhelms us so thoroughly that, like the air we breathe, it's easy to never think much about it. The United States alone raises and kills 10 billion sentient animals a year for food. The number is almost too staggering to contemplate. Right now, at this very second, hundreds of thousands of emotionally aware animals—animals that do not want to die—are experiencing, as conscious individuals, unfathomable suffering and despair. They are being zapped with electrical prodders, knocked in the head with bolt guns, having their throats cut open, jammed into cones to have their jugulars sliced. It's cool and hip in some circles to appear stoically insensitive to these realties, to deem them part of life, but they are—if you are honest with yourself—a tough reality to ponder. I can see why otherwise conscientious people avoid the issue of animal awareness. Still, in an age when we are coming to "know our farmer, know our food," the question should no longer be avoided: Why, despite holding values that clearly deem this situation abhorrent, do humans allow animal exploitation for food to persist?

No ethical checks and balances on eating animals exist. It is an instinctual and socially sanctioned, even celebrated, behavior. There's no immediate incentive to stop supporting suffering we almost never see or feel. We generally don't witness the pain and degradation required to bring animal products to our plate. It's all carefully hidden. Sanitized. Marketed out of mind. Instead, we see sunny pastures and happy animals, animals with space to roam and time to frolic, animals that eat natural diets and maintain bodily integrity. We cannot hear the pleas of these animals as they enter a slaughterhouse. We don't register their resistance. Whether they are on factory or small farms, animals are brutally exploited (unless you don't consider slaughter brutal), but they themselves never file official complaints. Lacking a cohesive and directly communicative language (at least one that we can understand), animals can't ask us to wake up and take stock about how they might feel about being pampered one day and slaughtered the next. So we eat them, too thrilled with their flavor to think about what we are doing.

I've opened this book with a chapter on animal emotions because I deeply believe not only that animals have emotions but that humans, who are inherently decent, have a deep capacity to connect with them. I believe that if we learn to thoughtfully observe and acknowledge animal emotion it will become the fertile starting point in reconsidering our decision to eat animals. Through these emotional expressions animals assert their individual capacity to feel and experience the pleasure and pain and boredom and thrill of life. Through emotion—which assumes the capacity to think—animals are showing us that they deserve not to be raised, killed, and turned into products to serve the unnecessary culinary desires of a species with a bigger brain, more nimble thumbs, and the exclusive ability to rationalize and ignore unnecessary violence. Through emotions animals speak to us. As beings gifted with a strong capacity to empathize, we should listen.

After all, we've rejected factory farming partially on the grounds that we think animals matter. We've said that animals do not deserve to be treated the way they are treated. We've been quite clear on this. But then we've manufactured excuses for eating animals while shrouding the truth of their suffering in the rhetoric of agrarian virtue. We dig into their flesh, purloin their milk, and crack their eggs, saying that everything's fine if the animal was raised with dignity. We say all is well if the animal lived a "natural" life. We point to our incisors and say we were meant to eat meat. We say simply, "Meat tastes good." We say, "I need my protein and omega-3s." We say, "I killed it myself." We say an awful lot of things to prevent ourselves from acknowledging the core ethical conundrum of claiming an animal has moral worth while, in the same breath, slaughtering that animal for food we do not need. We've said these things so persistently, and we've been acting so unthinkingly for so long, that we don't even bother to question our words or analyze our behaviors. Rarely do we wonder if we're making a colossal moral error when we continue to eat these creatures.

Factory farming has been exposed. We're outraged. Now, having become emotional about animals, it's time to do something equally necessary to proceed from thoughtlessness to thought. We must lift the veil on nonindustrial animal agriculture and take a harder look at what's happening inside the supposedly happy farms that claim to offer such a genuine, sustainable, and humane alternative to the industrial operations that, out of our honest concern for animals, we've deemed unacceptable. The first thing that we find, as the next chapter shows, is a contradiction. Call it the omnivore's contradiction.

THE OMNIVORE'S CONTRADICTION

There is no honest way to avoid certain moral questions.
—DAVID FOSTER WALLACE

Concerned consumers are well aware of the horrors of factory farming. What was once hidden is now exposed, and we've recognized it as deeply wrong. Books ranging from Peter Singer's *Animal Liberation* to Eric Schlosser's *Fast Food Nation* to Michael Pollan's *Omnivore's Dilemma* to Jonathan Safran Foer's *Eating Animals*, not to mention hundreds of influential documentaries and news exposés, have hammered home the lesson that industrial animal agriculture is a shameful legacy that must come to an end. While the overwhelming majority of animal products manufactured and consumed today come from industrial sources (to the depressing tune of 99 percent), never before has moral outrage against factory farms—and the corporations that run them—fomented with such rage. Impatience for change has never been more intense. Concerned omnivores are furious with what's happening to animals within these carefully obscured hellholes. With great emotion and ample justification, we want reform.

As we saw in the last chapter, our emotional relationship with the animals we eat is at best inconsistent. Thus, unsurprisingly, our moral consideration of them, and our behavioral response, has been equally unsure. Rather than confronting the reality of animal farming with a hard ethical cross-examination, we've chosen to alleviate our anger with industrial agriculture by appealing to a vast agrarian landscape of the imagination, a nonindustrial idyll where happy animals play on happy farms and, presumably, produce what one scholar has cynically called "happy meat."[1] Perhaps the best evidence of this response's flaw is that the so-called happy alternative requires us, in the face of an in dustry that profits from animals, to *keep eating animals*. That is, it asks us to continue supporting the very products that allow agribusiness not only to stay in business, but to thrive. The standard line—the accepted alternative—is that it's viable for concerned omnivores who are opposed to factory farming to keep eating animal products so long as they come from the right place and are raised the right way: outdoors, locally, organically, seasonally, through rotational (or "holistic") grazing, and by small-scale family farmers. This optimistic message has penetrated our critical consciousness, captured our hearts, and sold well in the court of public opinion. It comprises the dogmatic core of the ever-influential "sustainable food movement." Our decision has been to accept these alternatives unthinkingly, to ignore the deeper emotional and ethical implications of thoughtful observation, and to proceed as if these options were somehow fundamentally different from the one being offered by factory farms.

But they're not. In this chapter, I'll show how the concept of eating "humanely raised animals" is based on a contradiction. It's a contradiction that establishes the foundation for making factory farms stronger and animal suffering worse, all the while providing privileged consumers with the false sense that they are doing something meaningful to reform the food system. Choosing these alternatives might feel like an effective approach for guilt-prone humans to take. It is, however, of questionable long-term significance for the farm animals we claim to care so much about. Instead of blindly accepting the claim that the solution to industrial animal agriculture is nonindustrial animal agriculture, we should ask tougher questions. Can we expect to reform our broken food system if that effort is based on an intellectually inconsistent foundation that continues to support the slaughtering of animals for food we do not need? And if we fail to resolve this contradiction, can we really expect the burgeoning food movement to be a genuine force for change?[2] Might there be another, more effective, way to eat an ethical diet? To answer these questions it is essential to develop a deeper understanding of the omnivore's contradiction.

EMPATHY

What exactly makes us so angry about factory farming? It's worth paying careful attention to how we answer this question. Environmental and health-based concerns, as well as poor labor conditions, are certainly high on the list of reasons for wanting to end industrial agriculture. Distaste for corporate consolidation is also a popular reason for opposing it. However, for most concerned consumers, it's ultimately the way that animals are treated that makes us recoil when confronted with the graphic realities of industrial animal production. Their incessant abuse hits us in the gut and motivates us to fight the system and demand a change. The violence integral to industrial animal agriculture remains an ever-present and instructive source of anger against the pervasiveness of factory farming. It's not hard to understand, once we realize how animals are treated in these environments, that the current system bringing us cheap animal products is, by any standard, unsound. Most of us realize intuitively that no creature should ever be subjected to such a relentless regime of abuse.

Critics of industrial agriculture get this point and argue it well. They persuasively condemn the horrific treatment of animals, lamenting the manner in which animals on factory farms are mutilated (tail docking, dehorning, debeaking, ear clipping, branding), collectively consolidated (a chicken per square foot), individually confined (pigs and veal calves jammed into crates), sexually manipulated (female cows hooked to an artificial inseminator), and forced to wade knee-deep in cesspools of their own waste. Prominent writers and activists—big names with huge audiences and enviable media access—have dedicated considerable time, energy, and journalistic real estate to challenging the evils of this maligned industry. They routinely highlight and condemn these realities. The point they collectively make couldn't be any clearer: farm animals do not deserve to be treated the way they are currently treated. They are not objects. They have feelings. They suffer. Morally speaking, opponents of factory farming are, through a selective tapping of their emotional wellsprings, affirming that animals matter. Let's take a closer look at how these writers make this important case.

Epitomizing those sensitive to the plight of farm animals is the journalist Michael Pollan. Writing about pigs housed in concentrated animal-feeding operations (CAFOs), Pollan (in *The Omnivore's Dilemma*) engages in the best kind of emotionally grounded and thoughtful anthropomorphizing (although in other places he dismisses anthropomorphizing as sentimental). Just listen to his language and admire his genuine sensitivity to animal welfare. He notes how hog confinement results in a "depressed pig," a "demoralized pig," and a pig divorced from his "natural predilections." He goes on to condemn the way pigs in CAFOs are "crowded together beneath a metal roof standing on slats suspended over a septic tank." After visiting a free-range farm where pigs were being happy pigs, Pollan admitted that he "couldn't look at their tails [which were intact] . . . without thinking about the fate of pigtails in industrial hog production" (where tails are docked). Noting that pigs in confined circumstances experience a "learned helplessness," he comments, "It's not surprising that an animal as intelligent as a pig would get depressed under these circumstances."

Such remarks are easy to pass over. But they speak volumes. They are persuasive examples of Pollan's thoughtful observation of animal life. Whether intending to or not,

Pollan—due to his sharp anthropomorphic gaze—is emotionally connecting with pigs, poignantly reiterating that they have intrinsic worth, and acknowledging, in essence, that their lives matter at least enough for them not to be treated like objects, as they are in the industrial settings Pollan so eloquently despises.

Pollan is not alone in his admirable empathy for animals. Critics of industrial agriculture routinely highlight the emotional lives of farm animals in movingly affective ways. Mark Bittman, the influential *New York Times* food columnist, has in many columns observed the fate of animals enslaved in factory farms. Bittman routinely hits us with disturbing facts and figures. We learn that the number of cows housed in factory farms has doubled between 1997 and 2007, that the number of factory farmed broiler chickens doubled during the same time; and that the number of "large livestock operations" almost quadrupled between 1982 and 2002.[3] Our outrage gets stoked. At the same time, and more important, he connects these numbers to the emotional turmoil experienced by the animals trapped in these mills of exploitation. "Until a couple of years ago," he wrote in 2012, "I believed that the primary reasons to eat less meat were environment and health related." While acknowledging that such rationales remain quite valid, he adds, "But animal welfare has since become a large part of my thinking as well."[4] Bittman seems to have hewed to his own anthropomorphic tendencies, nurturing a habit of thoughtful observation while recognizing that animals are sentient beings rather than inert objects.

This decision has precipitated something of an epiphany for the *Times* columnist. As with Pollan, Bittman (who admits to being not much of an animal lover) has absorbed and aggressively acted upon his realization that the animals we eat are not objects. He notes that they enjoy richly emotional lives. An undercover Humane Society video of a Smithfield Foods' hog facility exposing the chilling abuse of pigs left the columnist, a thoroughly seasoned food writer, "pretty much speechless." He lambasted Smithfield Foods for it's "infuriating disregard for the welfare of their animals."[5] He even suggested that animal abuse in factory farming quietly damages the human psyche, exhorting readers "to look at how we treat animals and begin to change it."[6] The manner in which we treat and kill animals in industrial agriculture is so offensive to the welfare of the animals we choose to eat that, Bittman notes, it has reduced humans to "a warped state."[7]

Bittman's message about animals, like Pollan's, is as disturbing as it is encouraging. With eloquence and passion he's saying that farm animals feel pain, suffer, emote, and have an obvious interest in avoiding the terrible experiences to which we routinely subject them. He's saying that animals are not instruments and that, in our unthinking quest to eat them, we potentially—if not assuredly—harm ourselves (an argument made centuries ago by Immanual Kant). It's a remarkable thing for a columnist in a popular newspaper to write.

In addition to Pollan and Bittman, few writers have wielded a steadier influence on the public's disdain for factory farming than the novelist Jonathan Safran Foer. Foer's powerful book *Eating Animals* brought the condemnation of industrial agriculture into more literary and, in many ways, more detailed and thoughtful territory. Young people in particular were moved to action by Foer's nuanced but accessible analysis. His attention to the welfare of chickens was especially meticulous, guided by openly expressed anthropomorphic concerns. He slams factory farms for manipulating "food and light to increase productivity, often at the expense of the animals' welfare." He quotes an industrial poultry farmer who explains how turkey hens are killed after a year of life "because they won't lay as many eggs in the second year." It is, the farmer continued, "cheaper to slaughter them and start over than it is [to] feed and house birds that lay few eggs." This farmer, as Foer shows, was under no delusion about the morality of his behavior. "The birds suffer," the egg man acknowledged. Through telling anecdotes such as this one, Foer illuminates the chilling banality of animal objectification, showing how easy it is to overlook the suffering of animals raised on factory farms. After an overview of the egg industry, Foer concludes with an appropriate sense of disgust: "I didn't ever want to eat a conventional egg again."[8] Neither did millions of his readers.

Central to Foer's condemnation of factory farming—as with Pollan and Bittman, but even more so—is an explicit recognition that farm animals have meaningful emotional lives that we have a duty to recognize. Listing the negatives of factory farming, Foer pointedly includes "animal suffering."[9] He excoriates the "willful causing of unnecessary suffering" as well as "the indifference to it."[10] Mincing few words, he declares, "Nothing we do has the potential to cause nearly as much suffering as eating meat,"[11] and he makes those words veritably sing when he writes, "What is suffering? I'm not sure what it is, but I know that suffering is the name we give to the origin of all the sighs, screams,

groans—small and large, crude and multifaceted—that concern us."[12] Suffering, suffering, and suffering: this is Foer's
focus. Foer is a nuanced and sophisticated thinker, and I
hesitate to concentrate his thoughts about animals into a
single idea, but it goes without saying that he cares deeply
about the unnecessary suffering of sentient animals. He too,
thoughtfully, and at times brilliantly, anthropomorphizes.

Pollan, Bittman, and Foer represent what we might call
the thinking food world's leading tastemakers. They have
broad influence with a vocal minority of foodies interested
in seeing our food system reformed from the ground up.
Their anthropomorphic accounts of animal suffering on
factory farms are inspiring in their attention to the emotional lives of animals. They have, I would venture, pushed
the question of animal welfare into the vital center of opposition to factory farming. As a result, they've set the tem-
plate for a seemingly endless array of books, articles, films,
and blogs dedicated to the forthright exposition of abuse
endemic to industrial animal agriculture. Many of these
accounts are necessarily derivative and predictable, but a
notable point unifies the anti-factory-farm genre that these
writers have spawned: the recognition that animals have
moral worth.

THE NEXT STEP

Given the excoriation of animal abuse on factory farms by
our prestigious tastemakers, coupled with their emphasis on
animal sentience, one might reasonably conclude that the
days of eating animals among those who want to reform the

food system are numbered. Indeed, one might read these vivid accounts of animal sentience from our leading critics of industrial agriculture and reasonably decide that, should we act consistently with these findings, a powerful basis for abandoning the consumption of domesticated animals has finally fallen into place. Writers such as Pollan and Bittman and Foer—whether they intended to or not—could not have made a more persuasive case for the moral significance of the animals we exploit for food. Their relentless attention to the depression and suffering of animals, with their innate intelligence insulted by the cruelty of confinement, reiterates the lesson that, when we talk about farm animals, we're talking about sentient beings—conscious, social, intelligent, and self-aware individuals.

The importance of this emphasis on animal sentience cannot be overstated. What these writers and thinkers have accomplished through their writing is unprecedented: their condemnation of industrially raised animals has initiated a critical shift in the way humans conceptualize farm animals. There's thus good reason to assume that, should consistent moral logic prevail, enlightened consumers, given what we know about the fate of animals in factory farms, and given what we're learning about the emotional continuum we share with animals, would act in a way that respects the deeper reality of our bond with nonhumans. Which is to say, there's every reason to think that, as concerned consumers, we would not only stop eating animals from factory farms, but *we'd stop eating farmed animals altogether.*

But that has not been the common response. On the other end of these impassioned condemnations of factory farming we do not find a sustained appeal to eat a diet limited to plants. To the contrary, we find an appeal to eat animals. What the tastemakers propose as a solution to the problems they expose is the seductive but ethically questionable proposition that we can continue the consumption of meat, cheese, milk, and eggs. The reasoning goes something like this: As long as we avoid animal products from *industrial* sources, all is well. As long as factory farms are removed from the equation, then we're doing the right thing. Dig in. No regrets.

Our easy acceptance of these alternatives is the most tragic manifestation of our unthinking decision to eat animals. Whatever the underlying rationalization, it's a self-serving deception pregnant with detrimental consequences for the future of human-animal relations, not to mention factory farms and the future of ethical farming in general. Most critically, the nonindustrial option fails to acknowledge that if a farm animal has an emotional life, our chosen alternatives might well constitute an injustice just as horrific as factory farming itself. In both cases we are killing an animal for food we don't need. The popular endorsement of nonindustrial farms fails to explain how the ultimate violation of an animal's life—ending it—conforms with the moral worth we've conferred upon that being. Our blanket acceptance of nonindustrial alternatives thus undermines our deeper quest to honor animal welfare and create a truly just food system.

Proponents of animal welfare who eat animals have not been called upon to defend the unnecessary death of a sentient being. They've been protected by a culinary culture with little interest in allowing an ethical dilemma to stand between just food and tasty food. Ironically (but understandably), in a food culture that's increasingly asking us to think about where our food comes from, to *know our food*, omnivores have yet to confront the apparent contradiction they quietly perpetuate. They've yet to explain how killing an animal for food we don't need is consistent with that animal's welfare—welfare that they themselves have been so influential in promoting, so much so that they want to restructure the North American food system to accommodate it. The question at the core of the omnivore's dilemma is thus a deeply troubling one: How we can we claim to care about an animal's welfare and then support the killing of that animal?

Our default response has been (as is the case with most extremely difficult questions) to ignore it. Ponder the question, though, and you'll notice that it'll stump you a bit. I started thinking about it about a decade ago, at a time when I was a budding advocate for local farming, preaching the virtues of everything local and organic and whole, and once, on a crisp fall afternoon after teaching a history class, slicing the throat of my own chicken. I started to wonder, genuinely wonder, how is it that we can kill an animal to fulfill a luxury, no matter how the animal was raised, and call such an act "humane"? Could I truly reconcile that loaded word—*humane*—with that unquestioned act—killing? What, after all, does animal welfare really mean if we end up raising an animal with compassion and then turn her into an object, all because a chic restaurant wants to serve up some locally raised pork belly? How can we accept Pollan's claim that pigs are intelligent animals capable of experiencing depression and then seek social change that, while temporarily mitigating porcine depression, ultimately promotes gratuitous death?

SELECTIVE MORAL CONSIDERATION

The primary problem with condemning factory farming while continuing to eat animals from nonindustrial sources comes down to this basic point: doing so demands selective moral consideration.[13] This is another way of saying that eating "humanely" raised animals requires a double standard, with welfare standards applied differently to factory farms and small farms. Opponents of factory farming who support nonindustrial alternatives because they care about animals' welfare thus find themselves trapped in what seems to be a logical inconsistency. Let's bore into that inconsistency.

The rationale applied to animals in factory farms goes something like this: animals have feelings that are worthy of our moral consideration; animals are not objects; their welfare matters; therefore they do not deserve the abusive confines and unavoidable suffering of factory farms. These beliefs assume that animals have emotional lives, experience suffering as a result of being raised inhumanely, and thus have moral relevance. This recognition means that animals' capacity to suffer, while perhaps different in degree from our own, is nonetheless meaningful and familiar enough for humans to demand that animals be spared the abuses endemic to industrial animal agriculture. To reiterate a key point: that we believe these animals should not suffer in confinement affirms a basic respect for their existence as sentient beings. They *can* suffer, and we *should* avoid inflicting suffering whenever possible. The logic on this point seems tight.

But when we apply this moral consideration to nonindustrial farms, things fall apart. The moral standard applied to nonindustrial farms should be the same as that applied to factory farms. The core premises should still pertain: animals have feelings; they are not objects; their welfare matters; they deserve to live lives conducive to their general interests. These premises are (we will assume for now) often adequately met on small, sustainable, "humane" animal farms. Nevertheless, we must not forget that even on small, sustainable, humane farms, animals are raised for the ultimate purpose of being killed and turned into commodities. Matters therefore undergo an abrupt change when we extend moral consideration beyond the question of how animals are raised to the much more troubling question of their death. At this crucial crossroad in a farm animal's life—the human choice to slaughter the animal—the moral consideration we applied to factory-farmed animals suddenly—violently—disappears. And that's a problem.

Michael Pollan, who we've seen clearly affirm the inherent worth of farm animals, has dismissed the moment of an animal's death as essentially insignificant. He has said, "what's wrong with animal agriculture—with eating animals—is the practice, not the principle."[14] Death, in other words, is only one day. Give animals a good life, take them down when they least expect it, and these creatures will never know what hit them. We owe animals, not to mention humans, a better explanation than "death is only one day." Death is serious business that, for farm animals, denies them a future they'd otherwise have had. It also poses a major problem for the supporters of nonindustrial alternatives. Recall that in our application of moral consideration to factory farming, the animal's death is never mentioned. It doesn't have to be. The entire cycle of life on a factory farm is so abhorrent as to be dismissed outright as morally corrosive at every turn. Life is horrible for the animal; death is horrible for the animal; factory farming is horrible for the animal; the whole thing is horrible, horrible, and horrible. No more questions, no reason to draw a distinction between life and death, no reason to discern between how an animal is raised and why an animal is killed. The question of death is rendered moot and thus not considered when we condemn factory farms.

Now recall the primary reason concerned consumers believe farm animals should be raised in nonindustrial settings. They want animals removed from factory farms (at least in part) because they believe correctly that animals experience undue suffering on factory farms. Their suffering, as these critics see it, is significant. A pasture-based agricultural system is favored as an alternative to restore to animals a sense of dignity and the opportunity to live lives more or less free of human-imposed restrictions that cause suffering. I'm going to aggressively question this assumption in upcoming chapters, but for now let's assume that our desire for farm animals to be treated well is satisfactorily fulfilled on a humanely managed nonindustrial farm. Let's assume that animals have space to roam, can choose what to eat, and may even have sex under the warm sun on a breezy afternoon. They can, in essence, enjoy a more natural and pleasurable quality of life. This substantial reduction of suffering is fully consistent with our stated moral concern for farm animals, which led us to condemn factory farms and support their nonindustrial alternatives in the first place. The moral benefit of a nonindustrial farm is that it grants to animals the pleasure-inducing freedoms denied to them by factory farms. We believe they have a basic right to these pleasurable freedoms due to their sentience. So we grant them that right and feel good about doing so.

But then there's that moment that every animal producer and consumer must confront: slaughter. Recall that if our moral consideration for animals is genuine, we must apply that consideration to the entire cycle of the supposedly humane alternative. And that cycle includes an animal's early and intentional death. This inclusion reveals something troubling, if generally unrecognized in our common discourse on the tenets of responsible agriculture. It reveals that, on nonindustrial farms—just as in factory farms— farmers kill and commodify the animals they are raising. Intentional death is the essential feature of both systems. This claim is neither melodrama nor overstatement. It is a fact. Without systematic animal death, you have no animal farm—factory or otherwise, big or small, conventional or organic. It might take longer to get an animal to slaughter weight in the alternative arrangement, and that animal might have a lot more fun having sex and eating real food, but that animal's foundational and functional role in the system remains exactly the same as in the factory farm: to get fat fast, die relatively young, and feed people food they do not need to eat.

Our stated moral consideration for animals—and thus the moral argument for small-scale farms—crumbles on this point. To end a sentient animal's life is to suddenly objectify the animal after previously treating her as a subject worthy of moral consideration. That's inconsistent. That this decision is made well before the animal reaches even the prime of her life not only makes the "humane" alternative similar in its most essential aspect to factory farming, but is entirely out of sync with the moral consideration we've granted to animals in the first place. That the death is for the production of a commodity for personal profit cheapens the reality even more so.

We say we care about animals. We say it all the time. We say we care about them enough to urge a wholesale restructuring of the food system to promote their welfare as nonobjectified animals. We say it, moreover, because we mean it, because we're decent, because we have compassion. However, in a whiplash-inducing shift in moral logic, not to mention behavior, we suddenly ignore our concern and decide to end our consideration of these animals' emotional lives by killing them. No matter how you slice it, killing a healthy animal for food we do not need, no matter how the animal was raised, is never consistent with that animal's welfare. In the end, it mocks our original assertion of their moral worth.

This death, no matter how "humane," no matter how respectfully administered, no matter how thickly clothed in feel-good rationalizations ("it had a good life"), essentially negates the moral consideration that inspired us to condemn factory farms in the first place. You can't claim to truly care about an animal, alter her environment to demonstrate your care for that animal, and then, when the animal is nowhere near even the middle of her natural life, kill the animal for no vital reason. Doing so is morally and logically inconsistent. It's worse than ambiguous. It's wrong. It is, alas, the omnivore's contradiction.

EVASION

If my previous analysis is at all on the mark, we must confront this matter head-on. Rather than grapple with the omnivore's contradiction, however, the tastemakers with whom I opened this chapter want absolutely nothing to do with it. They've treated the omnivore's contradiction like a trip to the drive-through lane at McDonald's: they won't go there. Indeed, Pollan, Bittman, Foer, and other writers who have done such a noble job of highlighting the reality and power of animal sentience have ignored the deepest implications of that reality, opting instead to support unnecessary suffering, so long as that unnecessary suffering was inflicted in the proper venues—namely, on small farms by humane farmers. According to this solution, these writers suggest that it's deeply wrong to treat animals poorly, but that it's somehow okay to kill them when you are ready to eat them. These tastemakers, moreover, not only have wide influence, but they aim to use their influence to reform our broken food system. But to think that nonindustrial animal agriculture is going to reform our broken food system is—as the omnivore's contradiction strongly suggests—an idea beset with a huge problem. Advocating for a reform that essentially accomplishes the same end as the existing system—raising animals to kill them for food—does little more than obscure the status quo behind a veil of false virtue. It is therefore important to appreciate just how the tastemakers evade this contradiction.

Pollan eludes the omnivore's contradiction with Houdini-like efficiency. He does so by rhetorically shifting the focus of animal agriculture from death to life. His exclusive emphasis on an animal's quality of life is a sleight of hand essential to perpetuating the virtuous image of the nonindustrial option. Pollan explained to Oprah Winfrey that, after deliberating a bit about the legitimacy of eating meat, "I came out thinking I could eat meat in this very limited way, from farmers I could feel good about the way the animal lived."[15] Not only does Pollan dismiss the chance (in front of a gazillion viewers) to think and act consistently with his own confirmation of animal sentience, but, through his ongoing celebration of eating animals from nonindustrial farms, he dissuades his advocates from pondering the ethical aspect of eating animals. Left unresolved is the critical question: Is it even possible to ethically raise and kill an animal "in this very limited way"? This proposition demands to be resolved. Pollan doesn't do it.

Pollan respects those who choose not to eat animals. He does so, though, while framing it as a personal choice, a commendable but ultimately arbitrary decision to be deliberate about what we eat. Rather than acknowledging that vegans eat in a manner that's morally consistent with the core assumption that animals suffer when killed, Pollan doesn't just dodge the thorny question of killing animals he claims to care about. He encourages his readers to dodge it as well. He did so most recently by promoting the red herring that plants have feelings too. When *The New York Times* ran a widely criticized piece on plant communication, Pollan in all seriousness tweeted to his multitude, "Cool piece on how pea plants communicate with one another, possibly raising some tough issues for vegetarians."[16] Please. This is not a "tough issue." Pollan is just using a rogue hypothesis about emotionally aware pea plants to evade the truly tough issue that he and his followers won't face: the ethics of killing animals. Perhaps more distressingly, here we have the nation's most influential opponent of factory farming—the person who has done more than any other figure in American history since Upton Sinclair to raise awareness about the structural problems with our food system—sidestepping the genuinely difficult issue of eating animals by suggesting that chopping carrots and slaughtering pigs are analogous. Conscientious consumers deserve a more thoughtful response to the very question that Pollan himself initially inspired us to think about.

Mark Bittman has been more systematic in his efforts to grapple with the complex ethics of eating animals. He regularly raises the issue of slaughter in his columns and will occasionally explore the topic with authentic curiosity.[17] But he also skirts the "tough issue," driven as he is by the patronizing assumption that "meat eating may be too strong a habit for most of us to give up."[18] As with Pollan, Bittman studiously avoids confronting the contradiction of causing unneeded suffering to the animals he obviously cares about in ethical terms. He facilitates this avoidance by promoting the inherently illogical notion of what he calls "semi-veganism."[19] This malapropism centers on the false hope that recognizing the consequences of the "maltreatment" of animals will bring us to "a place where we continue to eat animals but exchange that privilege (that's what it is), for a system in which we eat less and treat [animals] better."[20] Embedded in this plan is the expectation that humans will gradually reduce their consumption of animals, producers will respond by designing smaller animal operations, and the overall suffering of farm animals will be meaningfully reduced. This all sounds sensible enough, and as a pragmatic tact, it strikes me as a legitimate short-term approach. Any change that improves the lives of animals is a change I support.

Still, think about Bittman's reduction hypothesis in more principled terms and a problem arises. Being semivegan is about as easy as being semipregnant. Just as one cannot call himself a nonsmoker and puff a few cigarettes after dinner, one cannot be a vegan and eat animals after six o'clock, as Bittman has said he does and as his book *VB6: Eat Vegan Before 6:00* advocates. Bittman understands the contradiction at play here. He's a smart guy who knows the difference between compromise and principle. However, rather than confront the omnivore's contradiction head-on and acknowledge it with an honest argument, he too has chosen to dodge it, and to encourage readers, in a quest to diminish their guilt, to look the other way, spend a little more, and eat fewer animal products, all sourced from "humane" farms, as if the moral points scored through such reduction will help revolutionize the food system. But it won't—because this choice conveniently avoids the core ethical dilemma, the omnivore's contradiction, presented in this chapter. Bittman, who brought in 2014 with a piece on the sublime nature of crispy pig cheeks, thus falls into the same trap as Michael Pollan.[21]

And then Bittman spins in circles. What we do not see, and what he (who, it should be noted, often writes meat-based recipes for *Times* readers to enjoy and says he loves hot dogs) will not directly show us, is how these good-guy nonindustrial farmers, just like the factory farmers, exploit and kill animals for their fluids and flesh when the time suits the needs of the market. Small farms that raise animals with dignity swaddle themselves in, and are swaddled by, an admiring media that comforts them in the seductive rhetoric of agrarian virtue. These are the good guys, we are told. These are the guys fighting the good fight. Support them. Forget that, at the end of the day, they have the same blood on their hands as the factory farmer. Overlook that ugly commonality. Ignore that all the meat we eat comes from an animal that did not want to be killed. In failing to show us the blood lining the pathway of part-time veganism, Bittman ultimately allows his genuine moral consideration to remain ever-conveniently selective, espousing principles that tolerate less blood rather than more. Frankly, it's hard to get fired up about a future food system based on such a lethargic assumption of what humans are capable of accomplishing.

Pollan and Bittman have encouraged hordes of consumers to reduce their consumption of animal products. That reduction has meant less animal suffering, at least in the United States.[22] Looking at matters in the short term, which they do, these writers have every reason not to confront the contradiction upon which they thrive. They are prominent figures with a large following of readers who would drop them like a bag of fast food if, acting in accordance with their beliefs in animal sentience, they took a morally consistent stance to not eat animals domesticated for food. (When I say "morally consistent," I do not mean consistent with "my morals" but rather with the morals their own appeal to animal welfare acknowledges.) If these writers advocated a plant-based diet devoid of support for small animal farms, their message would fall far afield of mainstream media expectations dependent on an ever-expanding audience that wants more than anything to keep eating farm animals while feeling morally exonerated as it does so. The consequence of leading rather than following the desires of a carnivorously inclined readership would be professional suicide.

The reality is, such that you probably cannot survive as a mainstream food writer today and not at least occasionally celebrate the sublime virtues of some sublime small farmer's sublime meat, cheese, and eggs. Michael Pollan's mantra, "Eat food, mostly plants, not too much," not unlike Bittman's clarion call to semiveganism, are marketing inspired slogans rather than genuine prescriptions for reform. They are gambits that brilliantly allow these gifted wordsmiths to do what they do so well—support the consumption of animals while conveniently acknowledging the ethical problems of factory farming. Speaking out of both sides of their mouths, they get to have it both ways: eat animals but don't eat a lot of animals. Unfortunately, they also obscure the fatal contradiction lurking in the shadows of widespread death and suffering: the contradiction of killing and eating an animal we've deemed, by virtue of our opposition to factory farming, deserving of moral consideration. As a result, the food movement they've founded will remain little more than a precious cult of well-heeled gourmands.

Of course, there is no necessary connection between professional self-interest and selective moral consideration. This brings us to Jonathan Safran Foer. Foer, who would surely recoil at being labeled a food writer, and has no skin in the game of foodie journalism. However, his distance from the genre hasn't prevented him from perfecting his own brand of equivocation. In October 2012, he responded to a question about the morality of killing animals for food by saying, "The answer doesn't really matter. Maybe it's fun, intellectually, to consider the question. But let's talk about what's actually in front of us." He added, "The question is the least relevant to the choices we make on a daily basis."[23] A few months earlier, the author of a book that likely drove more people into veganism than any other since Peter Singer's *Animal Liberation* could be found racking up hits on YouTube, clouding the logical implications of his impassioned call to recognize the moral significance of farm animals. He was hawking an online resource instructing concerned consumers *where to buy chicken.* Foer, having exposed the horror of death for chickens, wants us to eat the right kind of poultry because, one supposes, that's the question that's "actually in front of us." As I'll later argue, this kind of pragmatism has a limited role. Still, for those seeking more principled answers to the ethical questions of eating animals, this vision leads us nowhere. Alas, it's just another evasion.

I can understand where Foer is coming from in his above quote. By pushing for a more principled approach to the way we think and act regarding eating animals, I'm not outright dismissing the pragmatic possibility that calls for reduction might diminish suffering. The consumption of animals is so pervasive and systemic in modern society that any effort to lessen it may be worthwhile. When a fire is raging, every bucketful of water has value. My primary purpose in exposing the omnivore's contradiction is to highlight the need to situate all reduction efforts in the larger framework of eventually abolishing the consumption of farmed animals. Without this framework, any effort to support more "humane" alternatives and reduce consumption will do nothing more than shunt the killing of animals from big venues to small ones, from a centralized to a decentralized landscape of slaughter. And, really, what's the point of doing that?

CONSIDER DAVID FOSTER WALLACE

Not all high-profile writers have avoided the omnivore's contradiction. At least one has confronted it directly and concluded that to recognize animal sentience while eating animals cannot be resolved with proper moral satisfaction. This writer, the late David Foster Wallace, made this case not only in the pages of *Gourmet*, a posh lifestyle magazine that catered to the upscale tastes of gourmands who want food writing, like food, to titillate and indulge. But he made it by profiling a popular festival dedicated to the mass consumption of lobster—a crustacean so immune to basic human sympathy (unlike pigs, cows, and chickens) that rabid devotees in Maine dismiss them as "bugs." The article, "Consider the Lobster," which won numerous magazine awards, is notable not only as an emblematic piece of brilliant Wallace work, but as a rebuke to the writers profiled above, writers who have thus far refused to admit what Wallace, who stumbled into this topic out of nowhere and engaged the issue without pretense or disingenuousness, could not avoid admitting without compromising his intellectual integrity. (Wallace, not incidentally, was a former philosophy graduate student at Harvard.) What he argued in this *Gourmet* piece shocked the foodie establishment. He said it was morally wrong to kill *lobsters*.[24]

Wallace fully understood that food is culture and that culture is power and that people are uncomfortable about any of its being meddled with, especially when the pleasure of the palate is at stake. Moreover, he further understood that, as he explained to Kenyon College students as their 2005 commencement speaker, we are often at a loss to recognize and analyze the questions that are right under our noses. We are at a loss because these questions do not, in most situations, appear to be questions at all, but rather just the way life works. As Wallace put it, "The most obvious, ubiquitous, important realities are often the ones that are hardest to see and talk about." Despite all the good reasons for avoiding a forthright discussion about the difficult matter of slaughtering sentient animals for the glorified sake of pleasure, Wallace kept coming back to something that, "after all the abstract intellection," could not be erased from his mental archive: "the frantically clanking lid." That is, death. For unnecessary death, even that of a hard-shelled "bug," he could offer no viable explanation. And, having no tolerance for excuses, he was honest enough to leave it at that.

BEATING THE DEVIL

Animals suffer more than we can imagine on factory farms. Their suffering should be minimized as much as possible and ideally eliminated. However, the appeal to "humane" and sustainable alternatives does little to address the root cause of factory farming's existence: eating animals. Stop eating farmed animals and you do the most powerfully effective thing you can do to end factory farming. Stop eating animals and you start an authentic food revolution. Industrial animal agriculture cannot survive if consumers don't eat the products that industrial animal agriculture produces and thrives upon. The appeal to support nonindustrial alternatives, which we've been hearing about now for decades, has in no way shaken the confidence of factory farming. It never will.

Instead, our complicity has created short-term space for improved conditions for animals while situating a food reform movement on an intellectually dishonest foundation. Support for nonindustrial animal farms highlights the emotional significance of animal life while suppressing the most consistent ethical response to it—abolishing the consumption of all animals killed for food. I suppose this isn't surprising. Most consumers consider eating animals pleasurable and culturally acceptable. As a result, we're inclined, in the face of vivid exposés of factory farming, to follow the path of least resistance, allowing vague notions of "sustainability" to suffice as viable explanations for killing happy farm animals. We're instinctively attracted to a path of reduction that allows us to have our meat and eat it too, paying a little more for the indulgence, learning a thing or two about animal husbandry, and perhaps even getting to know our farmer and the animals under his care. We declare ourselves "vegan before six" without realizing that it's the same as "eating animals after six," all the while forgetting that animals don't care what time of day they're eaten.

The alternatives promoted by our foremost food writers and leaders of the sustainable food movement not only fail to resolve (much less even acknowledge) the omnivore's contradiction, but they make the mistake of trying to beat the devil at his own game. When we purchase animal products from small, sustainable, and more humane farms without explicitly understanding this decision as a step in the direction of abolishing animal agriculture altogether, we may actually be strengthening factory farming. The reason, which may not be readily apparent, is that consolidating animals in industrial settings is more efficient. Plain and simple, it pays.[25] Strangely, for all the advocacy of sustainable alternatives, we've yet to see a convincing economic argument for the long-term viability of nonconcentrated, nonindustrial farming in a globalizing world.[26] This economic reality is why we need to be extremely careful about promoting animals from small farms as a legitimate and permanent alternative to factory-farmed animal products. It might work for a privileged few who can afford to pay more to feel better about death. But it will never, even with the elimination of subsidies, work as a strategy for the meat-eating masses. Their trough will always be filled with agribusiness flesh.

One need not be an economist to grasp this point. It's common sense: economies of scale and density of production lead to cheaper animal products. Cheaper animal products mean more market share for producers able to bring their animals to slaughter weight faster and in greater volume than competitors. These economic realities automatically place small-scale animal producers at a permanent economic disadvantage, one that, barring drastic governmental intervention, they will never be able to escape. There will always be consumers who voluntarily pay more for a supposedly more humane option. There will always be consumers who opt for the value-added humane meat or carton of pasture eggs. But so what? No matter how many glowing articles in mainstream newspapers tell us how the small-farm movement is the wave of the future, the more expensive options will always remain popular only for a minority.

Jonathan Safran Foer tells us to look at matters as they now stand. Let's do that. The alternatives to factory farming have been available for several decades. However, only about 1 percent of the animal products Americans eat now come from them. When we support these nonindustrial alternatives, we are not supporting a realistic transition to a new way of raising and consuming animal products. We are, instead, supporting the very behavior most essential to the continued dominance of factory farming: eating farmed animals. Stop doing that and we'll see real change. Until then, it's hard to see choosing alternative sources of animal products as anything but a convenient salve for the problem we refuse to face in a morally consistent manner. This is what the pundits, in their studied evasion of the omnivore's contradiction, refuse to tell you.

We're human. Seeking alternatives that accommodate current eating habits is much easier, and perhaps more realistic, than exploring the deeper implications of an idea—avoiding all domesticated animal products—that demands a radical shift in personal behavior. Our unthinking response to the horrors of factory farming—eating animals from small farms—makes sense only in that this option appears to be nominally better for farm animals. In the short term, it may well be—and for this reason I've gone on record as supporting incremental welfare reforms within the confines of industrial animal agriculture.[27] Better, however, does not mean right. Better does not mean that it will ever be anything more than a limited response to an entrenched problem, designed more for consumers seeking a bit of conscience balm than for the animals they've made a big deal of caring for. Better is better. But when it comes to the long-term prospects of animal welfare and the reform of our food system, better isn't good enough.

HUMANE SLAUGHTER

What you are about to see is beyond your worst nightmares.

—*MEET YOUR MEAT*

Nicholas Kristof is a *New York Times* columnist who has dedicated his career to exposing suffering and abuse among the world's most vulnerable human beings. His work on this score is empathetic and profound. Occasionally, though, he turns his attention to farm animals. The results are usually disastrous. Never failing to remind us that he grew up on a cherry-tree and sheep farm in Oregon, Kristof asserts that animal agriculture can be delightfully humane if the animals are treated well. When animals are treated with dignity before they are killed, consumers can think of themselves as "benign carnivores." All they have to do is spend a little more cash to consume responsibly produced animal products. Everybody wins in this version of no-fault agrarian bliss—one that Kristof and so many other mainstream journalists promote in the popular media regularly for conscientious carnivores to enjoy over their locally sourced, organic, fair-trade, humanely raised, and welfare-approved plate of bacon and eggs.

To appreciate how uncritically Kristof evaluates small-scale animal agriculture, consider his September 2012 *New York Times* piece about "a high school buddy" of his who manages a dairy farm in Oregon. To stress how well this dairy farmer (Bob) treats his 430 dairy cows (yes, that is considered small), Kristof explains that Bob "loves them like children," "has names for every one of his 'girls,'"[1] and puts them out to pasture every day, where "they are much happier." This is all well and good. Until we get to paragraph twelve. There we learn that Bob is not running, as Kristof now puts it, "a charity hostel."[2] Though Bob works to keep his cows around, the economic reality of dairy farming remains: farmers, we are told, "slaughter them." And they do so when "they age and milk production drops."

So cows are not treated like beloved children after all. They are, instead, treated as objects of economic exploitation, beings whose lives are deemed less important than the whimsical human desire for a glass of milk. Kristof appears to be unaware that, in his Sunday-morning paean to small-scale animal agriculture, he has shifted from treating animals as sentient subjects to treating them as cold objects. He concludes that when we buy milk from Bob's farm, we should feel okay about the cow that produced that milk because, as he writes, "it had a name."

Like so many journalists who write about alternative forms of animal agriculture, Kristof thoughtlessly succumbs to the omnivore's contradiction. He treats an animal one moment with moral worth and the next as an objectified commodity while offering no explanation for the shift. In the space of a single article, Kristof confers moral worth on animals ("loves them like children"), approves of their killing ("farmers slaughter them") and confirms their sudden transition into a lifeless object ("it had a name"). In a piece intended to highlight the comparative benefits of small-scale animal agriculture, Kristof does something that's endemic to journalistic coverage of nonindustrial animal agriculture as a whole: he subsumes the serious ethical question of killing and commodifying a sentient being under the superficial rhetoric and titillating imagery of agricultural pornography. As with the writers profiled in the last chapter, he selectively stresses life, avoids death, and deems it all good, or at least better. No doubt the pressure to produce upbeat copy plays a role in this choice (yet another reason to distrust the popular media for a full and ethically nuanced presentation of something as complex as animal agriculture). Entertainment and simplicity too easily trump ethical inquiry, especially when it comes to agriculture and the reality of slaughter. Who wants to read about the horrors of an animal's death over a frothy morning latte?

Ethical whitewashing characterizes most food journalism. Recurring tropes dominate the landscape—blue skies, green grass, healthy-looking and happy animals, and an atmosphere of impossible pleasure populated with hip young people (or Joel Salatin) getting dirt under their nails and living the dream off the grid.[3] These seductive tropes shift the consumer's attention away from the inherent messiness of agricultural reality, hiding the most unpleasant aspect of small-scale agriculture—the animals' untimely deaths—behind a false but seductive veil of perfection. The popular media, not to mention these farms themselves, promote small-scale animal agriculture as a viable, sustainable, affordable, attractive, and humane alternative to the grim existence of industrial agriculture. They do so, though, by using the same distortions and marketing ploys that agribusiness deploys to convince us that all is well and good in the land of industrial animal production.

This chapter will show that, despite the conventional portrayals, not only is all not well and good down on the factory farm but, with respect to the most problematic aspect of all animal agriculture—slaughter—things aren't so great on Kristof's friend Bob's farm either. Ethically speaking, the small animal farm—despite being portrayed as a peaceful, healthy, and happy place—harbors considerable suffering. That suffering begins with a single and inevitable moment that the omnivore's contradiction refuses to reconcile: death in an abattoir. Discussing the death of farm animals in the abstract is relatively easy. It's when we take a closer look at how animals on small farms die in reality that things get complicated.

"WHAT I AM DOING, WHAT WE ARE DOING, IS WRONG"

Slaughter is a reality that honest farmers have no choice but to face without evasion. Most consumers, even conscientious ones seeking to "know where food comes from," don't have to undertake this task. They are spared the burden. It's a horrible job, so why would we face it if we didn't have to? Thus a paradoxical aspect of our widespread support for "humane" animal agriculture is how quickly consumers who've never stepped foot on a farm, much less a slaughter facility, will accept the whitewashing of death while many farmers themselves aggressively reject such a convenient portrayal. Consumer distance from agrarian reality makes us especially vulnerable to the humane mythologies promoted by the sustainable food movement. Thankfully, some nonindustrial farmers speak forthrightly about their work, providing a more sober look into the hard reality of slaughtering animals we claim to care about.

Consider another farmer named Bob, one that Kristof never interviewed. This one is the owner of Stony Brook Farm, a small pig farm in upstate New York. There's no doubt that Bob treats his animals well. They are, as Bob puts it, "as close to natural as possible in an unnatural system." Even more so, he explains, they are "as piggy as pigness, they are Plato's pig, the ideal form of the pig." Bob notes how within the media "there is celebration of the way I raise my pigs." He appreciates that the humane-sustainable-happy-meat people love him. To them, he explains, "I am honorable. I am humane. I am just." His pigs, if they could testify about their experience at Stony Brook, would surely sing Bob's praises because, as Bob summarizes their behavior, "they root, they lounge, they narf, they eat, they forage, they sleep, they wallow, they bask, they run, they play, and they die unconsciously, without pain and suffering." This seemingly self-congratulatory assessment by Bob the Humane Farmer about his ecstatic animals might sound familiar. But hang on to your overalls because this Bob is a different kind of farmer from Kristof's high school buddy.

Bob is tormented by his work. He rejects the entire idea of "humanely" raising an animal to kill her. He refuses to obscure the thorny ethics of his work behind some Jeffersonian veil of agrarian virtue. "As a pig farmer," he writes, "I lead an unethical life." His forthright self-assessment is rare. Bob the pig farmer calls himself "a slaveholder and a murderer." He's also acutely aware of why he's able, as a self-described murderer and slaveholder, to get away with his deeds: "The simplest way to put it is that slaughter is a socially permissible ethical transgression; societal permission does not make it ethical, it makes it acceptable, non punishable." The numbing effect of conventional wisdom, however, in no way distracts Bob from the fact that "out of the corner of your eye, in the blurry periphery of your vision, something dark, and something evil lurks: It is the truth: meat is indeed murder." As for Bob's own role in this carefully choreographed complicity, he explains, "I am balancing on the edge of a knife blade."[1] As if any doubts were left about Bob's ethical assessment of his professional handiwork, he concludes, "We have an obligation to eat otherwise. It might take incalculable generations of being hooked by and grappling with the ethics of slaughter to get there, but we have to get there, because again, what I am doing, what we are doing, is wrong."[5] In early 2014, Bob quit raising pigs and switched to growing only vegetables.[6]

Bob is not alone in his suffering. Barbara Fickle is a humane pig farmer in Missouri. She and her husband, Mike, raise an endangered species of hog called the Red Wattle. Their operation is small and their welfare standards are high. But the situation is hardly free of conflict. In a Facebook post, Fickle began to explain the discomfort that comes with loving and killing an animal. Of a sow she raised named Sue, she wrote, "She was so gentle, so kind. She had an amazing life while she was with us. She gave us two beautiful litters of pigs and many days of laughs. She once got out and waited for me to get back home . . . her and all 12 babies lying in the tall grass. As soon as I stepped out of my vehicle, they ran up to me snorting and grunting, as a group of dogs would. Well, as goes life here on the farm, Sue is now in the freezer."[7]

Fickle seems to wish she could rest the matter there— out in the freezer. But she cannot. She continues, "I will never forget the way she looked back at me as she was walked through the slaughter chute. I swear, I felt as if she were saying 'What? Why?'" Then Fickle's attention turns to Sue's daughter Rosie, who just had her second litter: "I went out this morning to feed her and my heart felt as if it caved in. You see, all but two of her babies have been sold and shipped off, squealing and shrieking." Fickle then unravels: "I raised Rosie and she loves me, I think. This morning she ran up to me and ran back to her hut, looked around and ran back to me. I know she is telling me that her babies are gone. The two remaining ones will not leave her side. I know I will be laughed at and hear all kinds of remarks from friends and family, but I cannot explain to you the deep sorrow I feel at this moment. I know in my heart I cannot change the past . . . but I can change the present. These three will NOT be eaten. And I am feeling extremely ill thinking of poor Sue. I cannot shake it. What has happened to me? I am sobbing uncontrollably."

Not every small-scale animal farmer is willing to testify so openly about the ethical conundrum at the core of her livelihood. Nonetheless, the general awareness that something is vaguely, and perhaps even fundamentally, wrong down on the farm is frequently echoed by other nonindustrial farmers, the very people who spend considerable time alongside the animals they name, know, and, in some cases, love much as they do their pets.

Bryan Welch, a small-scale livestock farmer (and media executive), treats his animals about as well as a farmer could hope to. He is, by his own assessment, "as humane as any livestock farmer can be." His actions seem to match his words. On Welch's farm there's no ear notching or branding, no confinement, no artificial insemination, no roping. There's endless fresh water, lots of socialization, and ample room to roam. Welch's personal relationship with his animals reflects the care with which he handles them. He explains of his current batch of rams, "Over the past nine months I've watched them grow from two-pound, curly-headed sprites into 80-pound monuments of ovine masculinity, created from grass. They are out there in the snow this morning, sparring and bucking, sharing a big bale of hay. Each of them has a personality and I care about each of them as individuals." There's much to admire in Welch's thoughtful anthropomorphism. Clearly, he's attuned to the problem of killing the animals he has raised. He's aware, indeed, of the omnivore's contradiction.

And it weighs on him. "In a few days," he writes, "I'll load five of my young rams into a trailer and take them to be killed. A few days after that they will be in our freezers." Never does he deny that they will suffer. He wonders, "Since humans can conceptualize the pain felt by our prey, should we nurture our empathy and refrain from eating meat?" The reason for Welch's insecurity is as obvious as it is poignant. He says of his rams headed to the slaughterhouse, "I held them when they were babies."[8]

A compassionate person does not easily forget such a bonding experience. Like Bob's, Welch's account has a clear and palpable sense that he knows there's an accessible answer to the ethical transgression he and so many others tolerate and, at times, even celebrate: "When I take them to be killed, I'll feel that familiar twinge." Tellingly, he adds, "It is a specific sort of pain I would not feel if I were a vegan." That even this "humane" farmer is questioning the ethical nature of his work, going so far as to raise the specter of veganism as an exonerating option, should give everyone—especially the consumers who salve their guilt by purchasing his products—reason to pause and reflect on what must happen for an animal to go from farm to fork.[9]

Many farmers are so psychologically tormented by their role in animal slaughter that they quit the business altogether. Harold F. Lyman, a fourth-generation rancher from Montana who has become a vocal vegan health advocate, is especially reflective about killing and eating sentient animals. "The ideal amount of animal foods in the diet," the former cowboy writes, "is zero." Countering the popular idea to eat "legitimate" animal products, Lyman notes, "There is no such thing as a clean, lean cut of meat—even if you buy it 'organic,' or blessed by rabbis, or hunt it down yourself." Lyman divides his life into two categories: "before the operation [to remove a potentially fatal tumor], when I was dangerously unhealthy, thoughtless, self-centered, and devoid of compassion for the animals I slaughtered," and after, "when the lessons I've learned about kindness and compassion have taken me on a journey that has restored my own health." Lyman may not cut to the ethical heart of the matter the way Bob does, but his frank recognition that raising animals for food degrades our own well-being is as evident, and every bit as instructive, as Bob's. That Lyman also closed his business and suffered the pangs of poverty as a result of his choice should serve as a powerful confirmation of his belief that killing animals for food we don't need comes with some moral accounting.[10]

The experience of Cheri Ezell-Vandersluis, a former goat farmer, is not dissimilar to Lyman's. Cheri was an attentive caregiver to her own goats, considering them, as so many small farmers do, "part of the family." Her farm was everything that sustainable and humane advocates would want it to be: free-range, pastured, and, compared to factory farms, all natural. Still, something didn't sit well with Cheri. Something left her ill at ease. No matter how well Cheri treated her animals, she couldn't allow herself to escape the fact that these sentient creatures would end up on someone's plate. The live animals she caressed and cared for and watched play and eat and sleep might, she knew, end up as stuffing for tacos, or perhaps a $12 appetizer at the trendy Cabrito Menu in Manhattan. The animals she nurtured would die, be cooked, and be tossed, as so much restaurant food is, into a Dumpster. Rather than rationalize away the implications of this dreadful reality, rather than participate in the emotional disconnect that so many producers and consumers rely upon to keep their conscience clean, Cheri confronted the cold reality of slaughter directly. She explained, "To watch a sentient being gasp for air and to look into his eyes filled with fear and to see the blood coming from his neck— it's the most heart-wrenching, awful thing."[11] And that was that. As Cheri reflected on this "most heart-wrenching, awful thing," the promise of humane animal agriculture quickly lost its appeal. Eventually, as with Lyman and Comis, she and her husband closed the business and eliminated animal products from their diet. They also turned their land into an animal sanctuary.

Another example of a small farmer choosing to grapple honestly with the ethical implications of killing sentient animals comes from Chris Kerr. Kerr grew up on a small farm in the Appalachian Mountains. He raised chickens, pigs, sheep, and ducks in nonindustrial settings. Kerr speaks of these animals as we might speak of our pets, recalling them as "part of the family." His parents were, like most farmers, studiously evasive about the ethics of killing the animals that Kerr came to love. He recalls, "We bought the sheep as lambs, raised them, sheared them, and then off they would go—no longer part of our lives. . . . There would be one conversation, and we were to understand that this was just how things worked." This explanation sort of sufficed when Kerr was young. It became less adequate, though, as he grew up. Realizing from his farming experience that "once you bear witness, you have a choice," Kerr too became vegan and has dedicated his life to developing companies that promote vegan options. Today he works as "entrepreneur-in-residence" at the Humane Society of the United States, helping to move plant-based product lines such as Daiya and Field Roast from conception to actualization.

A similar awakening overtook Harold Brown. Like Kerr, Brown came of age on an independent family farm. Also like Kerr, he would grow up to acknowledge that he was "indoctrinated" to accept the slaughtering of animals that he cared for as "essential to human wants and nutrition." Under the influence of his parents, his community, his church, and even his central-Michigan 4-H club, Brown came to appreciate the importance of treating an animal well. For him, 4-H was an especially pivotal experience. There he did his earliest thoughtful observing. "I saw many, many young people treat their animals as they would a cat or dog" only to "cry their eyes out when they auctioned off their animals at the end of the country fair." This emotional manifestation of the omnivore's contradiction was less repressed in children than adults, and the force of their expressions hit Brown powerfully. Eventually, like so many others, he decided to avoid the suffering altogether. "I can tell you as a former animal farmer," he explains, "that while it may be true that you can treat an animal kindly and show tenderness toward them, mercy is a different matter."

Like so many other people who open their eyes to the unpleasant realities of all animal agriculture, Brown had his awakening. He writes, "If I was going to be true to myself and live to my full potential I had to reevaluate, think, and choose. I chose life. So no, in my experience, there is no such thing as humane animal products, humane farming practices, humane transport, or humane slaughter." Compassionate carnivores who have never so much as smelled the happy farm producing their happy meat should take careful note of Brown's unhappy assessment of animal death, the courage it took to make that assessment, and the untold stories of unknown small-scale animal farmers who have looked slaughter in the face, turned away, and sought greener pastures.[12]

These transformative stories, all from small-scale animal farmers, are instructive. They remind us that, when it comes to the ethical conundrum of killing and commodifying a sentient being for food we do not need, farm size doesn't matter. Death is not just one day. Death is death. Sourcing animal products from a small farm does not resolve the omnivore's contradiction. If anything, as these accounts attest, it intensifies it. Consider that a smaller scale translates into more humane treatment for animals on the farm. If you buy this premise, then consider that the dilemma of treating an animal with dignity and moral worth for a couple of years and then transforming him into a pork chop when he's properly fattened. This act remains a serous ethical problem endemic to the small, "humane" model. When you kill an animal unnecessarily, the animal's having had a good life—if the aforementioned accounts mean anything—isn't a valid justification for causing death.

On the small farm, the moral consideration of animals is more than rhetoric, as it so often is on factory farms. It is grounded in the reality of daily interaction. Animals on small farms are often truly loved. They are provided lavish personal attention, emotional bonds are nurtured, thoughtful anthropomorphizing happens, and the animals' attachment to life becomes obvious for anyone willing to bear witness. Most small farmers deny and internalize the suffering of slaughter, rationalizing it away in savvy but false justifications. This is understandable. Only when a farmer extends his sense of compassion to *the full cycle* of an animal's potential life and opens his heart to the honest nature of his work does the "humane" supplier of animal products for "compassionate carnivores" become not a hero but, as "the other Bob" so soberly put it, complicit in a sentient animal's death. The problem of death remains, as it does in factory farming, at the vital core of the alternative solutions that are supposed to reform our food system, salve our guilt, and make the world a better place for animals. In fact, not only does the problem of death remain, it may even be emotionally magnified.

"IT'S AMAZING THE WILLPOWER THESE ANIMALS HAVE"

Death for a farm animal destined for sale usually requires that the animal enter the doors of an industrial slaughterhouse. The oft-touted "humane" nature of nonindustrial farms is challenged not only by the ethical conundrum of causing unnecessary death, but also by the precise manner of that death. Especially disturbing for most small-scale animal farmers is that the animals they have so loved and nurtured have to be transported hundreds of miles to an industrial slaughterhouse to be killed and processed. This is usually unavoidable. As the production of animals has increased, so has the consolidation of their slaughter. A large slaughterhouse is more profitable because it's cheaper and more efficient in transforming live animals into commercial products. The fewer slaughterhouses there are, moreover, the easier it is for the USDA to regulate them. A statistic from California, which has more small-scale animal farms than any other state, captures the aggressive nature of consolidation: in 1979, the state had seventy federally inspected slaughterhouses (for cattle); by 2011, there were twenty-three.[13] As a result, the vast majority of animals raised on small farms end up in the same industrial abattoirs, confronting the same underpaid and psychologically rattled stun-gunners and throat-cutters, as do the animals raised in feedlots.

Federal law in the United States (with a few exceptions) requires animal products destined for restaurants, retail outlets, or farmers' markets to be processed in a USDA-certified-and-inspected slaughterhouse.[14] The country has around eleven hundred of these facilities, most of them located in hinterlands, most of them of a relatively industrialized size, and all of them with alarming rates of worker turnover—often over 100 percent in a single year.[15] These operations survive not because they exist in obscurity. They survive because they work well. They are coldly efficient, processing thousands of animals a day, often at the pace of three hundred large animals an hour.[16] While four corporations slaughter roughly 80 percent of the cattle in the United States within these large slaughterhouses, small commercial producers—unless they use a mobile slaughterhouse (more on these soon) or sell the animal directly to consumers from the farm—often have no choice but to rely on them as well. While small commercial producers are not necessarily happy about this, it is an inescapable reality of agrarian life. While advocates for decentralizing slaughtering are working diligently to reverse this consolidation, chances are negligible, given the regulatory demands of the USDA and the prohibitive cost of building smaller slaughterhouses, that they will ever achieve more than a symbolic dent in the big business of slaughtering animals.

The critical point here is that the animals often portrayed as being humanely raised are more often than not still killed under brutal industrial conditions inconsistent with the values expressed on the farms from which they came.[17] Conscientious carnivores will often tell themselves that it's okay to eat animals from small farms because, as they so often say, "death is just one day." Well, let's take a look at what that one day looks like and see if we still want to accept such a rationalization for killing animals to produce food we don't need.[18]

On paper, a commercial slaughterhouse appears to be a model of efficiency, a clean blueprint of order and thrift. In reality, what happens inside these operations epitomizes the institutionalization of violence, so much so that, as we'll see, it psychologically rattles the humans who work there. There's that old saying "If slaughterhouses had glass walls, the whole world would be vegetarian." Perhaps. The reality is that it's culturally acceptable for consumers to turn a blind eye to this disturbing and largely invisible link in the supply chain. Nobody is asking us to think about glass walls when we eat animals marketed as humanely raised or welfare approved. The emphasis is on life, not death.

When animals reach the slaughterhouse grounds, whatever humane treatment they once received back on the small farm abruptly ends. The atmosphere of brutality is evident to animals before they enter. To a creature who was caressed and nurtured and treated with dignity throughout his life, it must come as a shock (literally) to suddenly be unloaded in a holding pen and forced, often by electric prod, to enter the slaughterhouse proper through a narrow chute called a squeeze pen. These chutes are commonly arranged in a zigzag formation to ensure that animals cannot see what's coming.

Prodding is still required because farm animals, especially hogs, recoil when they smell blood. These animals are already on emotional edge because they've just endured an arduous and unprecedented (for them) road trip banging around the back of a truck, deprived the entire time of food and water, petrified and yelling with fear. They emerge from these vehicles dehydrated, disoriented, and, on many occasions, having suffered broken bones. If they're pigs, they were likely poked in the anus or the eyeball with an electric rod earlier in the day when they refused—because they're smart—to board the truck. If they were chickens, they were yanked up by a leg and tossed like a football into a crate. Many animals are so agitated when they leave the truck for the slaughterhouse's holding pen that they lash out at their handlers. In July 2012 a farmer had his face broken by such a cow (who then escaped and took himself on a tour of the University of Missouri before being shot by the police). These animals even suffer stress-induced heart attacks as they're prodded down the line, headed for the next phase of the slaughterhouse experience: the knocking box.[19]

The knocking box is a small space where a worker wielding an eight-inch bolt gun spends nine hours a day shooting animals, serially, in the head with a retractable steel bolt to render them unconscious or dead. It's not always clear which.[20] To arrive in the knocking box, cattle are squeezed between two vertically mobile metal walls, immobilized, and suspended. They are then slowly elevated to the eye-level of the stun-gunner, who seizes the moment to pop the cow in the head, just above the eyes—eyes that the gunner must look between in order to make an accurate shot. If done properly, the stunned cow collapses into a heap. Timothy Pachirat, who worked undercover in a Nebraska slaughterhouse while researching a Yale dissertation, described the aftermath, which happens thousands of times a day within the confines of a single knocking box: "As the bolt retracts, gray brain matter often flies out of the hole in the cow's skull. . . . Seconds later, blood gushes out of the wound, bubbling up and out in a dark maroon stream as it oxygenates. . . . The cow's eyes typically take on a glazed look and its tongue often hangs limply from its mouth." The animal is now deemed either unconscious or dead. Often, though, he is neither. Often he remains conscious. One worker recalled how "a lot of times the skinner [working down the line] finds out an animal is still conscious when he slices the side of its head and it starts kicking wildly." When that happens, "the skinners shove a knife into the back of its head to cut the spinal cord."[21] Then he dies. Sometimes.

The gruesome reality is that animals, despite the apparatus of death in which they are caught, will fight their fate. Thus the knocking box frequently becomes a scene of rebellious mayhem as the will to live viscerally opposes the machinery of death. Pachirat recalls, "Sometimes the power, angle, or location of the steel bolt shot is insufficient to render the cow unconscious, and it will bleed profusely and thrash about wildly while the knocker tries to shoot it again."[22] Even then, the job often remains unfinished. "Sometimes," according to a slaughterhouse worker interviewed by Gail Eisnitz for her book *Slaughterhouse*, "they start yelling 'moo';

they're hanging down and still yelling moo; they pick up their heads and their eyes look around."[23] Workers have a hard time dealing with this.

Pigs are even harder to render unconscious. A former employee at a hog slaughterhouse recalled, "I've seen hogs stunned up to twelve times. Like a big boar would come through, they'd hit him with the stunner, he'd look up at them. go RRRAAA! Hit him again, the son of a bitch wouldn't go, wouldn't go. It's amazing the willpower these animals have."[24] Such a will to live continues to express itself even after the stun gun has supposedly knocked a pig into oblivion. A *Washington Post* reporter witnessed: "As [pigs] fall from the shock, a worker quickly hangs the pigs upside down on a conveyor belt, placing their rear legs in a metal clamp. Sometimes the stunned hogs fall off the conveyor belt and regain consciousness, and workers have to scramble to hoist the hogs' legs back into the metal clamps before they begin running wildly through the confined area."[25] No matter how aggressively these animals are treated like objects, their behavior mocks the ultimate attempt to objectify them, insisting until the end that we recognize these animals for who they are: live beings who are making a last-ditch struggle to avoid death.

Although farm animals often die once they are stunned, the official moment of death usually comes from the one-two combination delivered by the "pre-sticker" and the "sticker"—a tag team of workers who executes the next phase of slaughter. As animals stream by, hanging upside down and sometimes jerking involuntarily, the pre-sticker makes a small incision into each animal's neck. The sticker, standing a few feet down the line, goes into the incision and slices into the animal's carotid arteries and jugular veins.

Blood pulsates in thick streams. The animal—if he hasn't already died—approaches death. The carcass is then conveyed into a "bleed pit" to be shocked by "electrified metal cross bars." The purpose of this postmortem jolt is to jumpstart the heart just enough to squeeze residual blood from the arteries. Once the animal is totally "bled out," his carcass is passed on to the "tail ripper."[26] What was once a live animal is now, with the skin being stripped from his tail, a lifeless object on the verge of being disassembled into dozens of commercial products and by-products that will be shipped around the world to people who have no idea what just happened to make those commodities a reality.

The general outline of industrial slaughter sketched above is just that: a general outline. Much is omitted. There are macabre deviations. Chickens—whether they come from humane pastured farms or a cramped cage in a poultry warehouse—are, in industrial slaughterhouses, hung by their feet to a moving rail while fully conscious (this happens because chickens are exempt from the Humane Slaughter Act of 1983). They flail madly as they are transported to a large pot of electrified water into which they are submerged (still alive) to loosen their feathers so they pluck easier after death. Slaughter is accomplished either by gassing, throat slitting, or—no kidding here—rapid decompression (which causes the bends and, in turn, death).[27] Hogs are also occasionally gassed, a process during which "for thirty seconds the pig gasps and cries, and tries to climb the glass walls of the chamber to escape."[28] Rabbits destined for commercial consumption (whose slaughter is regulated by state rather than federal codes) are killed by "dislocation of the neck." Here is how the Mississippi State Extension Service suggests the job should be done: "The rabbit is held firmly by the rear legs and head; it is stretched full length. Then with a hard, sharp pull, the head is bent backward to dislocate the neck. The rabbit can also be struck a hard, quick blow to the skull behind the ears. A blunt stick or side of the hand is commonly used to incapacitate the rabbit. Both methods quickly render the rabbit unconscious."[29]

This overview of slaughter might seem gratuitously brutal. However, if anything, what I've presented is vastly understated. It doesn't even consider the increasingly rapid pace of slaughter within large abattoirs, which leads to egregious mistakes that compound the suffering and mayhem beyond our imaginations—imaginations that are too often preoccupied with the pleasant imagery of happy animals chilling out on small farms.[30]

Of course, not only the farm animals suffer in slaughterhouses. When we support "humanely" raised meat processed in a commercial slaughterhouse, we are also supporting systematic human suffering. It's difficult for human beings to subject animals to a gauntlet of violence—no matter how rationalized and sterile it may seem—and not suffer some level of psychological fallout. So gruesome is slaughterhouse activity that, as we have seen, even farmers who do not see what it does to the animals they lovingly raised suffer varying degrees of guilt and shame. Imagine, then, how the people in the slaughterhouse experience their work. Sometimes they tell us. One former slaughterhouse employee explained to a reporter, "Today, if somebody gave me a choice of going without a job or working for [a slaughterhouse], I'd go without a job . . . I'd do anything before I'd do that again."[31] Another investigator, upon visiting a pig slaughterhouse, wrote in *The New York Times*, "Slaughtering swine is repetitive, brutish work. . . . Five thousand quit and five thousand are hired every year. You hear people say, 'They don't kill pigs in the plant, they kill people.'" The *Times* editorialized, "What is most alarming at the slaughterhouse is not what happens to the animals. . . . It is what happens to the humans who work there."[32]

Considerable evidence supports these assessments. Statistically, slaughterhouses represent one of the most physically dangerous working environments on earth—if not *the* most. When the main tool of your trade is a knife honed to slice through bone like butter, and when the pace of work requires you to make accurate cuts every three seconds for eight hours a day, chances are good—in fact they're 51 percent—that you'll end up hurt.[33] It's no wonder that slaughterhouse turnover rates are commonly 200 percent for first-time workers.[34] The psychological scars can be equally painful. "The worst thing," recalled a former slaughterhouse employee, "worse than the physical danger, is the emotional toll."[35] Watching sentient beings repeatedly suffer and die is not a mentally healthy activity.[36] One study concludes, "Slaughterhouse work is very likely to have a serious, negative psychological impact on the employees."[37] Given that mental health professionals (and most of the general public) view animal torture as a symptom of psychosis, it stands to reason that workers who witness systematic violence against helpless animals—minute after minute, day after day—become psychologically disturbed. They may react in myriad ways: by brutalizing animals at work, drinking excessively at home, becoming emotionally disengaged,[38] or engaging in antisocial behaviors that impact the surrounding community. The influence of a slaughterhouse on local communities has been explored and appears to be quite pronounced. One study reports, "Slaughterhouse employment increases total arrest rates, arrests for violent crimes, arrests for rape, and arrests for other sex offenses in comparison with other industries."[39] The reason for this is simple, if disturbing: it's hard for people who naturally sympathize with animals—such as a family pet—to spend the day witnessing similarly self-aware animals die. This conclusion is not rocket science. It's common sense.

When we buy animal products from small farms, we are almost assuredly complicit in the slaughter-related problems described above. Through consumer choice, we become responsible for the suffering of animals and humans in the modern commercial slaughterhouse. This complicity is carefully orchestrated out of sight by highly selective efforts to help us "know our food." Highlighting the agriculturally pleasant links in the supply chain, the promoters of sustainable and humane animal agriculture leave death, the part that's most essential to bringing animals to the table, conveniently out of the frame. In a literal sense, it is true: death is just one day. But it is a gruesome day—for everyone involved.[40]

THE MOBILE SLAUGHTERHOUSE

A handful of small-scale animal farmers believe they have discovered a way out of this bind. To avoid the looming slaughterhouse, they've chosen the mobile slaughterhouse unit (MSU). These downsized, USDA-certified-and-inspected operations travel to the farm by appointment and kill a handful of animals a day—maybe eight to ten cows, twenty pigs, or forty chickens. Cooperatives of small farmers will often pool resources to fund this option, which is said to reduce processing costs for small growers. Although few in number, the existing mobile slaughterhouses are hailed by advocates as humane alternatives to the big abattoirs. [41] They are portrayed as rolling centers of salvation for the cause of local meat. The mobile option, however, is weakened by numerous factors that make it virtually impossible for these slaughterhouses (which are also called mobile meat-processing units or mobile harvesters) to offer anything more than a niche option for small animal farmers who want to avoid transferring their animals to the industrial abattoir. It is entirely unrealistic to think that a decentralizing system of animal agriculture could ever depend on this solution as a viable, safe, humane, and scalable alternative to the industrial slaughterhouse and the horrors that it represents.

Small farmers might save processing costs when they hire MSUs, but the macroeconomics of these operations don't work, particularly when pitted against highly consolidated and efficient industrial slaughterhouses. Typical beef slaughterhouses cost $2 million to build and can kill and process about 250 cattle an hour. MSUs, by contrast, can handle 8 to 10 animals a day and cost $150,000 to $400,000 to construct.[42] A commercial slaughterhouse is equipped to safely freeze and store meat for weeks at a time, while an MSU, which is known as a kill-and-chill facility, typically "cannot refrigerate carcasses for longer than a day."[43] Commercial slaughterhouses are able to fulfill their own curing, cutting, and wrapping requirements; MSUs must seek out government-inspected facilities to subcontract these tasks. The offal left after the slaughter is processed into a variety of by-products by industrial slaughterhouses, while MSUs have no standard procedure for offal disposal or processing. As one USDA report notes in a less than confidence-inspiring stipulation, "Farmers can make their own arrangements."[44] In some locations farmers are authorized to churn offal into the soil; in other places they can't, leaving the process subject to the whims of local regulations.[45] Either way, the solid waste can be, according to one report that supports MSUs, "a health or environmental hazard." If all the cattle now in industrial slaughterhouses were slaughtered in mobile units, undisposed offal would become, at the least, a contentious NIMBY issue.

The only USDA report dedicated to addressing how small producers can slaughter animals in a way that meets federal requirements while keeping products local leads to a sobering conclusion. It openly admits that mobile slaughterhouses aren't economically feasible. The study describes small producers of animal products as caught in a catch-22, explaining how "the small-scale characteristics of operations that produce, slaughter, and process locally sourced meat and livestock products inhibit the producer's and processor's ability to benefit from economies of scale." Unless the market-based structure of the meat industry is replaced by a state-run operation willing to place decentralization ahead of profit, this economic logic will be hard for the MSU, or any smaller and more local slaughter unit, to escape. Not that everything can or should be reduced to an economic explanation, but for now the scale of small animal farms, in a landscape of large ones, means that, as the report notes, "their small scale can also compromise the cost-effectiveness of the slaughter process, since more inputs are required per animal relative to larger fixed slaughter plants." It concludes, "Given the current slaughter capacity and the number of units in operation now, the extent to which MSUs can facilitate growth in local markets will be marginal."[46]

Water poses another problem for MSUs. Slaughtering and processing animals requires enormous amounts of it, no matter what the dimensions of the abattoir. A single cow carcass demands a minimum of four hundred gallons of potable water to be properly cleaned and processed.[47] So if an MSU slaughters eight cows in a day (which is normal), it will need at least thirty-two hundred gallons of water. It's not altogether clear where this water will come from. Municipal water systems are an option (not one that I want my tax dollars supporting), as are wells (but not during a drought). Water can also be transported in and out by the MSU in tanks, an option that requires extensive documentation of the water's source and potable quality.[48]

Although thirty-two hundred gallons of water is a hefty volume (what forty households use in a day), perhaps the real issue here is what to do with that water once it passes across the guts and joints of dead farm animals. MSUs generally lack access to municipal sewage facilities. All that the Food Safety and Inspection Service (FSIS) compliance guidelines have to say on this is that the MSU can haul the water away (to where goes unspecified) and that "blood and waste water might be dispersed on the producer's property well away from any stream or drainage, provided the local health

authority permits this dumping.[49] Vague. The MSU opera-
tor is required to provide a letter from the local health authority on wastewater handling at any operational site."[50]
To get a sense of the disaster that would ensue if all the animals we now slaughter in commercial slaughterhouses were
slaughtered in MSUs, imagine (if you can) 13,140,000,000
gallons of pink slaughter water being dumped willy-nilly
across agricultural land in the United States every year. It's
hard not to see this as an environmental problem.

Every mobile slaughterhouse must also somehow manage, without the more efficient disposal resources of an industrial operation, that thicker liquid known as blood. MSUs
slaughter animals outside the mobile unit, usually on a patch
of grass. About 768 pounds of blood are emitted from eight
cows—onto the farm's land.[51] According to an FSIS conference report titled "Considerations Unique to Mobile Red
Meat Slaughter," the pooled blood "creates an insanitary
condition," and "rumen contents are bulky and difficult to
deal with." The swamp of blood and other "inedible materials," according to the report, "attract flies and vermin if not
properly disposed." Because the rules for proper disposal
are ambiguous, an arsenal of insecticides must be deployed
(unless the operation is organic, then mineral oil is used)
to reduce pests that are quick to infest the viscera collect-
ing around an outdoor slaughter site.[52] The runoff not only
consists of multiple gallons of blood, but manure and wastewater are obviously environmental concerns as well, especially if the farm is located adjacent to streams or ponds.
The report simply leaves these issues to be "addressed"
later, while the more official FSIS compliance guide recom-
mends, but does not require, that blood be poured into a

"gravel bed" to prevent pooling and runoff.[53] As with water, we're talking about potentially dangerous volumes. If all cows in the United States were slaughtered outside (as they are in MSUs), a grand total of 25,261,659,000 pounds of blood would soak into American farms annually. That's about fifty-three hundred Olympic-size swimming pools of blood hitting the American agricultural landscape every year.

A final drawback against the MSU "solution" is psychological. The visibility of violence—something that we've seen can have a deleterious psychological effect on human workers—is even more prevalent in the MSU. Although too often downplayed, this factor matters a great deal to slaughterhouse workers. In his book *Every Twelve Seconds*, Timothy Pachirat describes the great lengths that slaughterhouse designers have gone to minimize (almost to the point of invisibility) human exposure to violence and death inside the abattoir. The "distancing and concealment of physically and morally repugnant practices," he writes, is part of the larger effort to "erase individuality and produce in its place a raw material."[54] However, the "technologies of distancing"—which are made possible by the scale, scope, and complexity of the industrial slaughterhouse—are not possible inside an MSU. The "alchemy of deception" (due to the tighter space) is exposed. In its place is the intimate and inescapable fact of death.[55] Promotional videos of MSUs—the ones that are ironically used to show how humane these operations are—do not reassure. They come off as undercover videos taken by animal rights activists. The deaths are every bit as brutal as what happens in the big slaughterhouse. As one former small-scale animal farmer has said, "I don't care if you say a prayer before they're slaughtered or if you simply send

them into the slaughterhouse. Their throats are still slit.
They feel pain. They gasp for air. I can't imagine what goes
through their minds."[56] Neither can I. But whatever it is,
I'm certain it doesn't much matter to them if the slaughterhouse does or does not have wheels.

Supporters of "humane" meat fawn over the way farm animals are treated while they are alive. Don't misunderstand
me: I too enjoy witnessing animals being treated with respect. This treatment appeals to an inner sense of justice,
the kind I was taught at an early age to nurture as integral
to my love of animals. However, when this respect and dignity is violated by the ultimate and final suffering—an intentional and unnecessary death—the celebration somehow
comes to an end. Those who promote the small guys as the
good guys are understandably seduced by the sharp contrast between happy animals on pastures and unhappy animals crammed into crates. Articles such as the one by
Nicholas Kristof (with which I opened this chapter) play on
this highly visible distinction to promote the truth of better
treatment as absolute justification for eating animals. But
it's not.

As we saw with the vignettes of small-scale animal farmers who are generally considered humane farmers, a farm
that treats animals better is in no way exonerated from the
ultimate perpetuation of unnecessary animal suffering at
the slaughterhouse. We have to include the entire cycle of
life *and* death in our analysis of animal agriculture. Not
only do most animals from small farms end up in industrial
slaughterhouses, but the ones that end up in smaller and

supposedly more "humane" operations, as my overview of mobile slaughterhouse units suggests, suffer as a result of inescapable ethical, economic, and environmental problems. At the beginning of the documentary film *Meet Your Meat* the narrator explains, "What you are about to see is beyond your worst nightmares, but for animals raised on modern intensive-production farms and killed in slaughterhouses, it is a cold, inescapable reality."[57] What consumers of animal products from small, pasture-based, nonindustrial farms must realize is that this assessment applies to all meat— their meat as well. Outsourcing slaughter—whether it's to an industrial abattoir or a small mobile unit—entails suffering for animals and people. In most cases that suffering is unnecessary. No amount of humane rhetoric or agricultural pornography should ever be allowed to obscure the fact that, for sentient creatures, death is a fatal form of suffering.

BACKYARD BUTCHERY

I thought I might cry or be too freaked to do the actual
killing. But I'm a meat eater. And I care about the
welfare of animals. Actually, I love animals.
—FRANKIE KIMM[1]

By now it should be clear that unnecessary death poses a problem when it comes to the ethics of eating animals. Still, there's an obvious way to avoid outsourcing the slaughter of animals. There's a way to downplay the complexities highlighted in the last chapter: you can do the deed yourself. Complete the cycle of life and death with your own hands. Of course, there might be barriers to this activity. You cannot sell the outcome of your back-porch butchery in grocery stores or in most farmers' markets, and for reasons that will soon become clear, only the smallest percentage of consumers have the internal fortitude to stomach this method of production. Plus, annoying municipal laws might limit the reach of your knife, or even more annoying organizations, such as Oakland's Neighbors Opposed to Backyard Slaughter, might harass you to find a new, preferably more remote, location to undertake your handiwork. Nonetheless, across the United States, backyard butchery is becoming an increasingly visible and popular manifestation of the localized extremes to which the sustainable food movement is pushing its carnivorous creed of nonindustrial animal consumption.

The popular quest to decentralize slaughter is as political as it is personal. Not only does do-it-yourself killing confront the cold alienation of a denatured food industry, but it confronts a recent history marked by a public health–driven effort to locate slaughterhouses in hinterlands so that urbanized folk can be spared the sensory onslaught of dead and dying animals. The anti-industrial justifications for backyard slaughter might strike us as empowering aspects of a sustainable food movement, aspects reflecting the popular desire to "take back our food system" from dominant corporate powers.[2] In a sense this is true. Backyard butchers are, with the exception of controlling the animal's genetics, taking almost complete control of the meat they choose to eat. Moreover, they aren't shy about touting their efforts in public forums.[3]

In taking charge of their protein source, however, these do-it-youselfers are, as I will argue in this chapter, unwittingly internalizing and abetting the same cynical message-manipulation that marks animal agribusiness. By making violence visible they are numbing themselves to the inherent cruelty of slaughter and perpetuating the same indifference that's necessary to keeping industrial meat production out of the spotlight. My guiding claim in what follows builds on this irony. It does so by showing how enjoying the taste of an animal that dies by our own hands not only entails considerable mistreatment of those animals, but also moral disengagement from the food that backyard slaughterers insist that we do everything possible to get to know. These people think that they are connecting with their emotions and addressing the omnivore's contradiction when they kill their own animals. In fact, they are burying that contradiction in layers of denial.

The material I've gathered on backyard butchery has a blunt way of speaking for itself. You would think the situation would be otherwise. That is, you'd think the perpetrators of such blood-soaked activity would be more inclined to keep matters on the down-low. Instead, the disarming self-promotional tone of backyard butchery revels in the exhibitionist tendencies of this vocal cohort of do-it-yourselfers.[4] For whatever reason, backyard butchers exhaustively archive their experiences in blog posts illustrated with graphic photo essays offering incontrovertible evidence that, yes indeed, violence and death happened and, no question about it, the blogger "did it myself." I had to work hard to suppress effusions of disgust—and sheer bafflement—at such displays as I researched these remarkably revelatory, if grim, documents. In the end, I was able (I think) to back up a bit and approach these posts as a literary critic might approach an alien genre of writing, identifying patterns and defining characteristics, intuiting motives and tracing tropes, all in an effort to make what I hope are useful observations about the problems that plague do-it-yourself slaughter. This chapter will show how personally killing an animal—although a radical departure from the industrial model—not only fails to resolve the omnivore's contradiction, but intensifies it, while, yet again, furthering the essential prerequisite of factory farming: the cultural acceptance of killing and eating animals we domesticated for that very purpose.

The narrative of slaughter revealed in these accounts consists of several commonalities, which I'll briefly outline here to make them easier to identify in the annotated accounts that follow. Like a Shakespearean play, the drama of a slaughter narrative moves through five acts.

- *Act I.* The typical self-slaughter account begins with self-serving justifications and articulations of ulterior motives for the impending death. These justifications and motives stress that the animal about to be slaughtered led a wonderful life. Slaughterers routinely argue that the animal is sacrificing himself so the slaughterer can reclaim the food system from the grasp of corporate evildoers. This idea is imbued with mythical and at times heroic notions of self-sufficiency. People call themselves "homesteaders" and praise the benefits of living off the grid. In some cases, they use slaughter to evoke an awkward legitimation of gender empowerment. Women are, in many cases, declaring to their peers, *Hear me roar*, suggesting, "I can handle inflicting death as well as any man can!" Interestingly, the majority of the accounts I found of backyard chicken slaughterers came from women. This was not the case with pigs or goats. Men killed those beasts.

- *Act II.* Often the narrative includes a poignant reflection about how the slaughterers reacted in the
  moments leading up to the slaughter. These emotions are typically a mashup of remorse, fear, and a
  rather strange sense that what's about to happen
  must happen, inexorably and for the betterment
  of everyone involved, including, somehow, the animal. The word *inevitable* is used a lot in this act.
  Confused as the logic may be, it is one of the more
  honest moments of the drama, offering snippets
  of psychological truth that provide rare insight
  into the emotional complexity of killing animals,
  not to mention the lengths people will go to escape
  its less savory implications.
- *Act III.* Invariably, a vivid description of the act
  follows, a money shot of sorts, emphasizing the
  horrifying messiness of slaughter and the self-
  promoted mental toughness required to deal with
  it. This moment is often punctuated with a picture. Most problematically, perhaps, this thread in
  the story line frequently reveals that the killers
  had absolutely *no clue*, technically speaking, about
  what they were doing. Botched slaughters abound
  in these narratives and are, be forewarned, disturbing. I had to walk away from this act several times
  and catch my breath.
- *Act IV.* Rationalizations emerge as slaughterers create distance between themselves and the corpse
  they produced. These rationalizations are sometimes leavened with nervous humor and, in an especially odd twist, the observation that the animal

did not, alas, mind the experience of dying. In many cases, the slaughterer responds to her butchery by referring to the killing as if it were a mundane and innocuous chore, like cleaning the gutters or knitting a hat. I've made up neither of these comparisons. You will see.

- *Act V.* Finally, the postslaughter pat-on-the-back and way-to-go comments celebrate the death of the animal with high fives and a photo of a man or woman holding the carcass in the air triumphantly before disassembling it into the same parts as would a commercial slaughterhouse. When the celebrations are more muted, butchers are likely to note the many noble reasons for doing what they had to do. "Now I know where my food comes from," they will say. In some cases, the backyard butcher experiences a gradual emotional letdown, a dull calm after a turbulent storm of excitement. But those emotions, in so far as they are verbalized, remain rare. Or at least rarely admitted. As is often the case in the best dramas, it's what's not said that holds the most power.

I could have built this entire book around these narratives. Wanting to delve deeply into all my collected accounts, however, I chose six to represent the whole. Taken together, the butchery profiled in this chapter represents a trend. The butchers are, I would argue, trapped in an unconscious but ingrained habit of moral disengagement. Although well disguised in valiant claims of bravery and activism, not to mention taking back the food system, the slaughtering of an animal that the person often knew well entails creating moral distance.[5] This disengagement has many facets that will repeatedly appear in the narratives that follow. Here's a quick overview of a few key elements.

- The first is marginalization. Dinner-to-be is often reduced in these accounts to an instrument. It's standard, for example, for a slaughterer, before undertaking the slaughter, to note how "it"— referring to the animal—"served us well." This linguistic strategy, one that sometimes has the ring of religious sacrifice, is frequently complemented by physical gestures that reinforce the verbal objectification. One man, for example, inserted his fists into the cavities of plucked and gutted chickens to deploy the carcasses as if they were boxing gloves. A friend took a picture.[6] That's marginalization.

- Marginalization is complemented by distortion. Butchers have a self-protective tendency to shield their psyches from the potentially jarring consequences of spilling blood. This habit is best glimpsed in the rationales that do-it-yourself butchers typically provide, such as "death is just one day," "it didn't know what was coming," and "it was making the ultimate sacrifice." None of these claims makes a whole lot of sense in terms of moral justification. As rationalizations, they would never withstand the most basic ethical scrutiny. But they work well as rhetorical bridges to a mentality of denial. In many respects, their repetition has re-

duced them to meaningless slogans and thus re-
minders that those who eat animals owe their critics
an explanation, rather than—as is so often the
case—the other way around.

- A final aspect of this disengagement is the prevalence of false moral justification. Backyard butchers often come off as heroes because they position
themselves against the nearly unfathomable horrors
of industrial slaughter. This juxtaposition makes
them look noble. But just because one form of unnecessary suffering is less egregious than another
hardly serves as a justification for that action. It
would certainly be better if I arbitrarily punched
an innocent person in the face rather than shot
him with a handgun. The right choice, of course,
would be to do neither. That option, however, is
absent from the stories that follow.

"THIS IS A JUDGMENT CALL WE LIVED TO REGRET"

On Saturday, January 9, the blogger Poor Girl Gourmet en-
titled her post "Not for the Faint: Killing It in 2010." The
"it" referred to was a chicken she'd been raising in her backyard. With the nervous humor typical of these reports,
Poor Girl warned her readers, "If you're offended by blood,
headless chickens, innards, or by discussion of those or any
related subjects, I'd advise you to skip past this post to another
more pleasant one." Justifying what she was now calling the
"New Year's Day Chicken Slaughterfest 2010," Poor Girl
noted how she and her husband aimed to "greatly decrease

the amount necessary to spend on food through the harvest season." She wrote, "At 39 years old . . . I have never slaughtered (or hunted or fished) my own creature for dinner, and it seemed like, so long as I had the option to completely understand what it takes to get that chicken to my plate, I should seize the opportunity." Any indication that Poor Girl ever seriously considered the idea that her quest for self-sufficiency required the exploitation of an animal who didn't want to part with her head was obscured in a popular aspirational claim. "We are," she wrote, "homesteaders." How homesteading absolves causing unnecessary suffering remains unaddressed. Fully addressed, though, is that she and her husband would do all the processing themselves. They would be pioneers. This task they were qualified to accomplish because "our wedding registry yielded a bounty of fancy cookware and small appliances."[7]

Homesteading today might be broad enough a concept to include the accoutrements from a wedding registry, but the essential reality of nonindustrial butchery hasn't changed. You have to know exactly what you're doing to minimize suffering when killing an animal under any circumstances. Poor Girl Gourmet, out in her backyard, hadn't an inkling. Here are the details of her first slaughter:

We came to believe that piercing the chicken's brain would be the least traumatic for all involved. Not so. On that fateful day, JR [husband] placed the chicken into the cone, where it promptly attempted to somersault its way out of The Guillotine, clawing furiously at the sloping plastic walls, pushing its head up as though it might get to see the sun again. JR took a pair of sharp scissors—this is a judg-

ment call we lived to regret; despite having an ice pick given to us for this very purpose, we went with the alternative sharp scissor implement. As it turns out, the chicken brain is a very small target, and one that is easily missed. I went from enthusiastic documentary photographer to gagging wife in the span of approximately a half a second. With camera now useless, and my retching instinct fully intact, JR grabbed his sharpened hedge trimmers. Oh, if only they were truly sharp, those sharpened hedge trimmers. The trimmers did not succeed in lopping off the head of the poor, tortured chicken. Instead, they folded its neck over itself in a zig-zag crease, which did, at least, succeed in breaking its neck, and therefore killing it.

Unless you totally desensitize yourself to what happened here, this is pretty harrowing stuff. Putting the chicken's death aside, what makes the tragedy especially senseless is Poor Girl's evasive emotional reaction to it. Rather than assess the inherent brutality she has inflicted, rather than contemplate an end to keeping and killing chickens, she wrote about how her act was confirmation of her inner tenacity as a strong and independent woman. She reiterated, in essence, her ability to hang with the boys under any and all circumstances, no matter how stereotypically masculine the context. She equated gender empowerment with her botched chicken killing, writing:

While watching JR remove the entrails from "his" chicken, I thought of early adult me, the woman who would enter into what was traditionally an all-men's tavern while the men bounced the c-word off of the walls to intimidate me, and I'd just sit and have my beer to show them I could (it was the law, after all—no discrimination based on gender). Or the woman who frequently had to pull over before leaving Boston for the hour-long drive home, get under her jalopy's hood and pour oil and antifreeze into her engine just to be sure she didn't blow the head gasket. Or the woman who just called it like she saw it (though, looking back, I do suppose there is something to be said for tact, particularly in one's professional life). The woman who was put off by nothing. If I felt it had to be done, it just had to be done. Suddenly, I realized how long-ago and far away that woman was.

Slaughter somehow brought it back. As for the chicken, which these small operations are supposed to treat with dignity, Poor Girl has not a word to offer. The chicken has become a lifeless object in her mind, a means to several ends. It would always be precisely that: an object to promote her security as a woman who could hang with the boys and eat a chicken whose welfare could not have been more thoroughly violated.

Poor Girl's slaughter delivers an even more revealing message. She was consciously engaging in violence that she knew on some level to be problematic. Her repressed belief that animals deserve moral consideration is never explicitly stated (in contrast to, say, Bob's in the last chapter). Nonetheless, the sentiment creeps into her narration. She rejects the "axe-and-stump method" on the grounds that "both of us agreed [it] was too much stress, not just on us, but also on the birds." She initially tried to pierce the bird's brain because, as she thought, "that would be the least traumatic for all involved." She lists the reasons she and her husband weren't slaughtering as often as they had planned to, noting "a lack of desire" as the first reason. *"Can you blame us?"* she added parenthetically. The implication, again, being that killing an animal is an emotionally burdensome job: *Can you blame us for not wanting to slaughter a sentient animal?* It's burdensome because, as she admits, "you're killing something. Something that lives with us." A kind of gallows humor seeps in to defuse this anxiety. Poor Girl repeatedly makes quips to lighten the weight of her action. She asks from the perspective of the bird himself, "Boy, don't you humans want to hunker down inside and make a nice *vegetable* soup?" Regrettably, Poor Girl had no idea that this was the most important question, by far, raised in her post.

The decision to make this event public highlights Poor Girl's slaughter experience as a performance for others to witness and, presumably, react to. Accolades for this botched slaughter poured into Poor Girl's comment box, effectively legitimizing her brutality while reflecting even more sharply its hypocrisies. NatureWriter noted that it's "important for people to remember where food comes from." Given this overriding imperative, this person suggested that the human-food connection could become even tighter if the killing was, no kidding here, *more violent than necessary.* NatureWriter approvingly mentioned friends who advised that the slaughterer "just hold the chicken in your lap and cut its head off because *you stay more connected that way.*" Forget the bird, it's all about your chance to "connect" with your food. A reader named Paula reiterated the benefits of making the violence visible: "I am considering keeping both chickens and rabbits and need to get desensitized somewhat so that I'll be able to slaughter them." Such are the requirements of humane slaughter.

"SHE STARTED TO LOOK LIKE FOOD ONCE THE FEATHERS WERE GONE"

In June 2011 the co-owner of Old Post Farm published the details of her first slaughter. In her introduction, after making "no apologies," she struck the familiar chords of justification for killing her own dinner, in this case a chicken. What followed, she warned with pride, would be gruesome, but "this is where our food comes from"—as if killing a chicken were a prerequisite to eating. She advised that the brutality of slaughter, which she conveyed visually and verbally, was "something you should probably accept." In case readers were concerned about the welfare of the bird, she noted, "This little bird had a good start and was killed quickly and processed with respect"—as if a dead bird cared how it was processed. For all her bluster, this "farmer" did admit to being "extremely nervous and anxious." Not just any kind of anxious but "freaking out kind of anxious." Deep down, no matter how hard she tried to convince herself otherwise, our farmer knew killing her bird was wrong. Her behavior, as much as it affirmed that feeling, was also carefully modulated to obscure it.

Early in the post it became clear that this person understood precious little about chickens. She understood even less about how to slaughter them. The birds she owned and raised on pasture were Cornish X's, an industrial breed of chicken designed to fatten quickly and move slowly and sparingly (they're what Tyson raises by the billions). When allowed to roam across a pasture—something that conscientious carnivores are increasingly demanding—they are prone to leg injuries, hence the condition of this woman's bird, who was hobbling. Throwing the claim to "humane slaughter" into question, moreover, was this woman's decision to forgo a killing cone. She rationalized this choice on the grounds that "we were only doing one little bird." (Not *slaughtering*, but *doing*.) The chosen method of slaughter went unmentioned, but, ominously, she "watched a few YouTube videos" in preparation for the butchery. Doing so, she had "gained confidence."

This slaughterer's report does an especially fine job of delineating the emotional choreography required for do-it-yourself slaughter, a choreography designed to identify the moral implications without internalizing them. She begins by saying of the bird, "She and I bonded a bit." What this meant in the immediate preslaughter moment was that the farmer "carried her around until I calmed enough to do it without shaking." Next, with feigned levity, she "told the duckies to turn away," simultaneously affirming and mocking their emotional sensitivities. Finally, the triumphant coup de grâce: "I did it." Photos accompany each of these steps. In the first, the bonding phase, she's holding the bird and making a kind of "I'm freaking out!" face, as if she were about to board a roller coaster. In the second, her pet ducks hover under a hutch in the backyard. In the third, instead of a dead bird, readers are treated to a photo of a blood-splattered tree stump—the "money shot" informing us that an ax was probably the weapon of choice (an especially cruel and inhumane way to kill a chicken) and the deed was done.

Inadvertently, the pervading theme running throughout this narrative, forced humor notwithstanding, is that the chicken's death mattered. It was not to be taken lightly. Why else act scared? Why else be "freaking out anxious"? Why else instruct the "duckies" to look away? I realize that this blow-by-blow conceit is intended by the author to convey tongue-in-cheek humor. But if a person feels the need to be tongue in cheek over something as serious as death, doesn't it indicate that the act carried moral weight that the individual had yet to face?

The "farmer's" response to the aftermath of the slaughter further confirms the need to emotionally and morally disengage from the violence. The writer's explicit observations reveal an implicit unease as well as the need to protect herself psychologically. The author seems acutely aware of what she's done. She writes of her bird, "She started to look like food once the feathers were gone." Processing the carcass into parts, she notes how critical it was not to contaminate the flesh by accidentally cutting "her" intestines. (The bird somehow gained a gendered identity *after death*.) Careful processing was also important so "her life wouldn't have been a waste," a comment that reveals the farmer's beliefs that (a) the chicken's life had meaning that could have been wasted, and that (b) her decision to eat the chicken is what gave the bird's life meaning. Notably, the butchers in these accounts rarely call themselves butchers. That term carries baggage. Par for this course, our slaughterer wrote that, after successfully dismembering her bird, "I felt like a real *farmer*." Once the guts were cleaned up and the deed done, the butcher-cum-farmer was left with a question, one that yet again confirms the repressed but emotionally vexed nature of slaughtering an animal unnecessarily. She asked, "Is it bad that at the end I said, 'Wow! She looks like real food!'?"

Readers' remarks seemed tailor-made to snuff out any residual anxiety that the farmer may have felt. "You are awesome and too funny," wrote Kim, assuring the slaughterer that the "the only really 'gross' picture is of the [sic] her alinging [sic], plucked wtill [still?] with feet." This is a revealing (if garbled) observation. When the animal is alive and bodily intact, nothing about the situation is "gross." When the animal is dead and dismembered across the butcher's table, her organs arranged like chess pieces, still nothing is "gross." Only when the object (chicken carcass) reveals residual evidence of the subject (a live chicken) it once was—through the presence of her feet—do matters become "gross."

Another commenter chimed in with "What a great job!" and "What a sense of accomplishment!"—presumably referring not to physically killing a chicken but to overcoming the psychological anxiety about doing it. Typical of these comment sections, the writer implicitly referred to the emotional nature of slaughter but highlighted the underlying reason that made such a sacrifice ultimately worthwhile. "I bet," she wrote, "it's going to taste delicious."

"HOW FAST . . . THE ANIMAL TURNS INTO THE RECIPE"

In May 2010, Jenna, who describes herself as an "8–5 corporate employee," stepped into her "personal bubble of agricultural ecstasy" (her backyard "freehold") and deemed the day ideal for killing chickens. Several red flags immediately emerge in Jenna's account. One is her observation that her birds evolved from "cute fluffy yellow chicks" into "white giants" not as a result of pecking grubs and eating kitchen scraps (which is an integral part of the backyard-bird narrative), but due to "two fifty pound bags of feed." A 50-lb bag of feed is likely the same feed used by industrial producers of caged birds and a reminder that what appears to be off the industrial grid is, for convenience, often directly linked to it (more on this in a later chapter). None of this bothered Jenna, who, as she stepped into the backyard to kill a bird, "felt as excited as a first date."

Jenna provides two rationalizations for slaughtering her chicken. They contradict each other and further reveal the moral schizophrenia in slaughtering an animal we know to be capable of suffering. First, she asks readers "who think this [slaughter] may be morbid or sad" to just get over it because her chickens are "100% food animals." In fact, she wrote, they would physically deteriorate if "they aren't killed swiftly for dinner"—indeed, her Rock Cornish hens were designed to get fat and be slaughtered, yet another genetic miracle perpetrated by the industrial food complex. For this inheritance they were, she suggested, better off treated as a commodity with a "use by" date than a living being with intrinsic worth.

A paragraph later, however, Jenna speaks of her dozen genetically fattened chickens not as objectified "food animals" but as sentient beings worthy of being treated as emotionally aware creatures. She writes, "Instead of growing up in a dark factory with 10,000 other birds these guys were living with 12 [birds] under my careful watch. . . . They were living exactly the life I felt farm animals should live: outdoors, on green grass, seeing sunlight, and chasing flies." A Rock Cornish, like a Cornish X, has no business on pasture for the very reasons Jenna mentions—their genetics don't support natural behavior. Nonetheless, this detail doesn't prevent her from arguing that her bird was, simultaneously, an object to be killed and a subject to be nurtured.

Then comes the slaughter. While many bloggers stress the messiness of slaughter as a way to underscore personal toughness, Jenna, interestingly enough, took the opposite approach: she opted for an implausibly sanitized depiction. After choosing "the fattest bird," she "held it by its feet (which lulls them into submission), and walked over to the chopping block." The notion that yanking a chicken by her feet instills submission—per Jenna's parenthetic remark—is a common fallacy. Picking up a bird by her feet does not instill submission. It instills terror. This terror is so striking that the bird, with blood rushing to her head, momentarily freezes, a reaction that could be exacerbated by aspiration and collapsing lungs.[8] Furthermore, the use of a "chopping block" instead of a "killing cone" reveals a basic disregard for animal welfare. This disregard is confirmed in the apex of Jenna's account: "I thanked the bird, almost at a whisper, then with one swift hatchet move all was done. No squawk, no pain." It is hard to decide which is more surreal: thanking an animal before whacking off her head or stating with such certitude that such an experience creates "no pain." I've obviously never had it happen, but something tells me that decapitation would involve a degree of discomfort.

Jenna's moral disengagement was as swift and transformative as her slaughter. Think about why. You've just grabbed a live bird by her feet, a bird you know has a unique person-ality, and you have just reared back with an ax and brought it down on her soft neck. The bird thrashes and blood splat-ters, and now you have to make sense of this mess. You might not *think* you have to make sense of it, but unless you have the emotions of a stone, the experience will likely lodge in a dark corner of your hippocampus and demand attention.

So you say your action didn't hurt the animal. Or you note how you said "thank you" to sanctify the act. But the ultimate rationalization that Jenna chose is the most com-mon. It's one that's endorsed by the food movement and the culture that celebrates it: "How fast," she writes, "the ani-mal turns into the recipe." Food! Indeed, what follows the kill is a gush of rhetoric culminating not only in a meal but in the observation that if you wish to "question the meaning of your existence" and "know how you fit into the story," you need only "buy a chick for [$]1.75 at Tractor Supply and follow a recipe." And if you think this recipe does not blend cognitive dissonance with a dash of denial, note Jenna's penultimate observation: "I was impressed with myself for pulling it off, but also shocked that what had yellow feet and clucked a few hours earlier now was on the end of my fork. I felt the same way I did when knitting my first hat." So there's an example of connecting with your food.

The commentary on Jenna's blog was unusually exten-sive. More than other accounts, this one demonstrated how the killing of an animal led to vicarious experiences that inspired readers to objectify animals in the name of oppos-ing factory farming. Consider the reaction of Paula, who wrote, "It's so funny. On one post you show adorable duck-lings or bunnies, and on another you write about dispatching a broiler [chicken] and cooking and eating it." This contradiction, which might have sparked a reconsideration of Jenna's "dispatching," had the opposite impact on Paula: "I go from dreading the idea of slaughtering poultry and rabbits to liking this idea very much." What a fascinating, if depressing, interpretation, one that confirms my earlier observation that killing animals undermines the human potential for compassion in ways we might not fully appreciate.

Paula was hardly alone in celebrating violence. Small farm girl, another commenter, expressed her empathy with Jenna's moral desensitization through culinary pleasure. "It was hard for me to kill the animals too," small farm girl admitted. "Chickens, rabbits; I just couldn't make myself do it. Then one day, like you, I told myself I was going to do it. So when it was time to deal the death blow, I said a little prayer. It was hard to do at first, *but the taste later made up for it.*" Another commenter wrote, "While I definitely dread the idea of the kill when we finally get chickens, I'm fairly certain that the *flavor of the meal* and satisfaction of knowing you raised that pure, healthy meat yourself will make it totally worth it." That Jenna equated killing her chicken with knitting a hat went unmentioned.

A reader named Sarah thought all this angst over death was a useless expenditure of sentiment: "I don't think the first kill is that traumatic. It becomes just another step in the process of reaching your goal." As Sarah suggests, Jenna also elicited from her readers a collective endorsement of death and violence and a desire to replicate it on their own. "Oh man," said Aimee, "that is so awesome, and I cannot help but feel just a tiny bit jealous." Another wrote, "You have inspired me to buy the rocks [chickens] for meat." Molly thought the account of the killing was "moving, touching, inspiring." Funny Ernie wrote, "I love this post. Our meat birds are six weeks old. I can't wait to harvest them." Zucchinimom too was among the converted: "I have seriously wanted to raise meat birds and I think we just might do it now!"

"ARLENE THRASHED FOR A BIT AND WENT STILL. MY HANDS WERE COVERED WITH BLOOD"

In September 2011, the writer for the blog *Working on Me* killed a chicken for the first time. After discovering that a hen she'd purchased for egg production was in fact a rooster (a common problem—sexing chickens is difficult business), the blogger decided that she'd "cull the rooster" herself. She did this despite her friends' frantic pleas to "give Arlene to someone who lives in the country." When one friend said, "I could never butcher one of my pets," the blogger simply retorted that the comment "pissed me off." Inspirations for butchering Arlene were, for the conflicted future butcher, easy to come by. One came from Barbara Kingsolver, whom the blogger quoted as saying, "You can leave the killing to others and pretend it never happened, or you can look it in the eye and know it." Another came from Michael Pollan, who buttressed the author's backbone by writing, "It seemed to me not too much to ask of a meat eater, which I was then and still am, that at least once in his life he take some direct responsibility for the killing on which his meat-eating depends." Completing the triad of influence was Novella Carpenter, whose book *Farm City* quoted the claim that "doing our own killing . . . teaches us humility." Collectively, these famous writers, through their work, convinced our initially skeptical butcher that she had no other choice but to kill Arlene because "slaughtering one's own meat has become a right [*sic*] of passage for Americans who are serious about food."

What comes through this account, though, is decidedly not a sense of empowerment. Instead, considerable doubt is followed by a protective layer of indifference. Novella Carpenter notwithstanding, not much humility is evident either. Despite whispering the motivational speeches of Kingsolver, Pollan, and Carpenter like an acolyte at the altar, the blogger ultimately found herself in a fit of confusion over what she was doing. She was unsure why she was killing her rooster. "What exactly is one supposed to glean from the experience?" she wrote. "A biology lesson? A deeper reverence for the animals that die for our dining pleasure? A decision to give up eating flesh altogether?" Her inner dissonance intensified as the day of slaughter approached. Although admitting "I kind of wanted to kill a chicken," the blogger first instructed members of her household not to touch the chicken for weeks (to deaden emotional ties) and then, as the day arrived, called upon her father, "who put himself through college working at a slaughterhouse," to do the awful task. The details of the killing confirm that her father, for all his supposed experience, was equally unsure about how to humanely kill a chicken. What follows was certainly more traumatic for the bird than had he gone to an industrial slaughterhouse:

At the sight of us, the chicken raced around the yard, squawking furiously, until, after a flying tackle, he was landed. A worthy foe, that bird. I let my father do the hard part. I held Arlene down on a stump and watched my father cut off his head with a pair of gardening shears. Arlene thrashed for a bit and went still. My hands were covered with blood.

One senses that the aftermath of the slaughter left this gradually troubled pseudo-butcher with more than a twinge of guilt. Trying hard to pat herself on the back, she wrote, "I didn't go 'ick' so I guess I get a gold star." She dutifully made chicken soup with Arlene's carcass but was "less than gung-ho about the meal." Her eight-year-old son assured her, "We're honoring Arlene by not wasting her." But our blogger didn't seem convinced. Although what she did was, she thought, "certainly cleaner and more humane than what happens at a Tyson plant," in the end the "paltry experience . . . didn't do it for me." The only way that her act made sense to her was if she framed it in "the gory whole of human history." In that context, she concluded, "Killing Arlene was messy and mundane." It was "like cleaning the gutters." One wishes she'd just chosen that option in the first place.

"THE PIG CONVULSED FOR ABOUT FIFTEEN SECONDS, THEN WAS STILL"

Backyard butchers slaughter pigs as well as chickens. On May 10, 2010, Jordan, who runs the blog *Front Yard Farmer*, slaughtered her own pigs in her own backyard with her own tools and her own "small army" to assist her with what indeed was, as she noted, "some very dirty work."[9] Familiar expressions of fear and doubt pervade Jordan's opening paragraphs. Because of the traumatic nature and scale of the homegrown butchery, she admitted that she was "afraid to write" about the experience. After an attempt to situate pigs on a vague hierarchy of existential significance (e.g., "They are smarter and much bigger than rabbits"), she delivers the clearest expression of selective moral consideration I've yet to find in these accounts:

> *There's a reason why animals raised for meat are kept in inhumane conditions. A pig in a cramped pen with a con-crete floor isn't going to get a chance to develop a personality, or at least express it. And it's much easier to kill a pig with no personality than the one that chews on the cuff of your jeans and rolls over to be scratched with a rake.*

Jordan's awareness not only of her pigs' sentience, but of her own dilemma, helps explain why, in the week leading up to the slaughter, she "woke up several times in the middle of the night, sweating, my ears ringing with the imagined sound of screaming pigs and blood." Still, for all the terror she experienced in anticipation of slaughtering an animal whom she knew intimately, Jordan bucked up: "I couldn't put off the inevitable any longer." How this impending event was inevitable never crosses Jordan's mind. But Jordan un-deniably knew that what she was preparing to do came with ethical consequences.

Slaughtering a massive animal not only requires bucking up, it requires planning. Jordan seemed to have taken all precautions. She sterilized steel tables, found some gambrels, sharpened her knives, and had a friend bring over a chain saw to cover the sounds of the .22 rifle that Jordan would use to get to know where her food came from. Then came the moment of truth—"Albert revved the chainsaw, Andy loaded the gun, and I grabbed some grain" to lure the pig into position—and Jordan's nightmares culminated in the reality of this experience:

> As soon as we approached, the first pig raised his head at the sound of the grain shaking in the can and that was the last thing he saw. The bullet from the .22 hit him point blank between the eyes. The pig convulsed for about fifteen seconds, then was still. The chickens (dirty birds) ran straight to the blood that dripped on the ground and started drinking it. Then we dragged the carcass to a cleaner spot and Andy stuck a knife between the collarbone and the neck and cut the aorta, sending a final gush of blood out onto the grass.[10]

It is difficult to imagine how, in the wake of slaughter, Jordan's obvious concern for her pigs coexisted peacefully with this violence. Jordan took solace in how well she'd treated her pigs while they were alive (thereby hiding behind the omnivore's contradiction). She wrote of his two pigs: "They . . . had a good time rooting and flopping in the mud, and I made those activities available to them almost every evening. I gave them the ability to just be pigs, which is, I think, what every animal wants: the freedom to express the traits of their species and their personalities." That they did not want to die eventually faded from Jordan's moral perspective. As she lost herself in the logistics of processing the pigs, she sensed that "the cloud of worry that had been weighing me down all week had been lifted." Two weeks of rendering lay ahead, but it was, she exclaimed, "time to celebrate, because the hardest part, psychologically at least, was over." It was time, she now declared, "to break out the mimosas."

"I FELT A BIT FUNNY AFTERWARDS"[11]

"Today, July the 12th 2009," wrote Danny, "I slaughtered my first goat." Danny's justifications for doing so built upon the cliché that "it was time to know where my meat came from." Aware that carnivores of the developed world were "disconnected . . . from where our meat comes from," Danny believed that by slaughtering a goat (with a knife that would prove to be too dull for the task) he would lend deeper meaning to "the ambiguity of the plastic wrapped meat displayed in such an appealing fashion throughout chilly meat aisles." His plan was to visit a nearby goat farm, choose a victim (male because "male meat is better"), feed him for a few days, and then kill him. Danny's plans would go badly awry, and his emotions would follow.

As Danny toured the goat farm to choose "his" goat, his general misunderstanding of these animals became immediately evident. "We entered a very spacious cage filled with about 40 goats, which, for whatever reason, were mostly huddled together," he wrote. The possibility that the goats were huddled together because a strange man (who wanted to slaughter one of them) had entered their pen never crossed his mind, but these goats were almost certainly huddling because of their basic shelter-seeking tendencies.[12] Danny's failure to understand even rudimentary goat behavior didn't prevent him from declaring himself to be gifted with "an innate ability to judge goats." After loading his chosen goat into a truck, however, Danny did become increasingly aware of how this experience might feel from the goat's perspective. As the goat "mehhed" in the back of truck, he noted that the goat "truly and understandably seemed sad to leave his world of friends, lady goats, open fields, and grass." As the magnitude of his forthcoming act sunk in, Danny admitted, "It was tough knowing that I had ripped this goat away from his life and was about to kill him." Before the moral heft of this observation sank in, Danny told himself that he should "take comfort in the fact that this goat led his life like a goat should." Then he projected happiness upon a terrified animal in order to assuage the impact on a guilty human: "He settled in and seemed to enjoy the very bumpy ride." Of course, no farm animal, even a goat, enjoys being jostled around the back of a truck.

One of the more compelling and confused reflections on do-it-yourself slaughter that I've encountered followed. When slaughter day arrived, Danny sat down next to his goat, fed him some leaves, and "began to speak to the goat," saying, "I am going to slaughter you in a few minutes and you must understand it is not because I hate you or disrespect you; quite the contrary really. You were put on this earth for two reasons, [to] become dinner and create more goats. You have achieved one with honor (or so the farmer tells me) and you will also achieve the second with honor." At this point, "the goat made eye contact with me." Danny continued his speech: "Goat you will not die at the hands of a stranger on an assembly line, you lived a great life for a goat, filled with fresh grass, room to wander and many goat girlfriends. You will be slaughtered by me, the man who is hand-feeding you at this very moment and your new friend." These were the last words the goat would hear. Within minutes, his "new friend" committed the following atrocity.

I put the knife to the throat of the goat (who for the moment, besides the occasional kicks, was laying [sic] quite calmly), and began to firmly saw at the flesh on his neck. After about seven back and forth sawing motions to the jugular (it is usually three but my inexperience and the relatively un-sharp knife made it a bit tougher), I cut the key veins and arteries and blood began to squirt projectily in a continuous, chunky stream into a wall nearly a meter away. It was at this point the goat let out a horrible scream. It was pain combined with a desperate cry for life. It still rings in my ears, it was truly the sound of death. Without a doubt, that noise was the hardest part of the experience.

The blood continued to squirt everywhere as the goat kicked and jerked for life. Blood was all over me including, literally, on my hands. After about 30 seconds from the first cut, the goat was still bleeding, jerking, and making gargled noises; to be sure to end the suffering, I cut deeper into the goat's exposed throat, nearly decapitating it. I then put one hand on it's heart and one on it's belly—looked it in the eyes and willed it to die. After a while his breathing slowed, his yells became murmurs, his eyes gently closed, and then . . . Nothing. The goat was dead.

Now it was time for Danny to process the experience: "I felt a bit funny afterwards. But there was no real flood of emotion." There was, though, a "dead goat laying [*sic*] inches from my bloody sandals [and] all I could think to say was . . . sorry goat, sorry." What Danny found to be "surprisingly relieving" was the realization that the goat, who "less than an hour ago happily munched leaves from my hand was now beginning to resemble food rather than a living, breathing animal." The power of "know your food" rhetoric on Danny's thinking was such that the mere use of the word *food* was enough to erase any doubt that what he'd done was wrong. Well, maybe not every doubt. "Some people," he wrote, "believe the goat will attempt to haunt me." Trying hard to convince himself otherwise, Danny explained, "I truly believe the goat has forgiven me." He made this assessment after he "tried to wash the smell of blood off my hands." In this last effort he was, Danny poignantly noted, "unsuccessful."

I could carry on with these narratives. I could carry on with narratives that are even more gruesome, more irresponsible, and more psychologically troubling than the ones here. No matter how many stories I included, though, an unavoidable problem would remain. When we're talking about documents as idiosyncratic as a backyard slaughter accounts, there's no way to avoid what critics will identify as a "sampling error." Is there a self-selecting bias in these accounts? I'm sure there is, although I cannot say in what direction. Still, what we can do, if we want to start understanding the deeper meaning of backyard butchery, is seek general patterns within the stories that have been made available for public consumption—bias and sampling errors notwith-standing. The stories that I've chosen to present in this chap-ter demonstrate a consistent and representational range of psychological and rhetorical tactics designed to clear ethical space for guiltless killing. These tactics appear repeatedly, throughout scores of accounts, and without any indication that they are in any way exceptional. So, if other backyard butchers out there approach their work differently, frame their handiwork within a different set of attitudes and prac-tices, and collectively deliver an entirely different message (and I'm sure there are), then I'll leave it up to other critics to uncover, present, and analyze their work, provide their own accounts, and correct my bias. I would love to be proven wrong. That said, let's revisit what I've discovered about backyard slaughterers and highlight why this highly personal approach to sourcing meat fails to offer a meaningful escape from the industrial production of animals.

These slaughter narratives demonstrate the convergence of three related sentiments: an awareness of animal sentience, discomfort with the idea of killing an animal, and the insis-tence that the killing was done to counter the influence of factory farming. Examples of each quality appear, in one form or another, in every post. When a slaughterer advises that "to prevent detachment I give generic names like 'extra crispy' and 'deep fried,'" he is, whether he's aware of it or not, confirming his awareness of animal sentience.[13] When a slaughterer says that "admittedly, slaughter is not an ap-petizing process," she is, whether aware of it or not, con-firming a feeling of unease.[14] And, finally, when a slaughterer justifies her act on the grounds that her animal had "a far better life than the meat I can get at the grocery store," she is, whether aware of it or not, justifying her act in relative rather than absolute terms. The problem here is that the first two qualities—awareness of sentience and personal discomfiture—do not lead to what they *should* logically lead to: a decision to spare the animal. That choice is the only way that the third quality—the quest to combat factory farming— would ever have any potency as an agent of change. Big Ag could not care less if you butcher your own animal. After all, they do a hell of a lot butchering themselves. Their only concern is that you keep eating the outcome of that butchery.

Evidence of the disconnection between the method of slaughter and the end goal of reform is evident in the most common excuse articulated by backyard butchers for killing the animals they raise. That excuse, in one iteration or another, goes something like this: "death is a part of life," "dead is dead," "they all want to live and they all will die," "it's a part of life," "death is only one day," and "everything dies." Every time the excuse is made it is preceded by the reminder that the animal "led a good life."

Advocates of backyard slaughter, in their repeated emphasis on the quality of their animals' lives before death, echo another set of voices from the world of animal production. These other voices similarly claim that they are "stewards of the animals," that they are always working to "enhance animal well-being," that they have a "proactive commitment to . . . animal well-being issues," and that they are dedicated to "proper handling." As this other group sees it, death is also one day, dead is also dead, and death is also a part of life. The difference, though, is that these latter voices are those of Tyson Foods (from which all the quotes in this paragraph come from). The organization with whom our backyard slaughterers share so much common rhetorical ground is one of the largest industrial producers of animals in the world. The similarity of the rhetoric reminds us of the similarity of the result: both groups benefit from dead animals.[15]

That brings us to the rub of butchering your own animal. The act is a crude, microcosmic approximation of what routinely takes place on an industrial scale. In fact, when the person doing the killing is inexperienced, which is often the case, or when something goes awry, as it often does, the slaughter is more inhumane than the cold but comparatively merciful efficiency of a commercial slaughterhouse. People who raise and butcher their own animals claim that they are opting out of—and, in turn, challenging—the business of industrial agriculture. Not so. As I have found through scores of cases and tried to show through representative samples here, backyard slaughterers affirm the most disturbing qualities that they claim to oppose. "Dead is dead" is equally true in the backyard as in agribusiness.

5

HUMANE CHICKEN

It doesn't even take a minute for things to become utterly sad and regrettable.

—JJ

The abstract moral inconsistency inherent in the omnivore's contradiction might have, at best, academic appeal. Many of us are easily able to recognize and appreciate moral inconsistency without necessarily feeling any urgency to rectify that inconsistency in our daily lives. For many thoughtful consumers, change happens as the result of an accumulation of concrete facts—an accumulation that reaches a tipping point and initiates a new way of looking at the world. The accumulation of concrete facts about factory farming led many of us to understand the moral failure of that system and to make decisions to support nonindustrial alternatives. The following three chapters depart from abstract argumentation about the morality of raising and slaughtering animals and focus instead on the concrete facts—the data, if you will—of agricultural life. Rather than exposing the depressing facts of factory farming, I'll highlight the hidden flaws of nonindustrial farming.

I'll start with chickens and eggs.

On March 13, 2013, mzgarden, an experienced keeper of backyard chickens, logged onto the website homesteading-today.com "to vent a little." It had been a rough week on the family farm. The farmer explained, "So, first we had to cull a juvenile, then a little chick died, then we find a juvenile hen in the coop this morning cockadoodle-doodling for all she, oops, he's worth (down one more future layer), a hawk got one this afternoon and one of the other chicks has pasty butt (a clogged cloacal vent)." This forlorn homesteader finished her post by adding, "I know it's nothing unique . . . but gee, maybe we could space this out a bit. I feel like I need to cover their pasture with a safety bubble. Maybe I'll crawl in too."[1]

Within minutes of her mini rant other small chicken farmers chimed in with similar assessments of doom. A chicken keeper going by the name Travifive explained, "I brood mine in my sunroom for the first batch of the year just in case we get a cold snap. Well, with these highs I've opened the windows to let in the fresh air (it gets kinda stale in there with 125 chicks) and of course I forgot they [were] open when I checked on them before bed. That coupled with a bout of diarrhea in some of the Cornish cross [an industrial breed of hen] from switching feed too fast ended in six laying hens and seven CCs dead." He concluded, "My own stupidity can be quite annoying." Mulegirl had her own chicken problems, lamenting, "We lost a laying hen to who-knows-what in the middle of the day last Friday, so it seems like it's one of those weeks."[2] Grandpepere joined the chorus, reporting, "I found 3 chickens dead inside of our coop this morning," an especially distressing discovery given that "2 chickens were killed by coyotes last week."[3] As we will repeatedly see in the pages ahead, mzgarden was right: none of this was "unique."

There's the bucolic image of the small-scale chicken farm and then there's the reality. The reality is messier than we're led to believe. It's hampered by problems that compromise any quest—no matter how small or seemingly attentive to welfare—to offer consumers a consistently humane and safe alternative to factory-farmed chickens or eggs. Consumers who oppose the industrial production of chickens are constantly urged to accept the imagery, ignore the reality, and eat guiltlessly. They're told to source their chicken products from their own hens or to buy only from small and local chicken farms. Family farms. Artisanal farms. Organic farms. Pastured farms.

The reasons for making this choice appear to be simple enough. Hens raised in industrial compounds are treated with ceaseless brutality. They're crammed into cages with four to nine other birds, forced into molting through periodic denial of food to the point of starvation (to speed egg production), fed industrial feed saturated with vaccines and antibiotics and growth hormones, deprived of essential nutrients, mutilated (through beak clipping) to prevent fighting, and denied a decent spate of sleep under the hard glare of ceaseless light.[4] A battery farm, as this operation is called, represents the deepest level of factory-farm hell. Here hens become the moral equivalent of machines. Machines that after churning out eggs are churned into dog food. Nobody wants this.

Eggs and chicken parts obtained from nonindustrial

settings are portrayed to come from veritable Gardens of Eden. These farms are seen to be more humane, safer, healthier, and free of the relentless despair of factory farming. Let's be clear: eggs sourced from smaller farms where birds are not crammed into cruel levels of confinement are eggs from birds who have lived a better life than those raised in battery cages. No argument on this point. The difference between being able to stretch your wings and not being able to stretch your wings is, I imagine, incalculable.

But the discussion does not end on the basis of this single distinction. It would be a terrible mistake to think that chickens producing eggs and meat off the factory farm are necessarily doing so in environments that are acceptably humane, safe, and healthy. Drawing on the testimony of small-scale chicken producers themselves, this chapter highlights the less obvious flaws of small-scale chicken farming—flaws that reveal habits and practices most concerned consumers would find unacceptable, if not abhorrent. The "happy" alternatives to factory-farmed eggs actually have more in common with them than the virtuous, relatively problem-free alternatives consumers assume them to be.

The problems outlined in the pages ahead are symptoms of our failure to confront the omnivore's contradiction. The deception at the heart of this dilemma should by now be familiar: consumers condemn factory farming on the partial grounds of treating animals poorly; we seek alternative animal products that are sourced from farms that are less industrialized and supposedly more humane; the ultimate

outcome of exploiting animals for food we don't need remains the perpetuation of unnecessary suffering and death;
and, finally, this contradiction (caring for and killing animals at once) is obscured in platitudes rather than confronted by sound moral logic. This scenario is the trap in
which sustainable animal agriculture currently finds itself,
a trap that ensures factory farms will continue to dominate
the production of animal goods.

The result of this unthinking process is that conscientious carnivores—although they claim to want to "know
their food"—get to feel good about eating animals they
never knew at all. While the animals may enjoy slightly
better conditions, in the end they are treated in ways all
too reminiscent of the factory farms we're so eager to condemn. We tend to identify overmedication, indifference to
animal welfare, unnatural living conditions, bodily mutilation, exposure to dangerous pathogens, and the use of
toxic chemicals as defining features of factory farms. But
these qualities are evident on small chicken and egg farms
as well.

ENVIRONMENTAL MIMICRY

Every problem identified in this chapter eventually comes
down to what we might call the arrogance of environmental
mimicry. Most domestic chickens, despite their radically manipulated genetics, behave (when provided the chance to do
so) the same way as their wild counterparts.[5] When egg farmers declare that they are raising chickens under "all natural"
conditions, or that their "chickens are getting to behave as

chickens," they are claiming that their birds live in an ecosystem conducive to their natural inclinations, that they are living a rough approximation of the life of their wild ancestors. This is a stretch. Consider the way wild jungle fowl live and you'll quickly see that a farmer could never contrive an environment reflective of a chicken's natural home.

In the wild, jungle fowl (who are native to the bamboo forests of Thailand) can live up to thirty years. They form tight cliques of a dominant rooster and two to five hens. These rooster-led harems are consistently on the go, interacting with other flocks (when it's safe to do so) to enhance security, reinforce hierarchy, improve breeding and feeding opportunities, and maximize playtime. Their seasonal itinerancy and social visits can play out over a twenty-mile range. Jungle fowl sleep at night within dense bamboo patches, about fifteen to twenty feet off the ground, with protective foliage above and below them offering an "easy exit in case of night prowlers." They are precise and insistent about this requirement. When it's time for a drink, dominant males lead females to a local stream, perching above their precious harems to keep an eye out for predators. When it's time to defecate, birds will often remove to one location (to avoid disease) and do their business there; when it's time to raise chicks, mothers will go to yet another location, often in isolation from the flock; when it's time to nest, roosters will seek out and approve appropriate sites for different hens.

This carefully choreographed system of movement—this behavioral topography of multiflock feeding, breeding, brooding, and protection—takes place across the forest floor. This matrix of activity requires patches of forest where there is a density of branches above small streams, and in regions where the predators are predictable, mostly avoidable, and practically known by name. The jungle fowl's natural home is a unique environment, one that could never be replicated by a "humane certified" farmer in Washington or Oakland.[6]

The essential behavior of chickens—what they eat, where they poop, when they mate, and how they protect themselves—was forged over thousands of years in this habitat. Chickens, domesticated or not, thrive best when they explore widely.[7] Their explorations, which demand considerable geographical range and diversity, foster their ability to make judgments about what to eat, with whom to interact, and about what specific chicken calls might signify. These explorations also provide opportunities for mothers to instruct chicks how to forage, perch, and range. A critical repertoire of skills designed to keep chickens well fed, as safe as possible, and attuned to natural surroundings—that is, to enable chickens to be chickens—is best honed under conditions in which social and familial relationships proceed with minimal human interference. That chickens can recognize upward of a hundred other chickens by face, create mental images sharp enough to locate long-hidden items, and even demonstrate an ability to anticipate future events reflects a genetic heritage forged in the dense bamboo forests of Southeast Asia.[8]

When chickens are condemned by Western consumers as "birdbrains," it is often forgotten that, even though these birds remain highly intelligent in domesticated settings (where they can recognize up to twenty human faces), they've been denied access to the natural environments in which their bird brains were made rather brilliant. When farmers move hens from factory farms to backyard farms, consumers assume that chickens are being placed in more comfortable ecosystems. In most cases, they almost certainly are. But, based on this relative improvement, we cannot simply conclude that chickens are able to maximize their welfare or intelligence under conditions that appear natural to us. Nor can we assume that the smaller system is any safer. In fact, the range of problems from which chickens routinely suffer on small alternative farms confirms something that we rarely take the time to consider: what humans conceptualize as natural is anything but natural to the birds, who continue to suffer under conditions that supposedly enable hens to live the good life. One should never assume that, just because a bird is spreading her wings and pecking grubs on a pasture, her surroundings aren't deeply contrived and ineffably foreign to her "birdness."

One chicken keeper, Lynn, seemed to get this point. She noticed that when her birds were on pasture, they seemed stressed. She wrote, "Freeranging involves risk, that's for sure. We have quite a few trees on our property and the girls seem to gravitate to the areas of protection. I have noticed them at times, RUNNING, over open areas, to get to another area of tree coverage."[9] Despite this behavior, Lynn reasoned, "I have had a few losses, but overall, I think the benefits outweigh the risks. My girls are so much happier when they are out and about."[10] Sounds great. But would the chickens see it that way?

"CAME HOME TO CARNAGE"

Death *is* a part of life. Predators kill jungle fowl in the wild. But undomesticated birds are not, like their free-range counterparts, set up for predation. They maintain access to their natural defense mechanisms. This is not the case for hens raised on small farms. Typically, nonindustrial farms alternate pasture time with coop confinement. Pastures rarely have the foliar density and roosting space that birds require to feel safe and protect themselves. Coops, when predators are afoot, can become veritable torture chambers for trapped layers. "They are," astutely explained one small-scale egg farmer, "subjected to the environment we have created, not nature."[11] As we saw in the opening of this chapter, raccoons, hawks, and coyotes kill cooped hens. According to the chicken attacks reported on the website backyardchickens .com—a sprawling clearinghouse of information for small-scale chicken keepers—raccoons accounted for 24 percent of attacks, hawks for 11 percent, and coyotes for 4 percent. Other culprits included cats, rats, skunks, snakes, owls, eagles, bear, mountain lions, weasels, opossum, mink, foxes, dogs (at 19 percent), and, at 5 percent, somehow or other, humans.[12]

When small-scale chicken farmers discuss predators, they do so with a combination of resignation and familiarity. Their tone suggests that deadly predators are as frustrating as they are commonplace in pastured systems. Comparisons of mortality rates between industrial and small-scale operations are fraught with difficulty, primarily because so much depends on management and breed selection. Nonetheless, a fair reading of the evidence indicates that the two systems, contrary to what we might think, have roughly similar mortality rates.[13] In addition to disease (more on this soon), a leading cause of chicken mortality on small farms is predation. As hundreds, if not thousands, of firsthand accounts reveal, these attacks are a terrifying way to die for the birds that we so often celebrate as having been spared the torments of the battery cage—a cage that would, ironically, have kept them from being torn to shreds by an animal they cannot use natural defense strategies to escape.

The stories that farmers share with each other in online forums can be as frustrating as they are macabre. Fire Pirate recounted how, as he was making his "rounds . . . I get to the Japanese bantam enclosure and find my proud little rooster without a head." Turns out "a cat is the culprit." The rest of the bird's body was stuck, headless, between the bars of the coop.[14] Show Me left her house for an hour one afternoon, and because a neighbor's dog had been a bit too curious about her hens, she locked her birds in the henhouse. "Not really fair to them," she explained, "but I wanted them safe." The plan backfired with fatal consequences. "Lost them all," the farmer wrote. "Came home to carnage. The dog/s chewed on house and managed to weaken the gate enough to get in. All four were brutally murdered."[15] A chilling report from BeckT recounted how "night before last I had my first coon attack." One of his birds was "attacked in his carrier by a family of coons" who "succeeded in pulling one of his legs thru the holes and ripping his leg off at the hip point." One commenter could relate all too well: "I fully understand. I had three coons pull three of my banty's thru a small hole in their coop."[16] Riceinhall14 described a bird "attacked by a fox" with "serious wounds on his back" and a "swollen and battered head."[17] "We had a hawk get one of our hens," wrote another farmer. "Just got a talon on it and split the skin open."[18]

In every one of these instances, the birds were maimed or killed *because they were denied access to their natural strategies of protection.* They were trapped in coops or set out on a pasture without access to dense foliage and secure places to roost and, as a result, became proverbial fish in a barrel. Chickens raised on pasture may be in greater danger than chickens raised in confinement. In December 2010, darin367 reported that he "went out to the coop and all 15 are dead." This discovery was especially distressing because "I've been fighting off the coons for months, my fence is dug down into the dirt almost a foot. But they dug under it." Although his wife was "devastated," Darin remained undeterred: "Gonna spend the next few days pooring [sic] a concrete foot around the bottom of the coop. . . . And then try and build a new flock."[19] An Illinois farmer named Mar reported that she "went to bed, had 39 chickens," but woke up to find "25 dead." Two others her husband had to "finish off b'cuz their insides were hanging out."[20] Her pain was felt by debillorah, of Northern Winds Ranch, who had "lost about 50 birds to a pack of coyotes" who stormed the coop one evening.[21] Hillary, from Front Range, Colorado, noted that "we lost our four girls last night to what we think was most likely a raccoon. . . . This morning we awoke to find the four of them scattered around the yard, all relatively intact, but all without their heads." A bulldog, explained one hen keeper, "came up in my yard, killed 19 of my chickens and I had to take care of one other because it's back was split open."[22]

These are not the stories of farmers who are neglectful about security. With so many consumers seeking nonindustrially sourced eggs, agricultural economists have finally taken note of the impact of these predatory mishaps. In the most comprehensive comparative assessment of mortality rates in caged versus cage-free chickens, F. Bailey Norwood and Jayson L. Lusk explain, when it comes to animal welfare, "There is no easy answer." They did, however, interview egg producers who raise chickens with and without cages. They report:

> *All of them state that hens were better off in the cage system. . . . These producers report much higher rates of injury, cannibalism, and death on cage-free farms. When we asked these producers about their perception of animal welfare in the two systems, they universally favored the cage system, asserting that animal welfare could not be high in a cage-free system where twice as many birds die.*[23]

Whether or not twice as many birds die in nonindustrial, cage-free settings is difficult to know for sure. What is known for sure is that keeping hens in what are at best seminatural conditions leads to their constant premature slaughter. It's therefore hard to see how this way of providing chicken and eggs is ultimately humane. We see chickens happily pecking grubs on a pasture and assume that all is well for those chickens; we assume that we're giving them the best life they could have. For all we know, though, the chickens live an anxious and depressed existence. Their access to more space, I would suggest, is a greater benefit to our shaky conscience than to the actual welfare of the birds themselves.

DISEASE: "DOES ANYONE KNOW?"

In the summer of 2011—roughly a year after the USDA recalled about half a million eggs suspected of being infected with *Salmonella*—*Food Safety News* reported that another multistate outbreak of *Salmonella* was under way. This time it was (according to the Centers for Disease Control) "tied to backyard poultry."[24] The outbreak left seventy-one people sickened and twenty hospitalized. Half of those both sickened and hospitalized were under five years old. A traceback investigation found that the infected chickens came from generic feed stores across the country—the places where most small farmers (who don't do their own breeding—few do) get their birds—and that the feed stores relied on a single hatchery in Ohio for the infected birds. *Food Safety News* further reported, "Most of those who are ill, or whose children are ill, reported buying the live poultry for either backyard flocks to produce eggs or as pets."[25] Speaking on CNN, Professor Michael Lacy, head of poultry science at the University of Georgia, reminded viewers that this event was, contrary to what people might think, hardly an anomaly: "There is no scientific evidence that free-range or organic eggs are less prone to S[*almonella*]. Enteritidis."[26]

Consumers often purchase eggs from small farms under the impression that they are necessarily safer than those being churned out of factory farms. Keepers of cooped and pastured birds, however, are well aware of the pervasive dangers of *Salmonella*. When they share information online, experienced chicken owners express considerable fear over contracting the disease from their own birds. Many are convinced that they've already done so. "Does anyone here have any experience with Salmonella? We are pretty sure that our 12 year old son has it," wrote one concerned keeper of backyard hens. Another farmer added, "My daughter had it." Another explained, "My husband had it once and my oldest son."[27] And yet another: "The two times I was out in the hen house with my hubby while he was cleaning it I got Salmonella. I was soooooooo sick for a week with it both times."[28] One farmer noted that she was "selling my eggs and don't want ppl [people] to get sick," to which another reminded her how hard it was to avoid *Salmonella* given that "it can be transmitted via rodent droppings" and that "flies can carry Salmonella between neighboring flocks."[29] These farmers also knew that *Salmonella* can come from contaminated feed and (as we'll soon see) that feed for small farmers comes from the same source that serves agribusiness. When contaminated feed was cited as the possible origin of a *Salmonella* outbreak on industrial eggs farms in 2011, small egg producers reacted with panic. "My questions are," one wrote, "when . . . was the feed contaminated (at the feed mill, or at the farms) and which feed is it? Am I possibly buying contaminated feed? I can find no answers at all online. Does anyone know?"[30]

Bacteria make it a point of being hard to know. *Salmonella* is a ubiquitous disease that every chicken and egg farmer, big and small, can best reduce—rarely with complete success—through diligent attention to sanitation. Locating egg production indoors, while certainly dreadful for the welfare of caged animals and in no way something I would ever support, theoretically allows the producer to maintain tighter control over sanitation. That doesn't mean proper sanitation will happen, but it does suggest that, when sanitation becomes a high priority for a producer, it can be better achieved than when birds are spread across a pasture. During the 2010 egg recall, while news reports were exclusively linking *Salmonella* to *industrial* egg production, *USA Today* ran a story about an egg facility in Illinois. The operation produced upward of eight hundred thousand eggs a day but, despite its industrial size, had never experienced an outbreak of *Salmonella*. The reason for this clean record was zero-tolerance biosecurity, a position made possible by consolidation and frequent testing.[31]

Small farmers and backyard chicken owners make a big deal about fanatical hand-washing and coop cleaning. This is excellent, and as it should be. But the decentralized nature of outdoor systems makes such rigid management virtually impossible to accomplish on smaller farms. It's difficult to control how roaming birds interact with wildlife, be it visible or microscopic. Farmers know this. "I realize letting them free range is risky," one farmer said of his hens. But, admitting the trade-off, he allowed it nonetheless because "they do so love it." Another farmer took stock of her sick birds and explained, "I have no idea what they could have gotten into, all the chicken free ranging during the day . . . has its own risks." (As for *Salmonella* testing on family farms, it's far too expensive for the vast majority of small egg farmers to do regularly—yet another advantage of an otherwise unacceptable arrangement.)

The anecdotes cited above attest to the presence of *Salmonella* (or at least fear of it) in birds and eggs raised in smaller, nonindustrial settings. A growing body of research suggests that these examples accurately reflect the larger picture. A 2005 study published in the *Journal of Food Protection* notes that commercial chickens processed from 2000 to 2003 had a *Salmonella* prevalence rate of 9.1 to 12.8 percent (according to the USDA). By contrast, researchers found *Salmonella* in 31 percent of the free-range birds they tested, and in 25 percent of the "all natural" birds in their sample.

The authors concluded, "Consumers should not assume that free range or organic conditions will have anything to do with the salmonella status of the chicken."[32] Not a single study has since negated this advice. More recently, a comprehensive 2012 evaluation of the presence of *Salmonella* in or on free-range and conventional eggs found "no significant difference" between the two systems.[33] A letter to *Feedstuffs* from a farmer who raised birds in both caged and cage-free systems captured this reality with some conviction: "What looks good to humans does not work as well for chickens." He noted, however implausibly, that a confined bird was a better-off bird because "safety pens protect hens from . . . eating their own feces, big temperature changes and diseases caused by lack of protection other systems fail to provide."[34] This sentiment was reflected within the chicken forums as well. One chicken farmer from Holland noted that caged birds "have like 3 percent problems with internal parasites compared to 86% of freerange [sic]." This was most likely an overstatement, but it at least confirms the on-the-ground awareness of a threat of which consumers seem largely unaware.

Salmonella isn't the only disease that plagues backyard birds and their disease-weary keepers. Nonindustrial farmers raising birds outdoors must deal with a widespread intestinal plague called coccidiosis. Chickens contract the coccidia parasites from soil contaminated with chicken feces—an unavoidable situation when a chicken is pecking and pooping in free-ranged but fenced-off space. Lethargy, droopy wings, and bloody stool are common symptoms of coccidiosis, which will spread like wildfire through an otherwise healthy flock of chickens. Thousands upon thousands of panicked reports to backyard chicken message boards suggest that, of the infinite problems that keep small-scale egg farmers on edge, coccidiosis may top the list. A typical account comes from Jarsheart, who claimed, "Coccidia is killing my flock, one by one—tried everything. . . . I have spent hundreds of dollars at the vet. My silkie chickens are dying one by one of coccidia. I had gone several weeks without a death, then had one today. He died at the vet in my lap. . . . I am down to eight chickens, and can't take much more of this." Of all the suggestions offered in response to her dilemma, the most practical one, ironically, would have made an industrial chicken farmer proud: "Might help if you get them off the soil up into wire cages without floors. Eliminating or greatly reducing their contact with soil/poop will stop cocci from re-entering their digestive tracts."[35]

Another common chicken ailment afflicting small chicken farms is called Marek's disease. Marek's is a herpesvirus that infects chickens with generally disastrous consequences. *The Merck Manual* calls it "one of the most ubiquitous avian infections."[36] It's untreatable and likely to kill not only the infected bird but about half of the flock as well. Symptoms include tumors, partial paralysis, diarrhea, blindness, a shriveled comb, and depression.[37] It's most prevalent in young birds and spreads rapidly through secretions, droppings, skin flakes, feather dust, and dander. The virus is both inhaled and ingested by birds. To small-scale chicken owners who know their birds well, the signs of this disease become immediately evident. "Three days ago," DWilkins wrote of her hen, "we noticed that she wasn't able to jump in the coop. The following day she was laying on her side in the lawn. Hubby picked her up and set her in the coop. I went out the following morning to feed them and she was laying in the same place with a wing sprawled out. . . . I feel it may be Marek's."[38] Betsy realized after the fact that Marek's was the source of her bird's sickness: "I am new to chickens and probably about three months ago a chick I had hatched got this weird leg deformity but was still eating and drinking so I separated it from the bigger chicks, put it with littler chicks so it wouldn't get run over and made sure it could get to food and water. Stupid me. The chick has since died but now I know it had Marek's Disease."[39] Livi wrote, "I recently lost two pullets, one I culled when she had a progressive paralysis in her leg without any obvious cause, the other lost her balance a week thereafter and I culled her too. They were 18–20 weeks, so pretty likely mareks: cry."[40] Sandee explained, "I too have had Marek's disease. . . . The first batch of birds, about 20, I lost all but two."[41] She planned to cull the rest of her hens. ChicKat's response to what seemed a tsunami of Marek's disease spoke accurately for all backyard chicken owners: "Marek's is awful and a heartbreaking thing to hit anyone's flock."[42]

Small chicken farmers and backyard chicken keepers must deal with a hit list of diseases beyond *Salmonella*, coccidiosis, and Marek's. They are inevitably bound to encounter conditions including (all of these are mentioned on a variety of message boards) bumblefoot, Newcastle disease, coryza, straddle leg, necrotic enteritis, worms, maggots, fatty liver, fowl cholera, egg binding, chronic respiratory disease, gapeworm, fleas, lice, scaly leg mites, nest mites, diarrhea, botulism, winking disease, crop binding, blackhead, hexamita, giardia, fowl pox, infectious laryngotracheitis (ILT), avian metritis, bird flu, crusty face, and whooping crud.

This litany of despair spawns its own list of symptoms that leave owners and their peers in a fog of diagnostic confusion. Chicken keepers go to other chicken keepers to seek advice when they find that their birds are demonstrating, say, "a swollen eye with bubbling liquid," "clear stringy poop," "lots of stones in poo," "maggots crawling in and out of her," "earlobe turned turquoise," "bloody behind," "fluid filled sac on rear end," "white poo," "BAD diarrhea," "tumor filled with liquid," "dark apple green colored pee," "brains exposed," "vent inside out," "eyes swollen and shut," and "lost voice." So maddening is this throwing of darts at a diagnostic dartboard that several veterinary colleges have designed Web sites where chicken owners type in a list of symptoms and the program spits out a series of possible answers.[43]

Chicken owners who have the option of undertaking such a search consider themselves fortunate. As often as a sick chicken will wobble and cough and secrete foul emissions from any and all orifices, she will, without warning, die. Sudden death is routine on small chicken farms, so much so that farmers repeatedly refer to "sudden death syndrome." "You will learn," wrote farmer Dustin Biery, "that they are prone to dying off without any warning or indicators as to what has happened to them." Story after story confirms this assessment. When Denise, for example, walked to her coop one morning, she found her daughter's 4-H hen dead. "I'm not sure how it happened," she wrote. "When I opened the big door this morning she was laying on her side right up against it, no blood or feathers missing, just obviously dead."[44] A chicken keeper named kcvalentine reported, "Went out one morning to service my coop and found one of our Rhode Island Reds dead with no trauma, and there was no sign of

previous disease. It was totally unexpected."[45] Ghetto Dunn
recalled, "I went out to feed this morning and all was good.
I just went out to give a head of cabbage to them and one of
my 7 month old's was dead. She had no markings on her.
This is the third hen I have lost." Hennyetta checked her
hens before she went to bed and they were fine, but then
"one was dead in the morning." The cause was unknown,
leaving her to remark, "Is there ever an answer in these
cases?"[46] Tburley lamented his suddenly dead birds by saying, "They all seem to be completely healthy and active till
they die."[47] Surveying these endless anecdotes of sudden
chicken death, JJ summed up the situation aptly when he
wrote, "Too many horror stories of folks who believed all
would be well and then tragedy struck. And it doesn't even
take a minute for things to become utterly sad and regrettable."

"DO NOT TEASE THE MICROBES"

Because easy answers to chicken health problems remain
elusive, many small-scale chicken owners resort to an arsenal of medications and chemicals to keep their birds healthy.
We tend to associate the systematic application of vaccines
and antibiotics to farm animals with factory farming, not
alternative farms, where conditions are perceived to be
"natural." But nonindustrial operations, even some organic
ones, frequently rely on vaccines, antibiotics, fungicides,
and pesticides as a cost of doing business. Consider the account of one chicken keeper whose flock came down with a
variety of conditions: "I haven't lost any. Been treating [the

mysterious disease] really well, but, I am out of Gallimycin [antibiotic that fights respiratory disease], till my order comes in! I am giving the 4 really bad ones LA-200 [another antibiotic] injections, and injections to the other sick pen. I have Terramycin [yet another antibiotic] in the water now, as well as Probios. I am also terrymincining [*sic*] everyone else as a precaution. All are getting VetRx [compound that treats worms and colds] at the moment too."[48] Through the use of medicated feed, vaccinations, antibiotic-laced water, potent pesticides, and a host of other drugs, small-scale egg farms routinely employ the same techniques used by industrial producers to prevent and cure bird disease. That they do so on a smaller scale is falsely reassuring.

The most common vaccine that hatcheries administer to chickens is the vaccine for Marek's disease. This drug contains strains of chicken and turkey herpesvirus, penicillin, and a fungiastic agent called Fungizone. The vaccine is given either embryonically or, more commonly, under the skin behind the necks of one-day-old chicks. The USDA forbids a vaccinated chicken to be slaughtered for consumption within twenty-six days of receiving the drug.[49] While some backyard chicken owners refuse to vaccinate their flocks under any circumstances, this is the exception that proves the rule. The consensus on every established backyard chicken forum—and certainly within the veterinary community—is to vaccinate for Marek's. When a woman asked a backyard chicken forum if she should purchase chickens that have been vaccinated for Marek's, the collective answer was unequivocal: "After what I've been through, I would vaccinate everyone"; "It's cheap, it saves lives, and there's really no risk"; "It is a TERRIBLE disease, and i

would think anyone stupid for not vaccinating against it!";
"It's a horrible disease and I only wish I had vaccinated. I
would have saved lives and saved myself alot [sic] of crying."[50]
In a word: yes, *vaccinate*.

Vaccination might seem to be an innocuous measure for
a small farmer to take. Nonindustrial reliance on vaccination, however, implicates small-scale animal farming alongside factory farms in the insidious cycle of viral resistance
that routinely makes the news as an endemic agricultural
problem. It fuels the pharmaceutical arms race we are so
quick to condemn as specific to industrial agriculture. A
2005 article published in *Expert Review of Vaccines* explored
this issue in some depth. It wondered if the use of Marek's
vaccines "could be driving the virus to greater virulence."
According to the authors, vaccinated chickens, while cured
of the virus, instead shed the antivirus, exposing the rest of
the flock, or a neighboring one, to Marek's. Because the disease persists, stronger vaccines must be created. These, in
turn, foster even stronger viruses. The authors hypothe-
sized that "the use of M[arek's]D[isease] vaccines could be
driving MDV [the herpesvirus] to greater virulence."[51] Established veterinary experts believe that this is already happening. Ahmed Anjum, a poultry specialist, notes that the
Marek's vaccine worked brilliantly when it saved the poultry industry in the 1970s, but in the 1980s, as one would
expect, "very virulent viruses emerged." Industry responded
by creating a more potent vaccine, which worked until the
1990s, when "very virulent viruses *plus*" developed.[52] Poultry experts, explaining that "during the last few years, Marek's
disease has impacted badly on the free-range sector," are
currently recommending double vaccinations.[53]

It's often argued that if chickens are raised under more natural conditions, such as the ones that supposedly prevail on small farms, then rates of disease will decline. This is decidedly not the case with Marek's. Chickens on pasture interact with wild birds (quail and pheasant, for example), which can carry Marek's disease.[54] Because the disease travels in airborne dust, it readily jumps from farm to farm, from one outdoor flock to another, and from bird to bird. As one authority on vaccinations wrote about small farms, "We don't have cramped or crowded conditions where disease festers and rapidly infects—but our chickens still coop together, drink the same water, mate and basically are in fairly constant close contact."[55] Even when farmers purchase vaccinated birds, there's no guarantee of bird health, a situation that's exacerbated by access to the great outdoors. The Marek's vaccination must be applied under unusually precise conditions, and because farmers typically don't do their own vaccinating, they are reliant on hatcheries that may or may not keep the vaccine at the right temperature, agitate it frequently enough to maintain its potency, administer it properly, and ensure ideal sanitation conditions. Summing up the situation of Marek's vaccination and small-scale agriculture, *The Natural Poultry Farming Guide* writes, "Although vaccines are commonly used in the commercial poultry industry, small numbers of doses cannot be purchased for use in backyard flocks. For backyard flocks, the best protection against Marek's disease is obtained by buying, from a commercial source, birds that have been correctly vaccinated." It then adds, "Vaccination alone will not prevent Marek's disease."[56]

Whereas Marek's disease implicates small-scale chicken farmers in the long cycle of viral resistance associated exclu-

sively with factory farming, coccidiosis does the same for
the equally troublesome cycle of antibiotic resistance. We
tend to think of chickens subsisting on grubs when we buy
pastured chicken. However, to prevent outbreaks of coccidiosis, alternative chicken farms commonly feed chickens
medicated commercial feed. According to an article posted
by the editors of backyardchickens.com, "Medicated chick
starter is like an insurance policy, aimed at preventing a single
disease called coccidiosis, caused by an intestinal parasite."
The active agent in this insurance policy is an antibiotic
called amprolium.[57] The demand for amprolium, according
to the article, was again actually exacerbated by outdoor access: "No matter how hard you work to keep the coop and
pen clean, as chicks scratch, peck and explore their world,
they ingest the coccidiosis in from the feces around them."
Theoretically, the prophylactic use of antibiotics is forbidden
on organic farms. Nevertheless, anecdotal evidence on forums suggests that many organic producers occasionally (and
quietly) use it as a temporary measure. Consider this comment, given in response to a question about using medicated
feed in organic egg farming: "This exact question was brought
up at our local feed store chicken seminar. We plan to feed
organic also, so we were concerned about the medicated feed.
The feed store manager said to put them on organic at laying
age, and it will take two weeks for the medicated residue to
purge out of their system."[58] Despite the farmer's effort to
raise chickens organically, medicated feed remains a staple
practice on small, non-organic egg farms, and, to reiterate,
it's often used prophylactically. As one backyard chicken website recently explained, "It is a preventative."[59]

The prophylactic use of antibiotics—one of the worst

problems in factory farming—not only happens for coccidiosis on small farms, but for a range of chicken sicknesses, or even vague signs of them. Within the chicken-farming community, antibiotic use leads to frequent and sometimes contentious discussion. Speckledhen regretted how "at the first sneeze, people dump Terramycin in the waterers." Another chicken keeper agreed, complaining, "When a newbie posts that she's scared about a runny nose or sneezy chicken a horde of responses tell her to throw antibiotics at them pronto." One veterinarian, Dr. Maren Bell Jones, knew all too well about antibiotic abuse on small farms. She explained how "someone gets a bottle of large animal Baytril (an antibiotic made by Bayer) for their calf with respiratory disease and then sells it to the guy down the road who raises chickens." The result: "It ends up as a meat residue in the food chain." Proof that Dr. Bell wasn't exaggerating comes from a farmer who told his chicken forum, "I used goat safeguard for my birds."[60]

Still, the "insurance" of amprolium is sometimes too comforting for farmers to forgo. "I use it," wrote Tec 27. "All my chickens are fine so I'll keep using it." Vickery added, "I'm thinking that people that have many chicks may NEED the medicated feed because there is just too many factors to manage to avoid infection." None of these farmers seemed terribly concerned with Dr. Bell's frankly worded warning that "constantly dosing animals with a low level of antibiotics in the food OR having certain antibiotics at the feed store . . . is exactly how we are selecting for the super bugs that kill people." Bell added, "As one of my vet school professors was fond of saying, do not tease the microbes."

Some farmers, though, seemed cognizant of the antibiotic impact. Calpsychic claimed that he'd no longer use the antibiotic Wazine "because there's so much resistence [sic] already," and dlhunicorn wrote, "I am questioning if giving her the same antibiotic a second time might perhaps be ineffective? (may even lead to resistance in the organism causing this?)"[61] Again, because of its scale, small farming is never considered a venue of antibiotic resistance, but many farmers within that rarely scrutinized line of work understand the case to be otherwise.

Another chemical that's common, and commonly unmentioned, on small farms is Sevin dust. If you've already heard of Sevin (aka carbaryl), it's likely been in the context of agribusiness, where it's deployed as a general-use insecticide. I first learned about it when touring a large apple farm in New York State, where it was the pesticide of choice. Sevin comes with the following summary from a University of Oregon/Cornell University chemical analysis: "Carbaryl is moderately to very toxic. It can produce adverse effects in humans by skin contact, inhalation, or ingestion. The symptoms of acute toxicity are typical of the other carbamates. Direct contact of the skin or eyes with moderate levels of this pesticide can cause burns. Inhalation or ingestion of very large amounts can be toxic to the nervous and respiratory systems resulting in nausea, stomach cramps, diarrhea, and excessive salivation. Other symptoms at high doses include sweating, blurring of vision, incoordination, and convulsions."[62] Not only is it of grave concern that small farms use Sevin regularly to control for earwigs, but that they do so at times with little regard for the insecticide's impact on chickens. One chicken farmer had purchased some Sevin to dust the perimeter of her farm. When, after coming in from applying the Sevin dust, she discovered a nest of earwigs in her barn, and poured the Sevin on them. She recalled,

> *Well of course my chickens came over to see what all the commotion was, and they started feasting on earwigs that all had a dusting of Sevin on their backs. The chickens would have none of me trying to shoo them away, and as I watched them all gorge themselves on Sevin dusted earwigs, I thought I'd wake up to dead chickens.*

She didn't, despite being *"sure I had killed my chickens."*[63]

This example suggests that Sevin, although recognized by at least one chicken keeper as "one of the very WORSE [*sic*] chemicals you can use," is nonetheless at least an occasional aspect of small-farm pest control that many producers believe is necessary to raising chickens. One farmer noted, "I put alittle [*sic*] 7 dust in my chickens [*sic*] dust bathing area's [*sic*] once a month. . . . Works really good."[64] Another added, "I put Sevin dust on the straw in coup [*sic*] and pen each time I replace it. My chickens have always been healthy. I pour lightly though." And another: "Good to hear that seven [*sic*] dust will do the job!" And finally: "Just wanted to say I just dusted my whole yard with the Sevin dust." To think that chemical usage is specific to agribusiness is, as these examples suggest, incorrect.

"IT'S NOT REVENGE, IT'S PROTECTION!!!"

Popular food writers and sustainable food advocates insist that we source our animal products, including chicken and eggs, locally and from nonindustrial farms. But they never reveal all the details therein. As the arguments in this chapter show, they never reveal that small farms are especially subject to predation, that they suffer from the same diseases and often use the same medicines and chemicals as factory farms. Instead, these writers and advocates resort to agricultural mythology, showing us hens on pasture acting as hens supposedly act in all-natural settings that enhance the "henness" of a hen. As one commenter on the CNN Eatocracy page explained, "The best eggs come from farms that have their chickens running free from the time they are chicks. Leave the door open, and let them run. Scratching bugs, dirt, cleaning themselves in the sand. A happy hen sings, runs to her roost singing loudly, squawking to let the world know she is going to lay an egg." The implication is that not only are these birds happier and healthier because they are living outdoors, but also their owners have a deeper sense of their animals' welfare. This chapter will end by drawing upon the accounts of farmers to demonstrate that this common assumption is not always true, either.

Many small-scale chicken farmers are explicit in their insistence that, when it comes to their birds, the bottom line is the bottom line. In a fascinating discussion that developed around animal welfare and Proposition 2 (the California initiative to ban battery cages—more on which soon), one farmer reiterated that, even for those who raised eggs on pasture, "I'm pretty sure it all boils down to economy and supply/demand."[65] One farmer refused to take her sick bird to the vet because the bird was "not worth a 100 dollar bill to me."[66] Although insisting that "we do treat our livestock with respect," another farmer explained, "In the end it is the money, we aren't doing this for a hobby."[67] When a chicken was attacked by a neighbor's dog, the farmer, although upset, chose not to make the sixty-mile drive to the vet because "I just don't have the energy to do it right now." A chicken keeper found her hen's feathers plucked to the skin and explained, "I'm not sure it's worth paying for a Vet."[68] When another woman's bird was attacked by a dog, leaving a three-inch gash in her neck, the woman avoided what she estimated would have been a $500 visit to the vet because "my husband would never go for it."[69] Yet another reminded the forum that, when it came to her animals, "we are going to take the best care of them that we can, because the bottom line is profitability."[70] This is, of course, not at all surprising. Money is money. But it's also not what they tell you about animal welfare when you buy "humane" products at the farmer's market.

One outcome of this business-is-business perspective is that farmers who are supposedly creating "natural" conditions for their birds to be birds often end up taking a murderous approach to any other animal threatening their investment. They might care about their chickens, but they come to despise the living beings that threaten those chickens. Economically speaking, this shift in perspective stands to reason. When humans own animals to exploit, they tend to calibrate welfare considerations to meet the imperatives of that exploitation. This behavior is confirmed repeatedly in the disdainful view that so many farmers have of the natural world around their birds. Killing an animal, wrote one chicken owner, "is considered protection of property. . . . Here's what justifies it for me. . . . If the animal is going to slaughter my animals, it darn sure is going to slaughter someone else's."

Thus it's best that the creature die. Another explained matter-of-factly, "Everything kills a chicken." This siege mentality is endemic on small farms that rely on coops and pastures. When a local cat killed a farmer's bird ("pulled him through the bars only enough to eat his head"), the farmer set out some tuna, lured in the cat, and, as he recalled, "I shoot him. 22 point blank and he gone." After the incident he admitted to having "a guilty conscience" but quickly surmised, "Who would want a chicken killer on their farm?" As with cats, so with dogs. After a dog killed almost twenty of her chickens, Jennifer, a chicken farmer in Griffen, California, wrote, "I killed the dog. Shot it dead." Other farmers were deeply empathetic with this choice. They wrote, "I'm shaking with anger for you," "Sorry about the chicken, good job getting the dog though," "So sad about your flock but I'm glad you took care of the problem," "Had you not killed it it would have been back," and, the most revealing, "It is always hard to lose a pet and then have to shoot the dog afterwards."[71]

Other animals besides pets are routinely (and literally) targeted as well. One woman recalled the fate of a raccoon that wandered too close to her coop: "Kent [husband] ended up putting 6 shots in him before he finally died. It took a second shot to the head. He kept moving around and that made it hard to take aim." When another farmer mentioned that he trapped and relocated raccoon and possum who lurked too close to the farm, he was told by another farmer, "There isn't a predator that gets caught or seen on this property that is re-located. I maybe [sic] cruel, but that's just how it is." Instead of relocation, he explained, "They get a lead injection [i.e., a bullet from a gun] and that's the end of it."[72]

But that's never the end of it. Wilderness abounds with

chicken predators. With chickens to protect (because, as we have seen, chickens are denied the chance to protect themselves) and sell, snakes are also deemed enemies worthy of a lead injection or shovel to the back, despite their effectiveness in rodent control. One farmer showed how quickly opinions about the natural world could change when precious eggs are at stake. She recalled, "I came across the prettiest 6 ft snake in my chicken house. He was after a rat so I let him alone. A few weeks later I saw him outside the house eating another rat. . . . Then 1 morning I went out to my babies cage & somehow he had gotten in. He killed 2 & 1 was in its belly. . . . Well my husband cut off his head & I will never let a snake live again." In case anyone missed the point of the endless slaughter of snakes, foxes, raccoons, hawks, coyotes, and other "deviants that are preying on my flock," one farmer reminded everyone, "It's not revenge, it's protection!!!" Such revenge might be perfectly justified from an economic point of view. But it would be remiss to call such a system natural or in any way designed out of love for animals and their habitats.

"I THINK THAT MOST PEOPLE BURY THEIR HEADS IN THE SAND"

One of this book's primary arguments is that nonindustrial animal production paradoxically promotes the underlying logic of industrial agriculture. When it comes to chicken and eggs, the support of small-scale alternatives might seem to be a bold expression of "voting with your fork" against the dominance of factory-farmed chicken and eggs. However, the endorsement of egg and chicken consumption per se ensures

that factory farms will always thrive in the business of providing cheaper and more accessible products for the vast majority of consumers to purchase. Many small-scale producers
grasp this point intuitively. They acknowledge that the prominent existence of factory-farmed products is exactly what allows them to stand apart from the herd and sell value-added
eggs and chicken parts to consumers willing to pay more for
products that come to the plate with a happier narrative. One
farmer lamented the economic logic working in his favor
when he wrote, "Most of us will agree it is somewhat inhumane to keep animals in confinement, but everyone must realize that the day of the mom and pop farms is long gone."
Consumers might want animal products from "grandma's
farm," but "grandma doesn't have enough room to produce a
semi-load of eggs." Only the elite few can afford to eat guiltless eggs. Still, the farmer was happy to oblige.

Consumers of chicken and chicken products from nonindustrial farms tend to think that their producers share
their ideological opposition to factory farms, battery cages,
and the harsh density of industrial agriculture. Considerable
evidence suggests otherwise. Small-scale farmers who bring
us "humane" chicken products do not always share in the
outrage. They may see their role as little more than a fash-
ionable pose. Many of these producers, especially ones far
afield of urban centers, identify ideologically with factory
farms while sharing with them a general disdain for groups
who wish to impose welfare-oriented rules on raising chickens. One farmer was tellingly explicit in his opinion that
backyard farmers could easily exploit this urban desire for
"happy" chickens to their economic benefit. She wrote, with
apparent bemusement, "I've seen Craig's List [sic] wanted ads

specifically asking for eggs from local, humanely-treated 'happy' backyard chickens!"

The punctuation here tells its own story: the quote marks around the word *happy* and the exclamation point that says, "Can you believe these yuppies?" "I think," the farmer went on, "that one has to live here [California] to fully understand the mentality (some of it a little 'out there' to me, even) of the people regarding their food."[73] None of this was going to stop this culturally perceptive farmer from selling happy eggs and chicken parts to these "extremist groups," no matter how "out there" they were. But it does suggest that hip urbanites who want "happy meat" are getting toyed with by those who know that such a product is a convenient and profitable fabrication of sorts.

Moreover, although many backyard chicken farmers are understandably eager to sell their products at a premium to welfare-minded urbanites, they hardly demonstrate a deep concern for animal welfare. Their typical punching bag is the Humane Society of the United States (HSUS). Because HSUS, according to a farmer named Julie, encourages consumers to "vote with their hearts," local farmers were warned to be careful because "someday they [HSUS] will be in Iowa trying to legislate how we care for our animals." She added, "These organizations want to put human characteristics on our animals, [so] that they be treated as we are." Another farmer (eggchel) was convinced that HSUS's "ultimate goal is to force all people to become vegan." She elaborated on what she (wrongly) perceived to be the organization's deeper strategy: "They have been unable to get lawmakers to pass anti-animal legislations so they have taken their agenda to the popular vote where there [*sic*] massive spending on misleading advertisements will convince animal lovers that the goal is to protect farm animals when the true goal is to eliminate farm animals and ban all animal agribusiness." Don't miss the irony here. This woman was selling eggs to people who were buying from her as part of an effort "to ban agribusiness."[74] One small-scale farmer was particularly clear about where welfare concerns stood with respect to his profit margin: "Since we are farmers and I see what it takes to make a living off the land, I'm not anti-big farm like so many people lamenting in the papers these days."[75]

The downsides of small-scale animal farming are there for those willing to put down the knife and take a look. But as one forum commenter noted, this is unlikely to happen anytime soon. "I think," she wrote, "that most people bury their heads in the sand."[76]

6

UTOPIAN BEEF

I seem to think we could be getting false hope.
—Anonymous

Behind every grass-fed steak lies a vision of utopia. Behind every utopian vision is a dream deferred by the messy reality of raising cows on pasture.

The utopian narrative that has developed around grass-fed or pastured beef is both recent and persuasive. For all intents and purposes it began with Michael Pollan's breathless introduction to Joel Salatin's postcard-perfect farm in Swoope, Virginia. In *The Omnivore's Dilemma* (2006) Pollan presented Salatin as the high priest of an ecologically progressive approach to cattle raising called rotational (or holistic) grazing. This land-extensive and labor-intensive approach to ranching requires farmers to periodically shift herds from one designated plot to another, often with the assistance of electric fences, in rapid but carefully planned succession. This series of rotations is said to obviate environmentally costly external inputs while limiting the system's primary source of energy to the world's cheapest source of energy: the sun.

As Pollan presented it, this natural cycle was elegant in its simplicity and execution. The sun grew grass; the grass grew cows; chicken poop fertilized the soil; and people drove in from around the state to break the cycle and haul home a side of beef or whole bird. The result, in Pollan's oft-quoted assessment, was the impossible agricultural feat of achieving a "free lunch." Salatin, for his part, has gone on to a career as a traveling agrarian hero, an ecologically inspirational evangelist preaching the gospel of grass to those who won't give up the dream of eating a guiltless steak.

It took about ten years for the Swoope revival to reach a global audience. The pivotal moment in this transition came in March of 2013 when the biologist and former Rhodesian parliamentarian Allan Savory delivered a now-viral twenty-two-minute TED talk that sent conscientious carnivores into unapologetic salivation. Savory, who was working with the same cycle-of-life principles promoted by Salatin, argued that the rotational grazing of cattle on the world's desert hardpan would not only lead to ecological reclamation but would *end global warming*. Savory insisted that what we had to do to reverse the largest environmental conundrum ever encountered (and created) by humans was to mimic "all of nature's complexity." Not some of it—*all of it*. Never mind that we could not possibly know all of nature's complexity. And never mind that, even if we could, it would be the utter peak of vanity to think we might somehow re-create it. Undeterred, Savory pressed ahead with his thesis that the environment could be saved if humans simply sharpened their knives and ate more beef. His talk evolved into a YouTube sensation. Chris Anderson, the curator of

TED talks, practically melted after Savory delivered his message. "I'm sure everyone here," he said, "wants to hug you."[1]

I'm sure they did. Conscientious carnivores have long sought a justifiable rationale for beef-eating environmentalism. As these examples suggest, though, proponents of pastured or grass-fed beef are prone to making grandiose claims (free lunch, ending global warming, etc.) without much to support them. Take a closer look at these schemes and you'll soon realize that what's not being said is more important than what is. What's not being said are facts that undermine the pasture-themed utopia consumers have rushed to embrace. Start with the free-lunch claim. The idea that, in a rotational system, the energy absorbed from the sun equals the energy embedded in the food is a deeply appealing ecological transaction. But it's also a fallacy.

The reality is much less elegant. What Pollan never tells us about Salatin's farm (and what Salatin, upon being questioned about it, conceded) is a critical cost within the pastured system: Salatin imports over 150,000 pounds of industrial feed for his chickens so they can fertilize the soil that grows the grass that fattens his beef. The oft-touted closed loop has a door, one through which Salatin imports the purloined nutrients of some other field's monocultural production. Salatin's fertilizer might be sourced from chickens, and such an earthy output might appeal to the ecologically minded consumer, but the chickens' manure is ultimately an odiferous mash of intestine-treated soy and corn grown somewhere in the Midwest. In the popular imagination, Salatin's farm epitomizes the energy-saving promise of rotational grazing, but its obscured linkage to the industrial supply chain goes unmentioned. That sin of omission means, for starters, that there's no free lunch down on the farm. Not even close. Salatin's lunch is subsidized.[2]

Even easier to topple is Allan Savory's pie-in-the-sky proposal. The gist of Savory's argument is that the exact replication of the ancient predator prey relationship (with cattle and humans playing their respective roles) on what are now plots of desert hardpan would green deserts worldwide and, in so doing, sequester sufficient carbon to let us off the global-warming hook. Such exciting news might drive conscientious carnivores to fire up the grill. Try to verify Savory's claim, though, and you'll discover something just as outlandish as Savory's promise to end global warming: his proposed method has never worked as he assures us it will. Trials of Savory's holistic grazing schemes have, according to several external reviewers, failed. Savory's claim that rotational grazing would turn the world's deserts into grasslands lacks validation by the scientific method. The single major trial undertaken by Savory took place in Zimbabwe during a time (1968–74) when rainfall was 24 percent higher than normal. Conditions were ideal to bloom the desert. Even so, Savory's high stocking density and rapid-fire rotation, according to one team of reviewers, "failed to produce the marked improvement in grass cover claimed from its application." Whereas Savory argued that frequent "hoof action" by added cattle would increase water filtration, yet another group of scientists found the opposite to be true, noting that North American experiments in holistic grazing "have been quite consistent in showing that hoof action from having a large number of animals on a small area for short time periods reduced rather than increased filtration." In his YouTube talk, Savory shows compelling before-and-after images to demonstrate the success of his hypothesis. However, as one critic flatly stated, "Savory's method won't scale." Savory's response to all of this criticism pretty much sinks his own ship: "You'll find the scientific method never discovers anything."[3]

Before we look under the hood of this system, a final example serves to highlight the disconnect between the utopia and the reality of grass-fed beef. This final case has to do with safety. It has long been claimed that when cows eat grass (as they do on pasture) instead of grain (as they do in feedlots), they are less likely to carry the deadly bacteria known as *E. coli* O157:H7. Writing in a 2006 *New York Times* op-ed, food writer Nina Planck aimed to set the record straight once and for all. She said of *E. coli* O157:H7: "It's not found in the intestinal tracts of cattle raised on their natural diet of grass, hay, and other fibrous forage. No, O157 thrives in a new—that is, recent in the history of animal diets—biological niche: the unnaturally acidic stomachs of beef and dairy cattle fed on grain, the typical ration on most industrial farms." Planck's statement is wrong. Deadly so. Between 2000 and 2006 researchers published over a half dozen reports demonstrating not only no correlation between grain or grass-fed and the prevalence of *E. coli* O157:H7, but that in many cases grass-fed cows had higher rates of the bacteria.[4] "Taken together," Dr. Paul Ebner of Purdue recently wrote, "the studies to date have not shown that grain-fed cattle more frequently carry *E. coli* O157." The *Times* never published a correction.[5]

These stories help establish an important premise: pastured and grass-fed beef are not as ecologically beneficial or safe as they are advertised to be. True, it's not factory farming; and true, it's certainly better for the animals than industrial arrangements. But pastured beef is not going to save the earth. Nor is it going to provide a risk-free and environmentally sound free lunch. Nor is it going to make you optimally healthy or create community cohesion. No matter how the cattle are raised, it will always be more efficient to use a plot of arable land to grow plants for people to eat than to grow plants for cows who will be eaten by humans. The land and water required to fatten cattle on pasture for people to eat will always far exceed the land and water needed to grow plants for people to eat. No matter how closely you or I might live to the point of production, whether or not we eat a fifty-mile or hundred-mile locavore diet, the resources demanded to produce and process and dispose of farm animals exceed those needed to grow plants, no matter how far those plants have to be shipped. These points have been well articulated in the existing literature and I will, when relevant, reiterate them throughout the following analysis.

The bulk of this chapter aims to demonstrate that, as with the production of pastured chicken and eggs raised on small farms, the hidden logistics of raising cattle on pasture involve endemic problems that the popular media rarely mention. The trials and tribulations of raising animals in a seemingly more natural and ecologically friendly manner for a growing market of consumers undermine the potential of this to be anything more than an endeavor enjoyed by a few who erroneously think it's a realistic option for the many. I do not argue that there are *no* benefits to raising animals on grass, but like all animal-based alternatives to industrial agriculture, I argue that, in the end, it will only support business as usual.

"AN ACRE OF FORAGE WILL CARRY JUST SO MANY POUNDS OF ANIMALS"

Advocates of pastured beef and milk proudly call themselves "grass farmers."[6] This is an inspiring idea. The logic is that, with agricultural resources going into the cultivation of healthy grasslands, thriving cattle and responsibly sourced beef will follow. I am not suggesting that raising cows on wholesome native grass cannot effectively reclaim degraded landscapes and nurture soil, grass, and cows. Under specific and localized circumstances, it can. Under specific and localized circumstances, it has. When rainfall is adequate, when grass grows free of disease and excessive weed competition, when cows avoid disease and deposit an abundance of evenly spread nitrogen-rich poop, when the temperature avoids extremes, when genetics are consistent with forage and climate, and, it seems, when the stars align, farmers can take some pride in producing beef in a way that, while hardly avoiding the omnivore's contradiction (or the commercial slaughterhouse), has an ameliorative impact on the landscape while supporting a cleaner alternative to feedlot beef.

But it almost never happens. Advocates of pastured beef

speak of rotational grazing as if it were only a matter of placing the animals outside and letting nature run its course. In fact, the endeavor, by virtue of its decentralized structure and exposure to myriad uncontrolled variables, resists the kind of predictability provided by cruel but efficient factory farming. As one grass farmer explained, "I once read that Edison was asked, 'How is it coming along with the development of the lightbulb?' And his response was 'Great, I know eight-hundred-plus things that won't work.' My attempts as a farmer are about the same."[7] Therein lies an important truth of grass farming. For it to work, every grass farmer has to accomplish the technological equivalent of reinventing the lightbulb.

The most obvious aspect of grass farming that "won't work" is land availability and quality. Raising cows on pasture requires an unsustainable amount of land to support enough grass to bring cattle to slaughter weight. In general, the fewest acres required to fatten the most cattle is environmentally ideal. A tight cattle-land ratio minimizes agricultural sprawl while preserving biodiversity (including rain forests). What we might call the curse of Joel Salatin, however, hovers over grass farmers who lack the dreamy agricultural conditions of Swoope, Virginia. Salatin boasts an ability to raise one cow per acre of grass "in his neck of the woods."[8] Two observations about Salatin's neck of the woods, however, demand amplification. First, one-to-one is nothing to write home about. A single cow reaching slaughter weight after seventeen months of eating grass and forage is a cow that occupied a relatively large amount of agricultural land for a relatively long time, emitted at least 50–60 percent more methane than conventional cows, and left the farmer a proud owner of a few hundred pounds of beef to process and sell. Second, and perhaps worse, Salatin's one-cow-per-acre ratio is about the best ranchers could ever hope to achieve. The land requirements beyond the idyll of Swoope are less than Swoope-like. In fact, they are, as grass farmers themselves are often the first to admit, comparatively dreadful.

Grass farmers writing on homesteading websites don't mince words about this situation. One writes, "Salatin may be able to raise 1 cow on one acre . . . however there are States out West where one will be hard pressed to raise 1 cow on 100 acres (too hot and dry, poor soils, little rainfall). . . . Without the benefit of supplemental feed and at least 90 days in a feed lot with a high grain consentrate [*sic*] feed, that cow will be nothing but a bag of bones."[9] Another wondered, "Do you think we could do grassfed finished cattle up here in Montana? Nope. They get sent south to be grass fed finished."[10] WildRoseBeef described conditions in California thusly: "For even [in] Northern California 3+ acres is not nearly enough to home a bovine, even if it's a miniature one. You will need at least 5 acres to raise and pasture even one bovine, more if you're wanting two, especially over a long-term period."[11] Another grass farmer in the American West noted that in the Sierra Nevada region "5,000 acres can only run 100 beef cows and their calves (total 200 head). . . . Location, location, location makes all the difference."[12] And if your location is the Texas Panhandle, you can understand this farmer's observation: "I recently visited Colorado and had to go through the northern parts of NM and noticed out there that many ranches were vast enough to follow the highway for 10 or more miles on each side of the highway for as far as the eye could see. I asked one gentleman in a fuel station in Dalhart, TX how many cow/calf pairs per acre and he just kind of laughed and said, 'it's usually about 400 acres per cow/calf pair.' I didn't take him seriously until he said 'I'm not joking.'"[13] When Francismilker learned that a fellow farmer was "running 100 head on 161 acres," he responded, "That's absolutely absurd in my area even if you did have the money for commercial fertilizer and use[d] irrigation."

A calculator helps put this problem in perspective. Of the about 90 million cattle in the United States, the vast majority of them—say, 97 percent—are penned in feedlots for most of their lives and fed grain grown in the American heartland.[14] As the references in the previous paragraph suggest, it's difficult to generalize about the acreage of grass required per cow. That ratio might range anywhere from 1 cow per acre to 1 cow per 400 acres. So let's work with ten acres. It's a made-up, and likely far too small, number of average acres required to bring a cow to slaughter weight, but nonetheless let's use it for the ease of calculation. Ninety million cows times ten acres means 900 million acres of land would be needed to raise today's cows on pasture. The United States has about 2.3 billion acres of land in total.[15] About 400 million acres of that are being used for crops, 600 million acres are forested, and another 300 million are in parks and wildlife. Let's say the forested land and parks are off-limits, in addition to the 60 million acres of land that's urbanized. Of the 400 million acres of cropland, about 150 million are in corn and soy. So let's say that this is land that could be turned over to grass (because it would no longer be used for animal feed).[16] If we turned all cattle in the United States out to pasture, we would have to use nearly every single acre of arable land, with maybe a few million acres to spare. And recall, this estimate is based on the unlikely minimum of ten acres per cow.

Further mucking up matters for the grass-fed option is what that nominal amount of leftover arable land would be used for—hay. Indeed, another glitch in the grass-farming scheme that's never highlighted is that pasture-fed cattle require ample and consistent supplies of hay. Hay isn't free. It's an intensively produced agricultural commodity grown on prime arable land that, when temporarily locked up in hay, cannot be grazed or used for the production of plants for people to eat. This allotment further increases the already expansive agricultural footprint of grass-fed beef production, again diverting arable land away from its most environmentally responsible and healthy use: growing plants for humans to consume.

When grass farmers talk among themselves—as they do in online forums—they spend much of their time discussing the troubling logistics of hay. One grass farmer pulled out a calculator to reiterate that "cattle eat a lot." He went on to explain that "a 1000 lb cow on just maintenance requirements consumes 2.5% of her body weight, or 25 lbs of *dry matter* ration (ration where all the water is removed) per day. Grass with a moisture percentage of around 70% means that that 1000 lb cow will be consuming 8.33% of her body weight per day, or 83.33 lbs of grass per day. That's a lot of grass."[17] Another farmer joined a discussion focusing on Joel Salatin's farm by noting, "Sorry I don't know Salatin or their [sic] process, I just know what works out here. Grass hay swathed, baled and put up for the winter."[18] Whereas

Salatin enjoyed his vaulted status as the grass farmer's guru, others viewed themselves as inferior acolytes reduced to mere hay farmers. Greybeard was forthright in his dependency: "You put out all the hay they can eat in 24 hrs and you do it for each 24 hrs. . . . Unless something is wrong with them, there should be hay in front of them every hour of every day."[19] Others mentioned providing "unlimited hay," "as much hay as he'll eat," and "I will continue with AM and PM hay."[20] Grass farmers would love to just graze, never importing hay or other feed. But doing so is impossible for most farmers. "I just don't think I can ever achieve the goal of being totally hay independent or anywhere close to that with the kind of place I own," wrote Agman.

The life cycle of hay, as these comments suggest, is costly. The water required to generate hay, the equipment needed to harvest it, the fertilizer and herbicides used to grow it, and the storage, transport, and processing costs—none of which are ever factored into the grass farmer's footprint— add up to a substantial environmental tab. Consider water. Almost all hay is irrigated. Water usage statistics vary, but in eastern Colorado, California, and Arizona (where studies have been conducted), alfalfa and "grass hay" demand more water than any other crop produced in those regions.[21] Much of that water is wasted. Some is transferred to alfalfa and exported to China. To better appreciate the energy expended in the production of hay, observe that, as the Minnesota Department of Agriculture does, "15 to 30 percent of the standing forage crop is commonly lost during harvest and storage. Field losses are greater for hay, while storage losses are greater for silage [high-moisture fodder]."[22] When stored for even minimal amounts of time, hay leaches out significant amounts of dry weight (water), protein, and energy.[23] Moving this hay consumes considerable energy as well. Then, when cows finally get their hay, the beasts are sloppy with it. According to the Iowa Beef Center, "Livestock trample, over-consume, contaminate, and use for bedding 25–45 percent of the hay."[24] Yet again, the inescapable reality of animal agriculture rears its ugly head: when you convert plants into animal feed—even if those plants are grasses—resources are lost in translation. We can talk all we want about a free lunch, but when you consider the less obvious stages of the animal supply chain, you always waste more than had you produced plants. Given the preciousness of global resources dedicated to food production, this distinction explains why there is no such thing as a beef-eating environmentalist.

Perhaps the most routinely touted benefit of eating pastured beef is that the animals were not fed what critics consider to be the bane of industrial animal agriculture: grain (or, more accurately, corn or soy). However, even this is not necessarily the case. If scores upon scores of accounts by grass farmers writing to each other on agricultural forums are any indication, grain is a routine and often unavoidable supplement to grass and hay. A small farm outside of Grand Rapids, Michigan, explained that its cows are "grass fed, some grain, no hormones."[25] Another said of his herd, "I grain and hay them year round. . . . Figure 100 lbs of grain per month, per head . . . plus the cost of hay."[26] One grass farmer was so dubious that another rancher could survive on all grazed grass or hay that he asked, "Does anyone have any pictures of cows coming out of a hard Winter without grain that I can view?" Farmers frequently speak of the conditions driving them to resort to grain. "I was the last person in the area that had to seek outside sourced feed," wrote a grass farmer with some pride, "but I hit bottom and had to buy feed." A grass farmer in the Sierra Nevada grazing a hundred beef cattle on five thousand acres mentioned feeding "good quality alfalfa hay plus grains" from May to November. He did so, as he put it, "in a feed lot." Another farming couple wrote how "the grass in the pasture is all but gone now. We are giving [the cows] two gallons of 14% grain a day and adding alfalfa hay as well."[27] Even one especially die-hard grass farmer admitted that "grain is a treat now and then," while the farmer noted that "1 gallon bucket of grain each twice a day is what I do." Joel Salatin tends to dismiss any deviation from his one-cow/one-acre measure as evidence of "Neanderthal" farming. But those who live beyond Swoope stockpile their grain and hay and call it reality. They also continue to call it "grass-fed."

"I WILL REMAIN AN ADVOCATE FOR ENDOPHYTE INFECTED FESCUE"

Raising pastured beef requires not only excessive amounts of land, hay, and grain, but also excessive amounts of grass. Nothing is more necessary to the system's proper functioning. The most important cool-season grass growing on cattle pastures in the United States is a nineteenth-century, inadvertent English import called tall fescue (or just fescue). Fescue is a high-yielding and protein-rich turf that's tolerant of variable environmental conditions. Today's hardy ecotype of fescue derives from a cultivar found in the 1920s by a local extension agent on a scraggy Kentucky mountaintop. Plant scientists began cultivating it in 1931. The University of Kentucky began to sell it as a pasture crop in 1943. It took off, quickly dominating grasslands nationwide, filling voids in the South where cool-season grasses did not grow in enough abundance to graze cattle productively.[28]

Fescue not only grows quickly and is tolerant of ecological variations, but it's unusually resistant to many insects. Called "the most important cool season grass in the United States,"[29] fescue is also known by experts as "most desirable grass to stockpile for late fall and winter grazing."[30] Given the popularity of fescue among grass farmers, it may come as something of a surprise to learn that not only is much of the fescue grown to feed cattle infected with a fungus that harms them, but many grass-fed farmers prefer and cultivate the fungus-infected fescue rather than its fungus-free counterpart. At the core of the grass-fed system we find a grass that harms the cattle whose welfare farmers claim to value. Grass farmers routinely tout their systems as natural. But eating an infected grass hardly seems natural.

The fungus that infects fescue is called an endophyte. Farmers tend to prefer endophyte-infected fescue for "its hardiness and good forage yields." Their support persists despite "its adverse effects on cattle well-being and yields." It is, according to one fescue expert, "a cool season perennial grass that cattle producers 'can't live with but can't live without.'"[31] Curiously, most of the grass farmers who actively participate in homesteading forums work to keep their fescue infected, eschewing opportunities to replace infected fescue with a noninfected variety. Agmantoo explained that his "farm grows only endophyte infected fescue and clovers and I feed the same forage 365 days per year." He notes, "The cows seem to relish the forage each day." Another grass farmer praised endophyte infection: "To date, the fescues that I know of that are endophyte free are not hardy." Yet another added, "Until convinced otherwise I will remain an advocate for endophyte infected fescue. . . . I just cannot find a forage with the [same] staying power." "Keep the fescue growing," chimed in a grass farmer from the South. A member of backyardherds.com reminded readers concerned about a clover that was causing deadly bovine gas, "There are several varieties of 'friendly' endophyte tall fescue like MaxQ out on the market. There are also endophyte free varieties, but the endophyte is what makes fescue so hardy." Although grass farmers might be tempted to opt for the healthy fescue, this member warned against making such a choice: "When they totally remove the endophyte, the grass isn't quite as good as the infected kind. They're finding the novel (or friendly) endophyte fescue is much better than the endophyte free stuff." The prevailing agricultural literature supports this farmer's assessment that infected fescue is a tough grass that yields well.[32]

What's good for the farmer's bottom line, however, is not necessarily good for the cows that eat it. Cows were "meant to eat grass," we are told over and over by advocates of pastured beef. But were they meant to eat endophyte-infected fescue grass? For one, consider why so much fescue is infected with endophyte in the first place. The relationship is symbiotic. The grass provides the fungus a safe haven in which to breed. In return, the endophyte provides grass hardiness, resistance to many insects, and—the key irony here—protection against consumption by herbivores, *such as cows.* Fescue formed an evolutionary relationship with endophyte so animals such as cows would not eat it. So, when it comes to whether cows *were meant* to eat endophyte-infected fescue, nature herself answers that question as clearly as she knows how to answer it: *No.*

It makes them ill. Cattle suffer from fescue-related conditions such as fescue foot, fat necrosis, and fescue toxicosis.[33] Fescue foot causes a rapid acceleration in respiration and body temperature, weight loss, gangrene that can lead to loss of extremities, eruptions of lesions on legs, and rapid hair loss.[34] Bovine fat necrosis causes reduced reproductive capacity, chronic discomfort from digestive turmoil, and depression.[35] Fescue toxicosis has been called "one of the most costly disorders facing livestock producers in the eastern US." Its impacts include the inability to produce milk, narrowed blood vessels, and severe birthing problems.[36] Because these diseases aren't infectious, and because their manifestations are often asymptomatic, farmers often don't act aggressively against them. But the cattle—animals who are said to be doing what they "were meant" to do—suffer the effects of eating what they were most assuredly never supposed to consume. If cows were meant to eat grass, why does this grass so often make them sick? How is that diet any more natural or unnatural than eating corn?

"A NONEMOTIONAL CULLING"

As we have seen, the practitioners of pastured beef call themselves grass farmers. But it would be more accurate to call them calf farmers. This point is rarely made when the numerous welfare benefits of pastured beef are touted, but grass farmers routinely shunt calves off the verdant pasture and into the industrial marketplace, thereby relying on industrial agriculture to enhance the small farm's bottom line. Perhaps even more important, they cull to maintain the critical and ever-shifting balance between flesh and grass out in the fields. Consider what one grass farmer writes: "The single biggest problem I have with the rotational grazing is my inability to balance the available forage to the needs of the cattle over a 12 month span." The quest to achieve a desirable ratio between cows and grass requires constant culling of cows. One farmer wrote, "Any heifer that requires assistance birthing at 24 months would be culled, no exception."[37]

But it's primarily calves that are culled. According to the farmer quoted above, "I market calves anytime I have a large enough load to justify sending them to market." His reasons were explicit: "cash flow" and "it also lets me vary the grazing load on the paddocks." He added, "I've heard that you get a better price at market if you have a group of calves that are the same size and age."[38] When we think about the quality of a cow's life on a grass-fed beef ranch, we tend to think that farmers are nobly avoiding the hard brutality of agribusiness, a brutality that separates calves from their mothers, treats the calves as commodities, and transforms them into milk machines or veal. Perhaps this impression reflects that we never get to see the pictures of terrified calves being dragged from their mothers and sold to the highest bidder at a livestock auction to help a farm's cash flow.

One farmer referred to the critical practice of undertaking "a nonemotional culling." This habit appears to be standard among grass farmers. Godsgapeach wrote how he was "confident that I can net more profit from the large tract with the large herd" because he could "cull and get the 'right size' cows." Goddess Kristie explained, "It does not matter that your calf hangs around a few weeks longer if your calf goes to market and sells in the top bracket." To those who might have thought this an emotionally cold way to handle calves, she reminded them of a critical caveat: "My operation is not a hobby." Another farmer chimed in, "If I get caught short of grass I have three options, sell calves lighter in weight, cull cows or buy feed." Culling and selling were her preferred options. The owner of Davis Farm explained of the excess in his herd, "You need to butcher them or sale [sic] them because you don't have the grass to keep them happy and fat."[39]

Doing so without emotion, however, was easier said than done for some farmers. "We're open to culling," wrote one grass farmer, while admitting that it would be hard to cull "a small no-name brand" who was "getting up in years." The reason was rather poignant: "When I go out and whistle she romps across the pasture like a dog." This farmer was hardly alone in his affection for the cows he so carefully fattened for slaughter. A contributor to localharvest.org wrote about how he could not eat his own cows because "they are like pets to me."[40]

When calves become the moral equivalent of cash, however, sentimentality becomes unaffordable. Grass farmers frequently evaluate the worth of their heifers explicitly in terms of their calving ability. One wrote, "With a 90% survival rate the big momma will send 9 calves to the sale." Worried that some of these calves might be too heavy for the market, she reasoned that even if the "price of calves drops," the "additional pounds" will ensure that they're "still profitable." When another grass farmer expressed concern about unwanted calves lingering around the pasture too long and consuming precious resources, he was advised, "It does not matter that your calf hangs around a few weeks longer if your calf goes to market and sells in the top bracket." Raising heifers on grass, as we've seen, demands a constant balancing act between grass and stocking density. "If grass is limited," a farmer explained, "I market the calves at a lower weight in order to conserve feed." Another added, "I do want to cull as much of the herd as permitted." Her advice to others was "Look at the calf, look at its mother. If the calve [*sic*] is OK and the mother is out of condition cull them both." The relationship between calves and "the market" is driven home without equivocation by one grass farmer's remark· "I market calves anytime I have a large enough load to justify sending them to market. I feel that instead of getting the high or low of the market I should get an average over time." This approach, he concluded, "gives a cash flow over the year and it also lets me vary the grazing load on the paddocks." One farmer purchased a new bull to "improve the calves that I send to the sale." This farmer too called himself "a grass farmer."[41]

As with so many of these grass farmers, it was calves that he was managing his operation to harvest. Again, while it is by no means a surprise that small farmers, just like large ones, are primarily concerned about profit, the blatant equation of calves and cash reminds us that, in both systems, animals are objectified for the purposes of the bottom line. And it's hard to treat them with respect when that's the case.

"NO RAINFALL"

Of the many problems that grass farmers face—grass quality, land availability, feed supplementation, balancing herd
density and acreage—none may be more critical than the
availability of water. Grass farmers can generally count on
the sun to shine. But rain is less predictable. Livestock production is already one of the world's largest consumers of
water. In conventional beef production it takes on average
about twenty-five hundred pounds of water to produce a
pound of beef. Cows need roughly two gallons of water per
hundred pounds of body weight a day, and that figure dou-
bles when they're lactating.[42] Nearly half the overall water
used in the United States is consumed by the cattle industry.[43] This is an ecological catastrophe. There's no evidence,
moreover, that grass-fed cows, despite their eco-correct
reputation, use any less water than grain-fed cows. In fact,
given that grass-fed cows need more time to reach slaughter
weight, it suggests that, pound for pound, they require more
water. Grass farmers are often the first to admit that theirs
is a water-intensive business.[44] On grass-farmer forums, water is a grave concern in raising cattle the way they "were
meant" to be raised.

The Salatin curse is especially pronounced when it comes
to water. Swoope, Virginia, home of Polyface farm, is in a
wet region, with an average of fifty inches of rain a year,
spread out over a hundred days. As grass farmers are the
first to note, the rest of the country isn't so fortunate
when it comes to the amount and frequency of rain. "Here
in the Far West," writes one grass farmer, "we have alka-

line soil, hard pan at the surface or just below it, [and] NO
rainfall from mid May to mid Nov." Another Californian
concurred, writing, "Here in Cali almost EVERYONE is
on what they call a 'dry lot' where you supplement 100% of
their feed . . . that's just the way it is here . . . dry dry dry . . .
we haven't had rain in months." Pastures with ponds or water tanks are standard, but it's not uncommon to experience,
as one farmer did, how "the pond almost dried up during
the drought." In hot weather, a farmer reported needing
"4500 gallons of water per day" for his herd, saying, "This is
where the challenge lies." She elaborated, "Got to get it
from somewhere. . . . We've just got to do some figuring. I
need to find out if any of the bored wells can still produce
or if we'd be better off having one drilled." Such genuine
expressions of frustration are common. "I have no irrigation and we have droughts of various magnitudes," a grass
farmer wrote. He thought he could make it through mid-
summer, "but I absolutely must have water in late Summer
and early Fall." In 2007 the "extended drought sent me down
the tubes."[45]

Global warming means a future of more serious droughts.
Serious droughts mean more ruined grass-feed farmers, especially in places such as Texas. Beginning in 2005, a drought
hit Texas and intensified well into 2012. Food writers who
for some reason see it as their job to promote the grass-fed
option typically downplay the impact of drought, often going so far as to suggest that grass farmers are better equipped
to handle it than their conventional counterparts. Writing
in *Grist*, Christopher Weber celebrated a Wisconsin grass
farmer's ability to hang on during a drought. He writes,

"A well-managed, ecologically diverse rangeland holds up in drought conditions."[46] Weber might have spoken to the owners of Fredericksburg Grassfed Beef, Texas farmers who have been in the business for over fifty years. Or he might have even just gone to their website and learned that "this drought has continued to intensify. We are not in production. I am writing this November 27, 2012. We still have a [sic] two calves to harvest in the fall of 2013. If the weather does not moderate we will not be able to finish calves for 2014."[47] The owners added, "Please pray for rain." Even artisanal beef websites understand how, as one put it, "grass-fed beef and droughts don't mix."[48] With climatologists predicting droughts will intensify into Dust Bowl conditions in the near future, it yet again raises the question of why conscientious consumers are so eager to pursue the grass-fed alternative when we could be growing plants that require a few gallons—rather than a few thousands of gallons—to produce a pound of decent food.

Sometimes the problem isn't a lack of water, but too much of it, such as with pugging.[49] This condition is created by repetitive hoof action by cows who gather in a wet place and hang out. The inevitable trampling of soil leaves behind damaging globs of mud around a pasture's water source—be it a pond, river, or water tank—where cows tend to stand when they're not eating. In and of itself, socializing cattle pose a fundamental problem for the grass farmer. One of the bovines' "jobs" is to evenly distribute rich manure to fertilize the pasture. When ancient ungulates roamed grasslands without the interference of a profit-driven grass farmer, the animals naturally spread their poop democratically. When confined in rotating pens, however, they tend to gather around designated water sources, where they deposit the highest percentage of their waste. The repetitive hoof action, moisture buildup, and concentrated manure create an anaerobic soup so dense that no grass can grow through it. The plot of land dies.

Making matters worse is that one of the critical requirements for effective grass farming—relatively reliable rain—makes it especially difficult to diminish pugging. As one New Zealand assessment of pugging reiterates, "It can be difficult to completely prevent pugging, especially in farming situations with heavy soils and wetter climates."[50] Grass farmers thus face a catch-22: too much moisture and the pugging becomes worse; not enough moisture and grass won't grow. Both conditions enhance the need for fertilizer and irrigation and thus keep padding the bill of what was supposed to be a free lunch.

"I HAVE NO IDEA WHAT I'M DOING"

Thus far I've only described a handful of the numerous problems endemic to grass farming. Advocates of pastured beef tend to downplay, hide, or ignore them. Nothing that I've written should in any way suggest that *every* grass farmer uses excessive amounts of land, imports external feed, culls calves for auction, relies exclusively on fescue, experiences constant bouts of pugging, and suffers from droughts. Instead, I'm merely trying to make the point that these mishaps happen as a matter of course on many grass farms. My goal is to highlight the inherent volatility of a practice that, to work effectively as a substitute for conventional beef, would have to operate at a consistently high level of efficiency. Given the brutal economics of grass-fed farming, the chances that even a large minority of cattlemen will transition from conventional to grass-fed production is minute. Even if they did, the chances that they could then raise cattle according to the rigorous standards required for this method to be even remotely sustainable would, if the accounts of the farmers themselves are any indication, be next to zero.

We cannot afford to indulge in agricultural fantasies. Time is short and too much is at stake with the global food system and the industrial giants that dominate it. Consider for a moment several problems that I'll only mention here in passing. As we saw with chickens in the last chapter, pastured cattle are routinely sick, exposed to predatory wildlife, prone to wandering off, dying without warning, and behaving in ways they were simply not supposed to behave. Even a die-hard supporter of grass farming admitted, "There are many risks involved when raising your own livestock—they can get out, get sick and die, hurt you, and you can get attached to them and then find it hard to butcher your pet!"[51] A quick stroll through any online forum of grass farmers will reveal that the commentary of despair and frustration— "She is loaded with parasites," "My cows have escaped 4 times onto the highway since I left," "She also has liver flukes and Coccidiosis," "I have no idea what I'm doing"— repeats like a broken record. None of this is to argue that growing plants for people to eat isn't beset with uncontrollable variables as well. It's only to note that, while there will always be ecological and ethical costs to growing food for billions of people, kale doesn't have to be sent to a slaughter-house. Kale doesn't have to be fed with forage grown else-where. Kale won't wander off to the highway and get hit by a semi. And if it dies a sudden death, rotten kale makes ter-rific compost.

Nevertheless, just for fun, let's end the chapter by going to fantasyland. Let's say that the people I opened the chapter with—Allan Savory, Joel Salatin, and Nina Planck—got their wish and waved a wand and saw a mass transition to grass-fed farming. What then? Considerable evidence sug-gests that even greater ecological problems than the ones we already confront would ensue. In her research exploring the carbon footprint of animal agriculture, Professor Judith L. Capper, of Washington State University, advises that we replace our "rose tinted spectacles" with a "high powered microscope." Peer into it and you will find, as Capper did, that "the increased land required for grass finished produc-tion renders the whole-scale conversion of the US beef pro-duction system to grass finished production practically impossible."[52] Her comparison of grass-fed versus conven-tional production, published in leading peer-reviewed jour-nals, found that, pound for pound, grass-fed beef had an overall carbon footprint that was roughly *20 percent higher than feedlot production.*[53]

Capper's findings are not those of a renegade crank. To the contrary, her recent work builds on a foundation of evi-dence that's skeptical of grass-fed beef's claim to environmen-tal virtue. In 2009 and 2010, Nathan Pelletier, of Dalhousie University, undertook research that led him to conclude, "We do see significant differences in the GHG intensities [of grass versus grain finishing]. It's roughly on the order of 50 percent higher in grass-finished systems."[54] He added, "It would appear that feedlot-finished beef products are less resource and emissions-intensive relative to management-intensive pastured beef production." So, even if you reject the analytical technique of this chapter—using real-life, on-the-ground accounts of grass farming to highlight its logistical inadequacy as a substitute for business as usual—the ecological promise of pastured beef is not supported by the numbers. This fantasyland would be a dark place.

The typical response to this argument from grass-fed acolytes will be twofold. First, they will appeal to *management*. Yes, grass farming can be sloppy and wasteful, but that's just because these farms suffer from poor management practices. Joel Salatin, in response to a piece I wrote for the *Times*, put it this way:

> *At Polyface, we call it neanderthal management because most livestock farmers have not yet joined the 20th century with electric fencing, ponds, piped water, and modern scientific aerobic composting (only as old as chemical fertilization). Hence, while his figures comparing the relative production of grain to grass may sound compelling, they are like comparing the learning opportunities under a terrible teacher versus a magnificent teacher.*[55]

Or just an average teacher. Every time you encounter an article or other news item praising the pastured option, note something critical: it's never "grass-fed" systems that are superior, but "properly managed" grass-fed systems that are superior. The qualification seems fairly innocuous, and perfectly justifiable, until you realize a critical sin of omission: nobody, not even Joel Salatin with his imported feed and industrial breeds, has been able to "properly manage" a grass-fed system in a way that is scalable and consistently replicable under various conditions. Asking consumers to wait for "proper management" to take hold and characterize a decentralized and geographically dispersed group of grass farmers is sort of like putting a person in a room, blindfolding him, spinning him in circles, and waiting patiently until he figures out how to throw a dart into the bull's-eye twenty feet away. You can say all you want, "Ah, he just needs a magnificent teacher," but he'll never consistently hit the target.

Second, advocates of grass will say that, no matter how hard it might be to properly manage a pasture, it's at least *better* than the horrible feedlot beef that now dominates the market to the tune of 99 percent. They will do this even while acknowledging the fatal flaws within the grass-fed approach. For example, consider that *Grist* piece by Christopher Weber. He writes:

> *Some folks will protest that the US lacks the land area to switch the beef industry to grass-finishing. While there's some truth in this critique, it misses the larger point: The beef industry and American agriculture as a whole have a lot to gain from rethinking their approach to land use, according to Fred Kirschenmann. "We have to remember that raising animals in confinement means we have to raise lots of corn and soybeans to feed them," says Kirschenmann. "A*

lot of that land could be used for grazing on perennials and raising alfalfa for forages, which would have significant ecological benefits."

But here's the question that neither Kirschenmann nor Weber nor Savory nor Planck nor Bittman nor Pollan nor any of the other big names associated with the promotion of the grass alternative will entertain: What would happen if, instead of comparing grass- and grain-fed systems, you compared grass-fed with the end of raising cattle altogether? People, after all, cannot eat alfalfa.

But they can eat kale and quinoa. The environmental writer Richard Oppenlander knows this well. While researching his book *Comfortably Unaware* he did a quick calculation and discovered something that captures the folly of trying to have our steak and eat it too.[56] He figured that if you had two acres of decent land and placed a cow on it, you would, after two years, have about four hundred pounds of edible beef. That same land, in the same amount of time, for much less of the cost, could produce five thousand pounds of kale and quinoa. This kale and quinoa could be obtained without the additional methane output or trampling impact and, most important, without the slaughter of sentient animals who would rather not be born in order to be killed and eaten by people with a warped sense of what cows were meant to do.

PAINFUL PORK

If animal lovers knew the facts . . .
—HEATH PUTNAM

The body of research currently being conducted on the behavior of pigs is something to behold. The basic rudiments of pig intelligence turn out to be deeply reflected in their everyday behavior. "They get scared and then have trouble getting over it," said the University of Bristol's Suzanne Held, who is doing pioneering work on the emotional lives of swine. "They can learn something on the first try and then it's difficult for them to unlearn it," she said.[1] These findings have bubbled their way into the popular media. "They are perhaps the smartest, cleanest domestic animals known," reported NBC news.[2] "The Joy of Pigs," an episode of the PBS show *Nature*, explained how "pigs are misunderstood in many ways"; while many people think of them as "portly and stupid," they are "smarter than any other domestic animal." Discussing the underlying reason for their intelligence, Dr. Lawrence Shook of the University of Illinois notes, "The pig genome compare[s] favorably with the human genome." This similarity, as Darwin observed over a century

before, confirms a number of "behavioral parallels." Cover-
ing this research for *The New York Times*, Natalie Angier
wrote how "pig hearts are like our hearts."[3] Interestingly,
Dr. Held, who agrees, explained, "I'm German and I love
sausage," while insisting, "I would never eat pork that isn't
free-range." On this last point—the free-range alternative—
the story of pork gets complicated.

I would love to know what Dr. Held would think if she
were present at Wind Ridge Farm, which raises free-range
pigs for personal consumption, on slaughter day.[4] The pro-
prietors, who maintain a website to assist other homesteaders in processing their own on-farm pork, evade ethical
concerns at the outset of their lesson with this nonargu-
ment: "What is a pet and what is for dinner is a matter of
culture." They then equate the slaughter of a pig with the
death of yeast. Bakers, they claim, similarly kill yeast when
they make bread. Having thus made their "ethical case" for
eating the animals that Dr. Held has shown to be smarter
than domesticated dogs, the farmers explain that the first
choice that must be made by any pig slaughterer is whether
"to skin it, scorch it, or scald it." No matter the option, they
explain (quoting, of all people, the rock-star-gun-nut Ted
Nugent), "You gotta kill it to grill it." Next, insisting that
meat tastes better when the pig is "bled out" while alive, the
farmers instruct readers how to "stick" a pig with a .22 rifle.
The purpose of this step is to shoot the pig "so that both
sides of the brain is disrupted" and he or she will lie still and
behave for the bleed-out. After what one would assume is a
terrifying, if not excruciating experience for the pig, the
farmers note that although "it will very quietly die from the
head wound," you'd be better off placing her out of misery

by slicing the carotid arteries or simply jamming a knife into the heart.[5] This is, I suppose, the farmers' idea of killing a pig as painlessly as possible, something they (ironically) suggest we all do. Of course, the only pain being minimized is the pain of having to watch an animal with the innate intelligence of a three- to five-year-old human fighting death.

I'm projecting here, but I would imagine that Dr. Held might leave the slaughter festivities with at least residual doubt about her free-range choice. She would be like many consumers of pork: a little confused. On the one hand, no other farm animal has so easily transitioned into the role of beloved house pet and earned the affection and respect of human companions. "Some pigs," we learn from "The Joy of Pigs," "are more welcome in the house than the barn." They "get along well with other domestic animals" and "enjoy lap visits and cuddling."[6] Breeders are breeding pigs to be smaller and smaller to cater to human desires to keep them indoors. An English breeder and pig owner told ABC News, "They are so intelligent, and they are so much fun. They will lay with you in the evening and watch TV, they love their belly scratched, and they are very, very loving."[7] Many pig owners even keep their pigs as pets despite city bans against it. One New Yorker does it "because they're really sweet and really smart animals."[8] A pig adoption organization explains how pigs "need lots of love and attention" and "make for a most affectionate pet."[9]

At the same time that we've come to appreciate the intelligence and affectionate nature of pigs, however, we've turned bacon into a fetishized luxury item. This fetish has become so ubiquitous that it has been elevated to a T-shirt slogan. Bacon T-shirts today declare such messages as GOT

BACON?, I'D WRAP THAT IN BACON, BACON ME CRAZY, MMMM . . .
BACON, EVERYTHING IS BETTER WITH BACON, BACON IS GOOD
FOR ME, BACON MAKES EVERYTHING BETTER, EXERCISE FOR BA-
CON, JEWS FOR BACON, and, for the minimalist, BACON. This
jejune glorification of taste for sliced pig can be seen in an
especially disturbing way on a recent video ad played at my
favorite source of satire, *The Onion*. In it, a well-groomed
man kneels before a beautiful woman while proffering a box
that appears to contain an engagement ring. The charming
paramour slowly opens the box to reveal two strips of crispy
bacon, a discovery that leaves the couple basking in an orgi-
astic glow. They will come together over bacon. The media
regularly promotes the supposed joys of eating bacon. The
British newspaper *The Guardian* published a befuddling
editorial in 2009 called "In Praise of Bacon." "There are
times," the paper's editorial board wrote, "that only bacon
will do." At the mere smell of bacon, "everything else slips
away into a happy haze." Their conclusion was no different
from Dr. Held's: "This should be a time to support (free-
range) British pig farmers."[10]

A familiar narrative pattern is being played out around
the pig. There's the hopeful recognition among concerned
consumers that, indeed, pigs matter. As with our dogs and
cats, whom we shower with affection, we know that pigs have
intrinsic worth, and as a result, we know that they deserve
moral consideration. But we also really like the way they
taste, so much so that we've practically created a separate cat-
egory of culinary ecstasy for the experience of eating them:
"*Mmmm . . . bacon!*" and so on. The popular solution to this
dilemma has been the by-now-familiar trope of "free-range."

Pigs on pasture have an opportunity to live as pigs naturally live, we are told. We are told that pigs on pasture are
healthier and safer to eat, less prone to *Salmonella*, trichinosis, and other pathogens that can seriously harm human
consumers. We are told that pigs living the free-range
dream are mercifully spared the mutilations required under
confinement. As we have seen with cattle and chickens, however, the realities behind these claims are driven by economic imperatives and, as a result, marred by practices that,
were it not for the comparatively horrific nature of the
factory-farming of pigs, would be unacceptable to consumers who claimed to care about the animals they eat. Once
again, the rhetoric and reality of the free-range option depart in ways that will be disturbing to anyone who claims to
give two oinks about the welfare of pigs.

SAFETY

Between 2001 and 2002 a couple of animal scientists went
into the field and studied the prevalence of "gastrointestinal
pig parasites" on conventional, organic, and free-range farms
in the Netherlands, a country known for well-regulated and
clean agricultural practices. They published their results in
the peer-reviewed journal *Veterinary Research*. Their findings might surprise anyone who thinks that, in terms of
safety, they're better off eating free-range pork than conventionally or organically raised pork. For the intestinal parasite coccidium, 88 percent of sows on the free-range farm
tested positive for it, as did 80 percent of those on the organic

farms. By contrast, only 44 percent of the sows on conventional farms had it. Roundworms, which can have "a devastating effect on human health,"[11] were discovered in half the free-range pigs but only 11 percent of the conventionally raised ones. This disparate pattern held true for other infections as well, leading the authors to conclude, "The presence of helminth [worm] infections of pigs on farms with outdoor facilities . . . is higher than in pigs on conventional farms."[12] Of course, these differences are not to suggest that we should all run out and buy our bacon from Oscar Mayer. To the contrary, it's just another reason to avoid pork. All pork.

Those with a financial and ideological stake in selling free-range pork insist that the extra space to roam in a paddock makes it less likely that the pigs will spread infections. This proposition would seem to make intuitive sense. However, this hypothesis, which downplays the remarkable sociability and curiosity of pigs, is not adequately supported by the evidence. A 2005 study published in *Applied and Environmental Microbiology* (supported by the organic industry) found that *Salmonella* contamination and dissemination was highly prevalent in "outdoor organic pig production environments." A summary of the authors' findings notes, "The organic rearing conditions and the low stocking density in the outdoor facilities do not prevent infections, probably because there is still close contact between the pigs. . . . Their rooting behavior is likely to pose a risk of ingestion of *Salmonella* from the contaminated environment." The authors note, "It cannot be concluded from this study that [outdoor] organic rearing conditions serve as protection against *Salmonella* infections, as a high infection rate did occur under some circumstances." The study found "a higher risk of meat juice samples from both organic and free-range herds being seropositive [for *Salmonella*] than from samples from conventional herds."[13] This result should not be terribly surprising. Free-range pigs, innately investigative and social creatures who are constantly exploring their environments, root with rare tenacity. It's virtually impossible to prevent swine from encountering soil contaminated with feces—their own and that of other species. A well-managed factory farm, by virtue of its cruel confinement methods, can better control the interaction between pigs and poop, albeit at a totally unacceptable cost to the pigs' welfare.

Evidence of trichinosis, toxoplasma, and *Salmonella* exposure in free-range systems has been documented in the United States as well. Wondwossen Gebreyes, a professor of veterinary medicine at Ohio State University, published a study examining the presence of pathogens in pigs raised in outdoor and "intensive indoor" systems. After testing hundreds of pigs brought up in both systems, he and his colleagues found greater evidence of pathogen exposure in outdoor than in indoor pigs. Over 50 percent of the outdoor pigs were exposed to salmonella, compared to 39 percent of the indoor pigs; 7 percent of outdoor pigs showed evidence of toxoplasma compared to 1 percent of the indoor pigs; and two outdoor pigs had trichinosis antibodies while none of the indoor pigs tested positive for it. Evaluating this research, Bill Chamcides, dean of Duke University's Nicholas School of the Environment, found the findings "quite believable," reminding skeptics of the obvious point that "free range pigs by definition live in a less-controlled environment that should lead to greater exposure to a whole variety of microbes and thus a higher incidence of pathogens." The Gebreyes team received funding from the National Pork Board to conduct its research. Nevertheless, Chameides appears to have followed the science rather than the money. He concluded, "For me the fact that the pork industry funded the study is moot," adding that it was "irresponsible" to suggest that Gebreyes fudged his results to please his supporters.[14] While the pork industry association is unfortunate, subsequent research has failed to undermine Gebreyes's results.

In 2012, researchers from North Carolina State University discovered that a leading cause of food-borne illness—antibiotic-resistant *C. coli*—was present in both conventional and outdoor (or what the authors called "antimicrobial-free," or ABF) production systems. And in much higher numbers. "We found," the authors wrote about young pigs, "significantly higher prevalence of *C. coli* on the ABF farms (77.3%) than on the conventional farms (27.6%)."[15] A similar study uncovered the same disparity between conventional and outdoor systems. From a sample of 889 pigs and 743 carcasses from both kinds of systems, researchers found *Salmonella* exposure at 15.2 percent in outdoor systems and 4.2 percent in conventional arrangements.[16] Again, although we commonly hear that pigs raised outdoors produce safer pork (even from animal rights' organizations),[17] we too easily lose sight of the fact that, as the Pig Site (which is sympathetic to all forms of pig production, including pasture-raised pork) puts it, "while these systems offer improved animal welfare they may create new problems for animal health and food safety." It adds, "Studies show that pigs raised from organic and free range production systems are associated with higher risk of *Toxoplasma gondii* (*T. gondii*) infection than the animals raised from conventional (indoor) operations."[18] Yet again, those within the business of animal production appear to be more cognizant of the dangers than the consumers they serve.

The most comprehensive study to date undertaken on the comparative safety of free-range versus conventional pork came out in 2011. The author, Peter Davies of the University of Minnesota, found since World War II "an 80-fold greater risk (per pig produced) of trichina infections resulting from eating niche market versus commercial pork products." What's unusual about Davies's work is not his findings, but rather his outspoken interpretation of them. "Misinformation in public discourse," he writes, "has achieved pandemic potential with the rise of blogging and other social networking tools." Discussions of food and agriculture, he continues, "are mostly ideological and heavily value laden." He believes that scientists must do more than practice sound science. They must exhort the "scientific community . . . to be more visibly engaged in refuting misinformation as well as presenting new information." Lecture delivered, Davies then gets to the point: "Available evidence does not support the hypothesis that intensive pork production has increased risk for the major bacterial foodborne pathogens." Nor does it support the opinion "that pigs produced in alternative systems are at reduced risk of colonization with these organisms." In fact, Davies explains, "Pigs raised in outdoor systems inherently confront higher risks of exposure to foodborne parasites."[19] None of this information ever seems to make it onto the front of a T-shirt.

WELFARE

Consumers can dismiss Professor Davies as a pork-industry hack and take some qualified risks, especially for the trade-off of pigs' being raised in an environment where their welfare is of paramount concern. If pigs have space to be pigs, consumers might reason, then it's okay to downplay a bunch of nitpicking studies by obscure scientists, some of who are funded by industrial interests seeking biased results. Fair enough.

But, as is almost always the case with nonindustrial forms of animal agriculture, what we imagine does not necessarily reflect life on the farm. Many consumers are surprised to discover, for example, that before pigs can be safely released into a pasture, farmers must mutilate them. Free-range pig farmers insert septum or nose rings into their pigs' snouts, thereby denying them expression of their second most natural tendency, rooting; and farmers castrate pigs without anesthesia, denying them expression of their first, the freedom and pleasure of reproduction. Farmers also accept conditions that allow mothers to roll over on their babies ("overlays"), allowing what farrowing crates reduce in factory farms, piglet death; and, finally, farmers kill their pigs at the end of the day—denying them the supposedly enjoyable life they had by sending them into a harrowing experience that, due to their tremendous intelligence, they will fully absorb before making somebody happy in the form of bacon strips.

These factors are a necessary part of the free-range reality. They should at least be acknowledged. Once they are appreciated for what they are—tactics that are reflective of factory farming—they demand that we keep thinking about, and rethinking, our decision to eat animals domesticated for food we don't need.

"AT A LOSS AS TO HOW TO STOP HER DIGGING"

A septum ring is a circular chunk of metal inserted into the snout of a pig. Many free-range pig farmers use septum rings to prevent pigs from tearing up their pastures. These rings cause pigs pain when affixed to their snouts and, afterward, deliver a sharp sting every time the pig roots. Pig farmers treat nose ringing as a matter of course. One farmer, Mudd, explained in a forum discussion, "The reasoning behind the rings [was] (1) if they are field raised (free roaming) they can't dig up the roots—therefor [sic] there is no need to re-seed the field [and] their food supply will always be available to them." Although another pig owner came to regret it (for welfare reasons), she inserted a ring into her eighteen-month-old pig's nose because she was "at a loss as to how to stop her digging up the backyard." Stevie G assured a skeptical new pig farmer, "Yes, nose rings are the most effective way to keep the ground from being dug up."[20] When another member of the forum expressed concern that the ring would restrict the pigs' ability to eat (a legitimate fear), he was reminded by Rhodie, "The 'Danish' pig rings, which are applied through the nasal septum . . . stops rooting but does not effect nesting or opening of self feeders."[21] When a forum member complained that his new pig, Harley, "was rooting terribly" and asked for suggestions to prevent it, he was told, "The simple fact of the matter is that nose ringing is the only way to stop pigs digging up the soil." When another member objected to this advice, claiming that it denied the pigs of their natural instinct, Stevie responded, "So if tanner wishes to stop the pig digging up the soil then tanner will have to ring it, keep it indoors, or sell it!!!!! Its that simple!!!!!"[22]

And that complex. This was not amateurish blather. Writing in his recent book *Animal Husbandry Regained*, John F. Webster explained, "There is no doubt that sows, given time, will reduce any pasture to the status of a badly ploughed field."[23] Few people who raise pigs dispute this. Although statistics are not available, much evidence suggests that the vast majority of commercial free-range pig farmers use septum rings to prevent rooting.

The reason for the device is clear enough. Jordan Graser, a pig farmer from Australia, explained to a local paper, "If I didn't use nose rings, they would be living in a dust bowl in summer and a mud pit in winter."[24] Producers such as those selling to the famed Niman Ranch, which has a reputation for animal welfare, permit its suppliers to insert nose rings.[25] An Iowa free-range pig farmer wrote that pigs "will tear up a field unless you put rings in their noses, which prevents them from digging, which some have suggested causes them to get depressed (and @ this point I would have to agree)."[26] Another US farmer writing on a farm blog about free-range pigs explained, "A farmer will put (pierce) their snout with a copper ring—about 3/4 inch in diameter . . . right in the tender end of their nose—so when they are tempted to root, they bump that ring—causing shooting pain."[27] The animal-rights attorney Piper Hoffman writes that nose ringing is a practice "which farmers inflict on nearly all free range pigs."[28]

Perhaps the best evidence that free-range pig farmers routinely use nose rings comes from the farmers who refuse to use them. Castigating those who do, they take the high road, suggesting that they are a noble minority. Rosery Farm, in Suffolk, England, explained on its website, "You'll also notice that none of our pigs have rings through their noses. Rings are put in to stop them from 'damaging' the land by rooting it up. . . . It's amazing to see free-range producers talk about welfare yet ring their pigs' noses."[29] Supporting this renegade perspective is academic research showing nose ringing to be a serious welfare violation.[30]

If concrete information on the exact percentage of free-range farms that insert nose rings is hard to come by, there's no doubt about the impact of nose rings on pigs: it causes them pain every time they put their snout to the ground. There's a reason that a number of welfare organizations—including Britain's Soil Association, the Farm Animal Welfare Council, Compassion in World Farming, the Humane Society, and the RSPCA—condemn the practice. The RSPCA explains, "As well as pain when the ring is inserted and the stress of handling, this practice leads to chronic pain. . . . Nose rings work by the action of discomfort and pain as the sow goes to root with her snout, causing her to stop."[31] The pain of insertion was effectively captured by a farmer named Brent, who wrote in a forum, "My last pig was ringed by the vet, its a fairly simple procedure but not for the faint hearted: the pig will make a hell of a racket."[32] He advised that farmers consult YouTube to learn how to do it. Animal Welfare Approved, a comparatively rigorous welfare label, prohibits nose ringing on the grounds that "allowing nose ringing is the easy option. We get a perception of good welfare, as the pig is kept on land with vegetation cover, but we have stopped the pig from performing part of its behavioral repertoire—and a key part at that." Additionally, "nose ringing causes acute and chronic pain which occurs during and after the operation to insert the ring. We also know that preventing rooting, which is such a key behavioral need, will cause the pig frustration."[33] Bruce Friedrich, formerly of PETA and now with Farm Sanctuary, explained to me, "Ringing causes psychological pain."[34] While it's impossible to quantify how painful nose ringing is for pigs placed on pasture, we can say with confidence that the intrusive and restrictive septum ring is not only common, but also illuminates yet again how the dream of humanely raised animal products is consistently compromised by an unrecognized reality that sharply undermines the spirit of the system. Spin the matter however you wish, but nose ringing is mutilation, and absolutely nothing about mutilation is humane. Until free-range farmers learn how to breed pigs that don't root, mutilation will always be the "easy option."

"CASTRATION IS AN ABSOLUTE NECESSITY"

If imagining what it's like to have the tissue in your septum pierced makes you cringe a bit, consider castration. *Without* anesthesia. Beau Ramsburg, head of Rettland Farm in Gettysburg, Pennsylvania, has contemplated the experience. Still, he remains unequivocal about the critical place of castration in every form of swine production. He wrote (in response to a piece I had written for *Slate*), "Castration is an absolute necessity for all male pigs, regardless of production system or philosophy." The reason: "Meat from an intact (uncastrated) male is inedible, due to the overpowering muskiness that is present in it." He's referring to "boar taint," which is caused by the accumulation of compounds in intact males. Producers with any interest in selling their pork will not allow it. Ramsburg refuses to use anesthesia, he explained, because "many consumers who seek out and purchase pastured pork do so because of their desire to have meat free from chemical contamination."[35]

But what about the impact of castration without anesthesia on the pig? Jennifer Small, co-owner of Flying Pigs Farm in upstate New York, has an interesting answer to that question. She insists that slicing open the piglet's scrotum and yanking out his testicles is no big deal: "My husband castrates them and I have to admit I was very surprised that as soon as you put them down they're running around like nothing happened. They might slow down a little bit for twelve or twenty hours, but it's surprising how little they seem to be affected."[36] Other farmers are less willing to whitewash the harsh reality of castration. Suzanne McMinn, a West Virginia pig farmer and blogger, recalled for her readers the details of castration day on her farm: "The pig man came out to 'cut' (castrate) Sausage this weekend. He brought the wife and daughter. Cutting pigs is a family affair. Even Jack [her son?] was interested. Till the screaming started. . . . There was a lot of screaming . . . and I mean SCREAMING. . . . Pigs can SCREAM."[37] A resident of Maryland recalled, "The worst part [about farm life] was when the stud pig was castrated. . . . Oh, I never saw anything like that; they would grab the pig and flip him over and cut them off. That pig would walk backwards for ten or fifteen minutes screaming."[38]

This may be the single most obvious sentence ever written, but, given the denial that many pig farmers conveniently indulge in, it must be said: castration without anesthesia is *painful*. Not only does every animal-welfare organization in existence oppose castration without anesthesia, but so does the comparatively conservative American Veterinary Medical Association (AVMA). It captures the catch-22-nature of the problem rather well. On the one hand, it notes, "Surgical castration involves cutting and manipulating innervated tissues and if anesthesia is not provided it will be painful as reflected by elevated blood cortisol concentrations, high-pitched squealing, and pain-indicative behaviors, such as trembling and lying alone. Some behavioral indicators of pain may persist for up to five days." It adds, "On-farm use of anesthesia is rare due to a range of economic, logistical and safety issues, both for the pig and the herdsperson."[39] On the other hand, numerous problems arise with both castration and, when it's used, anesthesia. The AVMA writes, "Potential complications associated with surgical castration include hemorrhage, excessive swelling or edema, infection, poor wound healing, and failure to remove both testicles. It has been suggested that surgically castrated barrows suffer from suppressed immunity, and exhibit higher incidences of inflammation, pneumonia and other diseases."

On the rare occasions when anesthesia is used on the farm, other problems can arise. Carbon dioxide "causes distress in piglets," "nitrous oxide is effective in inducing anaesthesia, but is not effective at preventing pain from castration," and "use of injectable general anesthetics is not recommended because of high mortality rates, and long recovery periods and risk of crushing by the sow."[40] When it comes to castration, there is no way to avoid inflicting the suffering that is routine on factory farms, where castration also happens as a matter of course.

In the trenches of the free-range pig forums, small farmers—those who tell us that welfare concerns are central to their work—remain generally indifferent to the physical and psychological impact that castration without anesthesia has on pigs. One farmer wrote, "Two important things I forgot to mention—make sure Mama Pig is secured in her stall while you're castrating the piglets and wear ear defendors!"[41] Another explained, "Yes, we have to wear ear defenders when we do them. They start squalloring the minute you pick them up and don't stop till you put them down!"[42] Beth recounted, "The vet came out and gave [her nine-month-old boar, whom she'd decided not to breed] some anesthesia and castrated him (About 12:00pm). He was doing good I checked on him for the last time at about 9:30pm he was walking around, still wobbly but not falling down just not steady. The next morning when I checked at 8:30am he was dead." A vet student responded, "Maybe he was bleeding internally and lost so much blood that he passed out (how did the vet castrate him exactly?)—sometimes you accidentally cut a vein during surgery and it doesn't appear to bleed at all . . . until after the wound is closed and it's too late."[43] Beth's eventual reaction was not to write about her emotions or to contemplate the boar's experience, but rather to note that "we were not able to salvage the meat because of the anesthesia so we had to haul our 330lb pig to the dump!!"[44]

"IF ANIMAL LOVERS KNEW THE FACTS, THEY'D PROBABLY BE IN FAVOR OF FARROWING CRATES"

In factory farming, no device may be as cruel as the farrowing crate. These cages house a lactating sow in quarters so close that she can only rest on her side and feed her babies, who nurse through metal bars. The cage is so constricting she cannot fully stand up. These stalls have been roundly condemned by animal-welfare advocates and concerned consumers alike. Both psychologically and physically harmful for sows, they have been deemed illegal in Sweden and the UK.[45] According to Compassion in World Farming, farrowing stalls "severely restrict the sow's movement and frustrate her strong motivation to build a nest before giving birth. They prevent the sow from being able to get away from her piglets, for example, if they bite her teats. It is common for piglets to have their teeth ground down or clipped, without anaesthetic, to minimize biting injuries."[46]

The RSPCA agrees with this condemnation of confinement, noting that sows in farrowing crates "have no opportunity to engage in exploratory and foraging behaviour, or to interact socially with other pigs." As a result, "they show high levels of stereotypical behaviour (repeating the same action, such as biting the bars of the stall and swaying their heads) and unresolved aggression."[47] Whole Foods, to its credit, bans pork sourced from pigs that have been housed in farrowing crates.[48] For all the popular and well-deserved condemnation of farrowing crates, though, an inconvenient point is rarely mentioned. Farrowing crates help prevent the death of piglets.

On pasture, sows routinely roll over and crush their

babies. The industry calls the problem "piglet overlay," and it's a major conundrum within free-range pig farming, where farrowing crates are verboten. The following testimony from a festival organizer writing at the Pig Site, and the commentary that follows, suggests the commonality of piglet overlays when sows aren't kept in tight confinement.

> *I am working at a Fall Festival and one of the pigs they brought in had 15 piglets last night. Two were dead when I arrived this morning but the rest seemed fine. A few hours later, after I clocked out, I was watching them and she proceeded to lay down on one of the babies!!!! I decided to try and get her to stand up, which she eventually did, and there was a lifeless, squished piglet laying there. I did everything I could (including mouth to mouth resuscitation) and, eventually, the little thing came around. My question is . . . is there a way of preventing this from happening in the future. She just plops down when she wants and doesn't seem to be aware if there are babies under her or not.*[49]

A senior member of the website explained to the festival worker, "Overlays are the most common cause of piglet mortality, hence the many designs of farrowing crates, and wall rails etc." A free-range pig farmer joined in, admitting, "I farrow outside and some sows are really good Mums and others are not and those that are not are sent to the meat works."

Other pig farmers went into considerable detail about how they had to spend hours upon hours observing their sows for the merest hint of farrowing and then, if they picked up on the right cues, had to monitor their behavior like a paranoid chaperone. One wrote, "It'll be three or four days before [the piglets] are fast enough to get out of the way and she can accidentally crush them at any time so you have to keep an eye on her and its difficult when you have work to do. This is why I think farrowing crates are better."[50] Rhodie highlighted the problem with consistent monitoring: "To keep the maximum number of born alive piglets surviving to weaning, there needs to be a constant, reliable, monitoring of the farrowing sows and young litters, to prevent overlays." She noted, "This is where most systems fail, as few people will carry out effective night monitoring, most stillborns and overlays occur at night when there is little or no monitoring."[51] A farmer in Washington State suggested that such observations were necessarily hit-or-miss: "The farmer never knows exactly when that sow will farrow, because he doesn't know when she came in heat. When sows farrow in the wrong place (easy to happen if you don't know when she'll farrow), the piglets die or suffer." The problem is, as is so often the case when farmers return to supposedly more "natural" approaches to raising animals, that moving away from the horrific conditions of the industrial model ends up alleviating some problems while creating others.

Losing piglets to outdoor farrowing can be painful and frustrating for all involved and it highlights the farrowing-crate paradox. Bruce King, a farmer in western Washington, captured the complex emotions central to this conundrum in a 2009 blog account:

> *Big momma farrowed in the woods at the edge of the pasture. 9 total, 2 stillborn. We ended up moving her from*

where she'd chosen into a shelter on the grass. Where she'd chosen was very damp and just moving around had converted more of the ground into mud, which was chilling the piglets. She lost 3 of them, so was down to 4 total when we moved them. Since the move sow and piglets are doing fine. This is the hard part of pastured pork. It's tough picking up the little ones, and having the sneaking suspicion that if this birth had happened in a farrowing pen you wouldn't have lost them.[52]

Responding to this post, Heath Putnam, who founded Wooly Pigs Farm, reminded readers, "Besides getting crushed, piglets die of exposure, infection and other causes." He hinted at the many secrets that free-range farmers must keep from conscientious consumers when he explained, "If the general consumer ever makes the connection that 'naturally raised' = unnecessarily dead piglets, we may see sentiment move against primitive pig keeping systems. At a minimum, if animal lovers knew the facts, they'd probably be in favor of farrowing crates."[53]

A recent petition on forcechange.com echoed a common feeling when it declared that we should "take a stand against animal cruelty in the commercial pig trade" by asking the USDA to ban the use of farrowing crates. Farrowing crates, it explains, are designed "to convert a living animal into a piece of production equipment." These sinister devices place sows "under an extreme amount of stress" and should be eliminated.[54]

I could not agree more. I even signed the petition. But, to reiterate what by now I hope is a recurring theme, to rectify the horrors of the dominant industrial system is not necessarily to address the underlying problem of animal exploitation in general. When free-range farmers abandon farrowing crates, they make life much better for sows. Of this there is no doubt. At the same time, though, they increase the possibility of mortality among piglets. When I asked Putnam, of Wooly Pigs Farm, to explain why so many small pig farmers he knew were returning to farrowing crates, he sighed and said, "They're tired of picking up dead piggies."

"I CRIED WHEN YOU SHOT THE PIG"

No farm animal wants to die. Every farm animal will fight death with unimaginable resistance to death. But something about pigs makes their slaughter especially poignant. Although it's probably unfair to express supplemental sympathy for one farm animal's slaughter experience over another's, a part of me has always wondered if pigs, perhaps because of their unusually high intelligence, might actually absorb the emotional terror of slaughter more acutely than other animals. I cannot prove such a claim. But the slaughter of pigs, even when witnessed by those who have a direct interest in their slaughter, clearly creates a heightened level of sadness and anxiety in humans, a reaction suggesting that we know something terribly wrong is happening while doing our best not to let it pierce our emotional armor. That vague sense of anxiety and sadness is evident in both industrial and nonindustrial settings.

Examples are evident in the vivid accounts that slaughterers publish in various venues. On CNN's *Eatocracy* blog,

managing editor Kat Kinsman described her eyewitness account of an "ethical slaughter" of two pigs, Porky and Bess.
It was "a grim, sodden day" on the upstate New York farm
where the "arguably less painful death" took place. Dutifully
listing all the economic reasons for not keeping pigs alive
on a farm—they don't produce eggs, their milk is of no use
to humans, no wool grows to scrape off their backs,
etc.—Kinsman, having salved her conscience a bit, writes,
"That doesn't make the act of their slaughter easier to watch."
Nor did it help that right before their fate was determined
they were seen "wallowing in the mud" and "nestling together in the cool of the shade." Observing the two farmers
in the aftermath of the slaughter, Kinsman was moved that
both men were crying. When one of them calmed down
enough to speak about the kill, he was "still wiping them
[the tears] away and was slightly choked in tone."[55]

Another eyewitness account of a pig slaughter was equally
attentive to its unusually intense emotional nature. Although
an experienced slaughterer of pigs ("I've done it all"), the
farmer/blogger admitted, as slaughter day approached, "The
night before slaughtering [is] the hardest, or one of the hardest parts of the process. . . . It is extremely hard when you've
kind of made pets of them." Despite this farmer's lifelong
experience slaughtering animals, she writes, "Personally,
this and the next part I hate. I'm not much of a blood and
guts person, and little things like this can make me start to
hyperventilate. I'll keep it mild, mostly so I don't make myself get ill."[56]

My hypothesis, one formed after reading hundreds of
slaughter accounts, is that pigs evoke a deeper and more
emotional response in us at the prospect of their death.

Perhaps this is because we have an inner sense that pigs know what we're doing to them when we send them to slaughter or kill them ourselves. Not only do they value their lives, but maybe they even understand betrayal. Anyone who spends time thinking about slaughter from the pig's perspective cannot help but entertain this thought. A farmer of heritage pigs asks herself of her hog Eddie, "How could I have spent so long with him, doing my best to nurture this sweet animal, and then leave him to die with strangers?"[57] Why was this farmer's "stomach in knots" as the slaughter-house truck pulled up the driveway to haul Eddie away? An animal-loving meat eater watches a documentary in which a pig is slaughtered and then finds himself looking at his cats and dogs and suddenly bursting into tears.[58] A family farmer recalls for an audience on a homesteading forum, "The last time we delivered pigs to the slaughter house, they were so terrified I cried the whole way home."[59] A woman recalls her first experience seeing the slaughter of a family pig and remarks, "He started off as a pet and then he was our meat. I cried."[60] These ruminations are commonplace, and for those willing to think about eating animals outside of the standard celebratory framework that dominates our dietary culture, they beg an important question: Why do it at all?

This is, however, rarely the question we are pausing to ask. Maybe it's because bacon is so damn good (yes, I once ate it, and, yes, I think it tasted good). Maybe it's because it has become so culturally chic to savor bacon, to wallow in our indulgence of it, to rise above the brutality of slaughter and say "death is death." Whatever the reason, faced with the co-nundrum of knowing somewhere deep inside ourselves that pigs suffer for the bacon on our plate, knowing that nothing is humane about shooting a pig in the face with a .22, no matter how lovingly he was raised, we equivocate. Throughout this book we have seen examples of otherwise thoughtful eaters stretching the boundaries of logic to have their meat and eat it too. This psychology is especially pronounced when it comes to pigs. The following remarks come from people who were complicit in the slaughter of a pig. Every one of them was cognizant of the suffering, but every one had an excuse, be it creating a closer connection to the meat we eat, indifference or desensitization to slaughter, the old claim that as long as the animal had a "good life" then the slaughter was "just one day," or the assurance that every part of the animal was consumed, that nothing went to waste, and that everything, therefore, is fine.

- Here is the farmer mentioned in a previous paragraph who cried after sending her pig Eddie to be slaughtered: "It sounds silly to say that a pig changed my life, but as I look back, that's exactly what happened. That sweet pig helped me in my journey as both a meat eater and an animal lover. I learned to take responsibility for the meat brought to my dinner table. And I don't think Eddie ever suffered."[61] Even his slaughterers "gave him the respect he deserved."

- Here is the account of an adventure eater who witnessed the slaughter of a pig named Hector, whom he then ate virtually every part of: "Having seen Hector die doesn't stop my discomfort with factory farming from growing, nor my resolve to find ways to opt out whenever I can. But I'm also not going to eat, or enjoy, meat any less. In fact, the next day, as we were tucking into our roasted Hector loin with romesco sauce, prunes, and figs, the table conversation segued into how we felt as if we'd made our peace with the slaughter long before the rifle shot. I mentioned to the woman sitting next to me, 'I keep forgetting that I'm eating a pig I watched being slaughtered.' I thought I should be feeling a more personal connection to this piece of pork, but it's just a good meal."[62]

- Here is the reaction of one man to the slaughter of pig shown in graphic detail on the show "Jamie [Oliver] Saves Our Bacon": "I too watched 'Jamie Saves Our Bacon,' and although the slaughter scene looked horrible, the pig had a quick, clean death at the hands of a professional, and the twitching was just nerve and muscle reflexes—it wasn't writhing in pain. . . . The way I (and many others see it—including Jamie) is that if the pig was cared for in life, and had a humane death, then eating its meat is justified."[63]

- Here is a woman who watched the same show: "I think it was a good decision on the program's makers to keep in the scene where the pig was slaughtered, after all this is what happens to every bit of meat that ends up on a table. At the risk of sounding a little hard (and I am really a big softie) I think that over the years we have become a little sentimental about animals and try to detach ourselves from what has happened to them before they end up on our plates."[64]

We say that the nonindustrial option is better. In the short term, I would agree. But I think pigs deserve better than better. If our emotional response to pig slaughter is any indication, I think they deserve some long-term consideration. There's no reasonable consolation for the perpetuation of unnecessary death, and the sample of excuses shown above are just that—excuses. They have topical appeal, they are reducible to sound bites, and they certainly confirm our bias for eating animals. But they do not hold up to the kind of thoughtful scrutiny that we are otherwise being asked to bring to the food we eat.

Beyond this moral inconsistency is something less abstract: the damning data of the experience of raising nonindustrial pork. As we have seen with cows and chickens, raising pigs on a smaller scale and in outdoor settings, while nominally more pleasurable for the animals, is not nearly as safe and humane as the practice is typically made out to be. There are unintended consequences. By having already limited ourselves to nonindustrial alternatives, we have made it clear that we are thinking seriously about our food choices. When are we going to bring the scrutiny we have brought to bear on industrial agriculture to the alternatives that we are gradually coming to embrace? The future of food hinges on how we answer that question.

OUR UNTHINKING DECISION

Humans, like many other animals, are omnivores. We have the most well-endowed frontal lobe of any species in the history of evolution. We use it, every now and then, to mediate our savagery. Healthy humans have the will and the ability to make conscious choices. We can justify those choices on the grounds of heady concepts such as justice and fairness and moral equivalence. When it comes to making decisions about what we put in our mouths, we have lately been exercising the frontal lobe rather productively. Perhaps the greatest revelation to emerge from this zeitgeist— one largely driven by what we identify as the sustainable food movement—is the moral value of rejecting animal products that come from the horrific factory-farm system that churns out the overwhelming majority of the flesh and milk and cheese we eat to excess.

Conscientious consumers are, instead, opting in greater and greater numbers for animal products sourced from kinder and gentler methods of production. We want the animals we eat to have lived on pasture, to have been spared the mutilations required for industrial production, to be free of vaccines and antibiotics and growth hormones, and to have been cared for in ways that the mechanistic demands of the factory farm render impossible. We've pursued these values by voting with our forks, and as a result, the nonindustrial alternatives continue to make meaningful inroads into that environmental and ethical disaster known as the standard American diet.

This change has been marginally beneficial for farm animals. Millions of sentient creatures who would otherwise have been raised in terrifying confinement have now been provided a modicum of freedom to roam pastures, eat a more natural diet, play around, and have sex on their own terms. These animals have been allowed to live their lives, however truncated, as the creatures they are, indulging their instincts and making their choices and pursuing whatever version of happiness is available to them until the slaughterer turns out the lights.

This comparative improvement, while obviously far from perfect, is difficult to oppose when it is juxtaposed with the practice of factory farming. Accordingly, an entire movement has cohered around the transition to small-scale and pasture-based animal agriculture. Progressive agricultural values have been codified in the language of sustainability, welfare, empowerment, and enlightenment. Conscientious consumers are increasingly choosing the nonindustrial, small-scale, pasture-based options. They seem to have initiated a cycle of compassion, one in which human consumers seeking sustainable and morally responsible choices choose animal products from systems that are attentive to animal welfare, thereby propelling the food system into a brighter future.

This future, I have argued, is ultimately an illusion. The food movement, to its great credit, is premised on thought—often sophisticated thought. We are exhorted by the leaders of this ambitious revolution to get to know where our food comes from, to examine every link in the farm-to-fork supply chain, and to ask hard questions about food access, welfare, and justice. Books, academic journals, and university classes have mushroomed around this quest. However, for all the emphasis on critical thought regarding the sources of our food and the methods behind its production, we have been hesitant, perhaps willfully so, to bring the same habit of curious investigation to the nonindustrial alternatives.

Our failure to think critically about the environmental and ethical consequences of nonindustrial animal agriculture has many causes, but one of the most important, as I discussed in this book's opening chapter, is our stunted emotional response to the animal world. By refusing to make the human-animal emotional bond a central point of discussion in our larger debates about ethical eating and food reform, we open ourselves up to being ambushed by what I call the omnivore's contradiction (discussed in the second chapter). The omnivore's contradiction encapsulates our aspiration to grant animals moral status and yet eat them. Our failure to resolve this conundrum, much less acknowledge its existence, generates a laundry list of unthinking myths and rationalizations for slaughtering animals (overviewed in chapters 3 and 4). These myths and rationalizations clog the arteries of food reform, collectively reducing our earnest efforts to sound bites and slogans rather than thoughtful observation and analysis. The omnivore's contradiction threatens to rot the food movement from within, primarily by compromising the habit of thought so essential to the existence of any movement that hopes to have lasting and transformative power.

Although I've spent much of this book illuminating the hidden problems of nonindustrial animal agriculture, I've occasionally hit the brakes and noted that the small-scale systems, for all their problems, are still better for animals than the factory farm. This might have seemed confusing, so allow me to place a frame around this claim before proceeding with my concluding thoughts about the nonindustrial options and how we should ultimately respond to them.

Eating animals is endemic to modern life. I hope this will not always be the case, but for now it is. As much as I would like to simply plant my flag and declare the end of eating domesticated and hunted animals, and conclude the discussion, my experience as an advocate for animals has (through some hard knocks) taught me that most people undergo behavioral changes in gradual stages rather than heroic leaps. They do not want to be conquered by logic or ideology so much as provided realistic options to explore through the exercise of free will. The nonindustrial operations profiled in this book provide some of those options. They are hardly ideal, but in the short term they offer a nominally better life for animals and a nominally better choice for humans. Recall what Jonathan Safran Foer said: "Let's talk about what's actually in front of us." What's in front of us, immediately, right here and now, is a population of consumers seeking to make better choices when it comes to eating animals. That's huge. And the small-scale option, compared to factory farming, is, given the reality in front of us, a better choice. Hence my condemnation of the nonindustrial animal farm is not 100 percent. Too many people need that stepping-stone, and I am in no position to kick it away.

But we must also ask, where will those stepping-stones lead? This question brings me back to my primary project of highlighting the intractable problems of nonindustrial animal farms (chapters 5, 6, and 7). Foer is correct in that we must face what's in front of us. But we must also look beyond the moment and glimpse some sort of endgame. My strategic rationale for dismembering the myth of humane farming is to encourage consumers to conceptualize their better choice not as an end in itself, but as a layover on the way to the eventual and complete elimination of domesticated animals from the human diet. I'll confess something important here: for all the time I spent in these pages developing the omnivore's contradiction, my hunch is that most open-minded consumers are unlikely to be persuaded by it alone. For many it will be too abstract, too divorced from our experience in the shopping aisle or what we read in the news, too foreign from what's in front of us. Too academic.

Instead, most ethically inclined consumers—the ones prone, however mildly, to consider eliminating animals from their diets—are going to be persuaded by, to steal a term from Immanuel Kant, "the data of experience."[1] The data of experience is hard information that, as it accumulates, appeals to common sense, the same common sense that has driven so many of us to withdraw our support for animal products sourced from factory farms. With enough revelations and exposés and documentaries and bestselling books, the data reaches a point at which it quietly convinces us to make new decisions. The balance gets tipped. This is already happening with industrially produced meat. It should now happen with nonindustrial meat. If this book has accomplished anything, I hope it helps to initiate this process.

The overview of on-farm troubles described in the second half of this book is integral to the task. It should not imply that life on small farms is a constant firestorm of disaster. My rationale for demonstrating that small farms experience many of the same problems endemic to factory farming, and even a few new ones, is simply to show that they exist. Regrettably, such a task, however perfunctory, is necessary. The whitewashing that characterizes the vast majority of small-farm promotions— which is endemic to so much food writing today—obscures daily realities of on-farm life that concerned consumers should know about. Critics might find my portrayal selective. Well, sure. But the objective here is not always to make a case about the commonality or representativeness of the problems I've highlighted—death, disease, medication, mutilation, etc. Instead, it is to suggest that their mere existence (and I think many of the problems I found are quite common) dashes any hope we may have of achieving a nonindustrialized system of animal production that offers a viable alternative to the dominant models of animal agriculture. Only a small percentage of our animal food today is sourced from the kind of farms I explored in chapters 5 through 7—maybe 5 percent. Imagine, as the food movement wants us to do, if these farms were producing 25 percent of our animal food? The problems I exposed here would be greatly magnified, and as a result, all our efforts to reform our food system would be greatly undermined. That would be tragic.

When I first began to criticize small farming, a number of critics (most of them small-scale farmers) roundly condemned me for supporting agribusiness. In my favorite example to date, Joel Salatin, who figures prominently in the grass-fed-beef chapter, condemned my "love affair with confinement hog factories"! This reaction, while wildly inaccurate, is nonetheless important to take seriously. Most notably, it's almost comically indicative of how narrowly we have framed our options. Joel was serious. His accusation shows that by constricting our choices to animal products sourced from either industrial or nonindustrial operations, by holding up the animal-based alternatives to industrial agriculture as our only alternative, we have silenced discussion of the most fertile, most politically consequential, and most reform-minded choice: eating plants. This alternative to the alternatives changes the entire game of revolutionizing our broken food system. It places the food movement on a new foundation, infuses it with fresh energy, and promotes the only choice that keeps agribusiness executives awake at night.

What I'm asking you to imagine is thus a movement that requires us to become more emotionally in tune with animals, ethically consistent in our behavior, and better informed about the evolutionary heritage we share with sentient creatures. This movement, whether we join it all at once or gradually, with immediate zeal or reluctantly, will, in the end, triumph over industrial agriculture because it will be, above all else, a bloodless revolution based on compassion for animals, the environment, and, ultimately, ourselves.

NOTES

INTRODUCTION: THE AGENDA

1. Charles Darwin, *The Descent of Man* (London: John Murray, 1871), 1:105.
2. Ibid.

CHAPTER ONE: GETTING EMOTIONAL

1. By far the most incisive exploration of this phenomenon is by the social psychologist Melanie Joy. Her book *Why We Love Dogs, Eat Pigs, and Wear Cows* (San Francisco: Conari Press, 2011) introduces the idea of carnism, which Joy defines as "the belief system, or ideology, in which it's considered ethical to consume certain animals."
2. It's worth noting that, every now and then, they do. In October 2012, a farmer in Oregon entered his pigs' pen and was eaten by them: http://newsfeed.time.com/2012/10/02/oregon-farmer-eaten-by-pigs/. And, another

source on this topic could be: http://www.npr.org/tem plates/story/story.php?storyId=129551459. See also http:// www.sfgate.com/news/article/Authorities-Oregon -farmer-eaten-by-his-hogs-3910403.php/. For a more systematic look at animal-on-human violence see Jason Hribal, *Fear of the Animal Planet: The Hidden History of Animal Resistance* (Oakland, CA: AK Press/CounterPunch Press, 2010).

3. See Matthew Scully, *Dominion: The Power of Man, the Suffering of Animals, and the Call to Mercy* (New York: St. Martin's Press, 2002), 398: "Animal welfare is not just a moral problem to be solved in statutes, but a moral opportunity to fill our own lives with acts of compassion." When opponents of animal rights argue, "I care about solving human problems before animal problems," they forget that the capacity to care for animals has a positive impact on our capacity to care for humans.

4. The idea that we are, as a culture, becoming more psychopathic and narcissistic is expressed in Kevin Dutton, "Psychopathy's Double Edge," *Chronicle of Higher Education*, October 22, 2012, accessed October 27, 2012, http://chronicle.com/article/The-Psychopath-Makeover/135160/.

5. Donald Griffin, *Animal Minds* (Chicago: University of Chicago Press, 2001), 259; Lorraine Daston and Gregg Mitman, eds., *Thinking with Animals: New Perspectives on Anthropomorphism* (New York: Columbia University Press, 2005), 178. Griffin here is quoting N. K. Humphrey. Another researcher who has explored this same idea in special depth is Jonathan Balcombe. See his book *Second Nature: The Inner Lives of Animals* (New York: Palgrave Macmillan, 2010).

6. Griffin, *Animal Minds;* Datson and Mitman, *Thinking with Animals*, 3.

7. Bernard E. Rollin, *Animal Rights and Human Morality*, 3rd ed. (Amherst, NY: Prometheus Books, 2006), 66, 241, 259.

8. Marian Stamp Dawkins, *Through Our Eyes Only? The Search for Animal Consciousness* (New York: Oxford University Press, 1993), 3. 9, 180.

9. Virginia Morell writes, "In human psychology, there's no longer a question about whether cognition operates separately from the emotions. It doesn't. . . . The same is probably true for all vertebrates, possibly some invertebrates." *Animal Wise: The Thoughts and Emotions of Our Fellow Creatures* (New York: Crown, 2013), 21.

10. Meg Daley Olmert, *Made for Each Other* (Cambridge, MA: Da Capo Press, 2009), 72; Hal Herzog, *Some We Love, Some We Hate, Some We Eat* (New York: Harper, 2010), 88.

11. Olmert, *Made for Each Other*, 217.

12. Herzog, *Some We Love*, 88; James Serpell, *In the Company of Animals: A Study of Human-Animal Relationships* (Cambridge, England: Cambridge University Press, 1996).

13. For example, see John Homans, "The Rise of Dog Identity Politics," *New York*, February 1, 2010, 20.

14. Ibid., 82.

15. Meg Daley Olmert, "Dog Good," *Psychology Today*, May 5, 2010, accessed October 9, 2012, http://www.psychology today.com/blog/made-each-other/201005/dog-good.

16. The young primatologist Jane Goodall experienced this pressure when she considered publishing her observation that chimps thought and expressed emotions. She wrote, "Yes, it doesn't make much sense to say they aren't

thinking or don't have emotions. Most of us studying animals in the wild see things like this all the time. But we've learned to be careful." Morell, *Animal Wise*, 8. In this respect, Louis Leakey, Goodall's mentor, always thought that Goodall's lack of formal training was a good thing.

17. This is not to say that considerations of animal behavior and mood do not sneak into the scientific literature. One animal scientist noted in a research article, "The idea of 'behavior needs' crept into the scientific literature without any scientific evidence." Despite the author's apparent disapproval of the appearance of these unscientific materials, he wrote, "There is now increasing evidence that domestic fowl do have certain 'behavioral needs.'" Not enough, though, for the author to toss the scare quotes. See Ian H. Duncan, "Behavior and Behavioral Needs," *Poultry Science* 77 (1998): 1766, http://www.poultryscience.org/ps/paperpdfs/98/ps981766.pdf.

18. It really is a safe assumption. In 2012, leading cognitive neuroscientists declared at a University of Cambridge conference, "Humans are not unique in possessing the neurological substrates that generate consciousness. Nonhuman animals, including all mammals and birds, and many other creatures, including octopuses, also possess" these qualities. Morell, *Animal Wise*, 22.

19. Daston and Mitman, *Thinking with Animals*, 5.

20. "Philosophy is a dangerous thing," writes Mark Rowlands. "It can get you to believe all sorts of ridiculous things." From *Animals Like Us* (New York: Verso, 2002), 3.

21. The idea of thoughtful observation, as I'm developing here, owes a debt to Darwin's student George John

Romanes, who introduced the idea of "inverted anthropomorphism" in his book *Animal Intelligence* (London: Elibron Classics, 1886).

22. The best recent book examining the inner lives of animals is Jenny Brown, *The Lucky Ones: My Passionate Fight for Farm Animals* (New York: Penguin, 2012).

23. http://www.huffingtonpost.com/2011/07/14/humpback-whale-video_n_898859.html, accessed May 1. 2014; more general reference to animal communication with humans, see Marc Bekoff, *The Animal Manifesto: Six Reasons for Expanding Our Compassion Footprint* (Novato, CA: New World Library, 2010), 97.

24. Jeffrey Moussaieff Masson, *When Elephants Weep: The Emotional Lives of Animals* (New York: Delacorte Press, 1995), 95.

25. "Echo: An Elephant to Remember," *Nature*, PBS.org, premiered October 17, 2010, http://www.pbs.org/wnet/nature/episodes/echo-an-elephant-to-remember/video-full-episode/5920/.

26. Bekoff, *Animal Manifesto*, 54.

27. Megan Cross, "Cow Proves Animals Love, Think, and Act," GlobalAnimal.org, April 13, 2012, accessed May 22, 2012, http://www.globalanimal.org/2012/04/13/cow-proves-animals-love-think-and-act/71867/.

28. Masson, *When Elephants Weep*, 91.

29. Bekoff, *Animal Manifesto*, 68.

30. It would be tempting, and quite satisfying, to fill the rest of this book with examples of animal emotionalism. One case might be the two Tamworth pigs who, as the truck carrying them neared the slaughterhouse, unlatched the door to their cage, leaped from the truck,

crossed a river, and disappeared into the English country-
side, running in terror every time their owner, who angrily
chased them, appeared in the distance (he eventually let the
pigs go and they ended up national porcine heroes living in
a farm sanctuary). Another example might include the female monkeys in Thailand who were recently documented
actively teaching their children how to floss their teeth,
spending twice the amount of time flossing when their
children were watching them than when they were alone. I
could also discuss the example of sperm whales who, when
they dive for food (which can take an hour), arrange for
babysitters to watch their calves when killer whales have
been seen nearby. One could fill volumes with these revealing examples of emotionally informed decisions, which are
a privilege for humans to thoughtfully witness and appreciate with emotional openness.

CHAPTER TWO: THE OMNIVORE'S CONTRADICTION

1. Gary Francione: http://www.abolitionistapproach.com
   /happy-meatanimal-products-a-step-in-the-right-direc
   tion-or-an-easier-access-point-back-to-eating-animals
   /#.U3lj7a1dXOg, accessed May 1, 2014.
2. Jonathan Safran Foer, *Eating Animals* (New York: Little,
   Brown, 2009), 35.
3. "Is the US One Big Factory Farm?," markbittman.com,
   December 3, 2010.
4. Mark Bittman, "The Human Cost of Animal Suffering,"
   Opinionator (blog), *New York Times*, March 13, 2012,
   http://opinionator.blogs.nytimes.com/2012/03/13/the
   -human-cost-of-animal-suffering/.

5. Mark Bittman, "Is Factory Farming Even Worse Than We Know?," markbittman.com, December 15, 2010, http://markbittman.com/horrific-animal-abuses-un covered-at-smithfiel/.

6. Bittman, "Human Cost." Bittman's work has been so sensitive to ethics that I would not be surprised if he did go vegan himself and defy the message I'm delivering here. I hope that happens, as I'd loved to be proven wrong. On the connection that Bittman hints at between animal abuse and human degradation, it's worth recalling Sue Coe's comment that "barbarity inflicted on animals can spill into a hatred of our own species." See *Cruel: Bearing Witness to Animal Exploitation* (New York: O/R Books, 2011), 23.

7. Ibid.

8. Foer, *Eating Animals,* 59–60.

9. Ibid., 34.

10. Ibid., 53.

11. Ibid., 76.

12. Ibid., 78.

13. If I've learned one thing in the years I've been writing about animals and food, it is that any argument against eating animals is bound to provoke defensive responses from people who eat animals. As a result, it's important to note before proceeding that, despite the aggressiveness of what follows, I do not intend it to be a personal accusation, just part of a larger exploration into the ethics of eating animals.

14. Michael Pollan, "An Animal's Place," *New York Times,* November 10, 2002, http://faculty.smu.edu/jkazez/ani mal%20rights/an%20animal's%20place.html.

15. "Michael Pollan Talks Meat," oprah.com, February 1, 2011, accessed June 27, 2012, http://www.oprah.com /oprahshow/Michael-Pollan-on-Eating-Meat-Video.

16. "Pollan, Vegans, and Plant Suffering," vegan.com, April 30, 2012, accessed June 27, 2012, http://vegan.com/blog /2012/04/30/pollan-vegans-and-plant-suffering/.

17. At the same time, he will remain oblivious of the welfare implications of his topic. In a column he wrote against the consumption of milk, he based his entire argument on his heartburn's having ended when he stopped drinking it. Nary a mention was made about the suffering that milk cows endure. Mark Bittman, "Got Milk? You Don't Need It," *Opinionator* (blog), *New York Times*, July 7, 2012, http://opinionator.blogs.nytimes .com/2012/07/07/got-milk-you-dont-need-it/.

18. Bittman, "Human Cost."

19. Mark Bittman, "No Meat, No Dairy, No Problem," *New York Times Magazine*, December 29, 2011, 44.

20. Bittman, "Human Cost." *Privilege* is an interesting word choice here. *Privilege* comes from the French *prive lege*—"private law." So, in a sense, Bittman is right in that those who eat animals get to follow a private law, one that is not rooted in ethical consistency, one that makes imposing unnecessary suffering "legal" for a few. I'm not sure if this is what he meant to say, but it's accurate.

21. Accessed January 2, 2014, http://markbittman.com/crispy -pork-cheek-belly-or-turkey-thigh-salad/.

22. Well, sort of. Between 2010 and 1012 Americans reduced their meat consumption by as much as 12 percent. But in China, the meat market is just now industrializing, and it is doing so at a rate to allow billions a steady diet

of pork, chicken, and beef. See Wayne Pacelle, "Rising Meat Consumption Threatens Animals and Our Environment," *A Human Nation* (blog), Humane Society of the United States, October 22, 2012, accessed October 23, 2012, http://hsus.typepad.com/wayne/2012/10/china-meat-consumption.html.

23. The exchange is recounted in "Does Jonathan Safran Foer Believe It's OK to Kill Animals?," thebeeteating-heeb.com, October 24, 2012, accessed October 28, 2012, http://thebeeteatingheeb.com/?s=foer.

24. David Foster Wallace, "Consider the Lobster," in *Consider the Lobster and Other Essays* (New York: Little, Brown, 2006), 238–54.

25. The best economic analysis I've seen of factory farming comes from the authors of a book that's highly critical of the welfare practices on factory farms. See F. Bailey Norwood and Jayson L. Lusk, *Compassion by the Pound: The Economics of Farm Animal Welfare* (New York: Oxford University Press, 2011), 93–100.

26. Case in point: the *Times* did a piece on the "new business model" for small farms, but somehow never got around to, well, explaining what that business model was: Kirk Johnson, "Small Farmers Creating a New Business Model as Agriculture Goes Local," *New York Times*, July 1, 2012, http://www.nytimes.com/2012/07/02/us/small-scale-farmers-creating-a-new-profit-model.html?_r=1&ref=us.

27. James McWilliams, "Vegan Feud," slate.com, September 7, 2012, http://www.slate.com/articles/life/food/2012/09/hsus_vs_abolitionists_vs_the_meat_industry_why_the_infighting_should_stop_.html.

CHAPTER THREE: HUMANE SLAUGHTER

1. Note what ecologist Marc Bekoff says about naming animals: "A name immediately, and almost by definition, confers subjectivity and sentience. Names don't lead us to mistake animals for people, but they lead us to take their sentience seriously, whether or not it resembles ours." See *The Animal Manifesto: Six Reasons for Expanding Our Compassion Footprint* (Novato, CA: New World Library, 2010), 111.

2. This kind of remark, one that tends to follow comments that say how important it is to treat animals well, is all too common. When a discussion broke out on my blog about Green Mountain College's decision to slaughter two oxen from its teaching farm (despite an offer by a local sanctuary to take them free of charge), a defender of the decision wrote, "We're not running a bed and breakfast."

3. For a more sustained look at the connection between food and sexual pornography, see Carol Adams, *The Sexual Politics of Meat* (New York and London: Continuum Books, 1990). "Part of the battle of being heard as a vegetarian," writes Adams, "is being heard about literal matters in a society that favors symbolic thinking" (105). The symbols of agricultural pornography, I would suggest, distract us from the literal material processes that bring meat to our forks.

4. "The Grapple of Ethics," accessed September 24, 2012, http://mcaf.ee/tosh4.

5. Ibid.

6. Bob Comis, "Here's My Plan to Quit Pig Farming, And Start Living Ethically," The Dodo, March 24, 2014, https://www.thedodo.com/my-plan-to-quit-pig-farming-an-490419846.html. Accessed May 22, 2014.

7. https://www.facebook.com/barbarafickle?hc _location=stream.

8. Bryan Welch, "Rancho Cappuccino Case Study: Is It Fair to the Livestock?," *Mother Earth News*, February 28, 2012, accessed October 2, 2012, http://www.mother earthnews.com/beautiful-abundant/rancho-cappuc cino-case-study-is-it-fair-to-the-livestock.aspx.

9. Ibid.

10. Howard F. Lyman, *No More Bull!: The Mad Cowboy Target's America's Worst Enemy: Our Diet* (New York: Scribner, 2005), 94, 61, 8. Also see Corine Bowen, "Kind Cowboy," *Veg News*, September–October 2012, 47.

11. Corine Bowen, "From Autopsy to Sanctuary," *Veg News*, September–October 2012, 49. Also see Cheri Ezell-Vandersluis, humanmyth.org, undated, http://www .humanemyth.org/cheriezell.htm.

12. Brown's account was published at HumanMYTH.org, accessed October 10, 2012, http://www.humanemyth .org/haroldbrown.htm.

13. David Ferry, "Slaughterhouse Shortage Stunting Area's Eat Local Movement," *New York Times*, April 7, 2011, A23, accessed October 22, 2012, http://www.nytimes .com/2011/04/08/us/08bcslaughterhouse.html ?pagewanted=all&_r=0.

14. One exception to this is with chickens. If a producer is slaughtering fewer than twenty thousand chickens a year, he can rely on state inspection and can, as a result, theoretically do his own slaughtering.

15. "Slaughterhouse Workers," Food Empowered Project, accessed April 4, 2013, http://www.foodispower.org /slaughterhouse_workers.php.

16. Jennifer Dillard, "A Slaughterhouse Nightmare: Psychological Harm Suffered by Slaughterhouse Employees and the Possibility of Redress Through Legal Reform," *Georgetown Journal on Poverty Law and Policy* 14, no. 2 (Summer 2008): 2.

17. Writing in *The Seattle Times*, Maureen O'Hagan notes that the industrial slaughterhouse "is the only way [for small livestock farmers] to go if you want to sell to grocers, restaurants or at farmers' markets, or even sell a steak to your neighbor." See "Slaughterhouse on Wheels Aids Locavore Movement," *Seattle Times*, August 11, 2011, accessed October 29, 2012, http://seattletimes.com /html/localnews/2009636109_slaughterhouse11m.html.

18. Lyndsey Layton, "As Demand Grows for Locally Raised Meat, Farmers Turn to Mobile Slaughterhouses," *Washington Post*, June 20, 2010, accessed October 2, 2012, http://www.washingtonpost.com/wp-dyn/content /article/2010/06/18/AR2010061803509.html.

19. Timothy Pachirat, *Every Twelve Seconds* (New Haven, CT: Yale University Press, 2012), 47; Gail Eisnitz, *Slaughterhouse* (Amherst, NY: Prometheus Books, 1997), 68; Peter Singer, *Animal Liberation* (New York: Ecco Press, 1975), 150; "Pig Transport and Slaughter," Peta.org, accessed October 3, 2012, http://www.peta.org/issues/ animals-used-for-food/pig-transport-slaughter.aspx.

20. This may be by design. Workers don't want to be sure that they were the exclusive cause of death.

21. Eisnitz, *Slaughterhouse*, 29.

22. Pachirat, *Every Twelve Seconds*, 54.

23. Eisnitz, *Slaughterhouse*, 134.

24. One reason that larger hogs aren't hit with more power

from the stun gun is that it can damage their flesh and harm the quality of their meat.

25. Singer, *Animal Liberation*, 150–51.

26. Pachirat, *Every Twelve Seconds*, 56–57.

27. Sue Coe, *Cruel: Bearing Witness to Animal Exploitation* (New York: O/R Books, 2011), 141. Fewer chickens from small farms are slaughtered in industrial slaughter- houses because of an exception that allows those who process fewer than twenty thousand chickens a year to build their own slaughter facility to be approved by the state. These structures, however, are usually pro- hibitively expensive for small farmers. See Clara A. Wise, "Small Poultry Farmers Grapple with Lack of Slaughterhouse," *High County News*, January 24, 2011, accessed October 21, 2012, http://www.hcn.org/issues /43.1/small-poultry-farmers-grapple-with-lack-of -slaughterhouses/article_view?b_start:int=1&-C=.

28. Coe, *Cruel*, 64.

29. "Slaughtering and Dressing Rabbits," Mississippi State University Extension Service, https://msucares.com/live stock/small_animal/slaughter.html.

30. "Slaughtering and Dressing Rabbits," accessed October 21, 2012, http://www.poultry.msstate.edu/extension/pdf /rabbits_slaughtering.pdf.

31. Eisnitz, *Slaughterhouse*, 77.

32. Matthew Scully, *Dominion: The Power of Man, the Suf- fering of Animals, and the Call to Mercy* (New York: St. Martin's, 2002), 282. One study found that "common ailments among slaughterhouse workers include back problems, torn muscles and pinched nerves, as well as more dramatic injuries such as broken bones, deep

cuts and amputated fingers and limbs." See "Sustainable Table [Food Processing & Distribution]," Grace Communications Foundation, accessed October 29, 2012, http://www.sustainabletable.org/issues/processing /#worker. *New York Times*, Feb. 6, 2005, editorial

33. Dillard, "Slaughterhouse Nightmare," 2–3.
34. Michael Broadway and Donald Stull, " 'I'll Do Whatever You Want, but It Hurts': Worker Safety and Community Health in Modern Meatpacking," *Labor: Studies in the Working Class History of the Americas* 5 (2008): 27.
35. Ibid., 1.
36. Jocelyne Porcher et al., "Affective Components of the Human-Animal Relationship in Animal Husbandry: Development and Validation of a Questionnaire," *Psychological Reports* 95 (2004): 275, 286.
37. Dillard, "Slaughterhouse Nightmare," 8.
38. This can happen to the reporters who write about animal slaughter as well. Here is Kathy Gustafson writing in *The Huffington Post*: "I'll spare you the gory details here (though they're included in the book), but I can say that as a former vegetarian I was surprised to find that watching the slaughter was minimally traumatic. It was all so routine—so organized, controlled and exact—and designed to include as little mess and suffering as possible." Katherine Gustafson, "Mobile Slaughterhouses Help Meat Go Local," *Huffington Post*, May 14, 2012, accessed October 26, 2012, http://www.huffing tonpost.com/katherine-gustafson/mobile-slaughter houses-sustainable-food-meat_b_1515217.html.
39. Amy Fitzgerald et al., "Slaughterhouses and Increased Crime Rates," *Organization and Environment*, 2009, 1–27,

http://www.animalstudies.msu.edu/Slaughterhouses
_and_Increased_Crime_Rates.pdf. The blog *Honest Meat*, an obviously pro-meat website, admits the same, writing, "These industrial slaughterhouses have helped resurrect dying small towns, but brought with them a host of new problems from environmental contamination to transforming the cultural and social fabric of these places. Postville, Iowa, site of the infamous kosher processing plant Agriprocessors, Inc., went from a town of just a hair over 1,000 residents to over 2,200 residents in twenty short years. The town now enjoys gangs, increased drug and alcohol abuse, domestic abuse, overcrowded classrooms with limited English speaking pupils, and other phenomena." See "Slaughterhouse: Series: Part Two," honestmeat.com, September 2, 2008, accessed October 29, 2012, http://www.honestmeat.com/honest_meat/2008/09/slaughterhouse.html. As might be evident, this account has a whiff of xenophobia.

40. Eisnitz, *Slaughterhouse*, 68.
41. As of August 2012, one comprehensive catalog of working MSUs included seven that were able to slaughter cattle: accessed October 30, 2012, http://www.extension.org/pages/19781/mobile-slaughterprocessing-units-currently-in-operation. These seven MSUs were able to kill about sixty cows a day, total. To put that in perspective, the number of cows killed per day in the United States is around one hundred thousand. It thus is more than misleading when high-profile food writers ask if these operations provide a solution: Marion Nestle, "The Slaughterhouse Problem: Is a Resolution in Sight?," *Food Politics*, May 25, 2010, http://www.foodpolitics.com

/2010/05/the-slaughterhouse-problem-is-a-resolution-in -sight/. Not when they can only handle about .1 percent of the demand.

42. Jane Morrigan, "Mobile Abattoirs: Benefits and Challenges, Part 2," Organic Agriculture Centre of Canada, http://oacc.info/DOCs/NewsArticles/MobileAbattoir Part2.pdf; Nate Traylor, "Mobile Slaughterhouse Project Aims to Help Local Farmers," *World*, November 15, 2010, accessed October 29, 2012, http://theworldlink .com/news/local/article_af683c48-f0eb-11df-a8fa -001cc4c002e0.html.

43. Morrigan, "Mobile Abattoirs." This discussion is about MSUs in Canada, but the criticisms hold true for the United States as well.

44. Stephen Thompson, "Going Mobile," *Rural Cooperatives* (USDA Rural Development), November/December 2010, accessed October 29, 2012, http://www.rurdev .usda.gov/rbs/pub/nov10/going.htm.

45. Ibid.

46. Rachel J. Johnson et al., "Slaughtering and Processing Options and Issues for Locally Sourced Meat," Economic Research Service/USDA, June 2012, accessed November 7, 2012, http://www.ers.usda.gov/media/820188/ldpm216 -01.pdf.

47. J. L. Becket and J. W. Oltgen, "Estimation of Water Required for Beef Production in the United States," *Journal of Animal Science* 71 (1993): 821, accessed October 30, 2012, http://www.journalofanimalscience.org /content/71/4/818.full.pdf.

48. What's unclear about this option is that, according to the USDA, MSUs can only carry five hundred gallons

of water to a site. See Greg L. Sherman, "Considerations Unique to Mobile Red Meat Slaughter," FSIS Net Conference, n.d., accessed October 30, 2012, http://www.extension.org/mediawiki/files/9/95/Consider ations_Unique_to_Mobile_Red_Meat_Slaughter _FSIS_webinar_GSherman.pdf.

49. It is no surprise that cooperatives of small farmers who wish to use MSUs seek exemptions from wastewater laws. See this report, page 5, for an example: "Slaughterhouse Feasibility Report," accessed October 30, 2012, http://www.uvm.edu/~susagctr/Documents/Slaughter houseFINALREPORT.pdf.

50. USDA, Food Safety and Inspection Service, "Mobile Slaughter Unit Compliance Guide," accessed October 30, 2012, http://www.fsis.usda.gov/PDF/Compliance _Guide_Mobile_Slaughter.pdf.

51. Information on blood volume for cows: "Mammary Macro-Structure Dairy Cows Udder Anatomy," Independent Study Modules for Animal Sciences Classes, University of Illinois, accessed October 30, 2012, http://classes.ansci.illinois.edu/ansc438/mamstructure/anat omy_7.html. Average weight of cow: twelve hundred pounds.

52. This is from the "Mobile Slaughter Unit Compliance Guide," page 6: "Pest control substances must be approved by the Environmental Protection Agency (EPA) for use in food processing environments and be used in a manner that does not adulterate product or create insanitary conditions. Under the Federal Insecticide, Fungicide, and Rodenticide Act (FIFRA), EPA reviews pesticide formulation, intended use, and other

information; registers all pesticides for use in the United States; and prescribes labeling, use, and other regulatory requirements to prevent unreasonable adverse effects on the environment, including humans, wildlife, plants, and property. Any meat or poultry establishment using a pesticide must follow the FIFRA requirements."

53. USDA, "Mobile Slaughter Unit Compliance Guide."

54. Pachirat, *Every Twelve Seconds*, 28, 40.

55. The death, moreover, is not enough to become numbing. One way that slaughterhouse employees psychologically protect themselves is by imagining the animals as objects. This objectification is possible because hundreds of animals are handled in assembly-line fashion. Killing eight animals a day is different, especially when these animals have names and will be led to the truck by farmers and families who may have formed emotional attachments to them.

56. Ezell-Vandersluis, humanemyth.org.

57. Michael Broadway and Donald Stull, "The Fight for Rights: Animal Welfare vs. Worker Welfare," *Corporate Social Responsibility Newsletter*, CSRSWIRE.com, July 12, 2012, http://www.csrwire.com/blog/posts/462-the-fight-for-rights-animal-welfare-vs-worker-welfare].

CHAPTER FOUR: BACKYARD BUTCHERY

1. "Raising Ducks: Butchering the Drakes," *Makin' it with Frankie* (blog), June 2, 2012, accessed November 4, 2012, http://frankiemakes.blogspot.com/2012/06/butchering-at-eight-weeks.html.

2. The cri de coeur for this power-to-the-self-slaughterer message has its most recent origins in Novella Carpenter's *Farm City: The Education of an Urban Farmer* (New York: Penguin, 2009). Carpenter calls the post–World War II, 1960s, hippie-driven quest for self-sufficiency "a cultural virus" (106)—a good one, I guess, one that clearly infected the city of Oakland, where Carpenter lives and acts as a guru of sorts to the backyard slaughter movement.

3. For a whiplash-inducing example of the paradoxical moral shift underscoring the self-congratulatory nature of self-slaughter, see the work of *The Ethical Butcher*, ethicalbutcher.blogspot.com. The name alone is remarkable in that it takes one of the most ethically challenging questions at the core of historical and modern philosophy—is it okay to kill animals needlessly?—and blithely assumes it to be true, honoring the idea with a website and a celebration of all things DIY slaughter. I say "almost complete" because most backyard butchers are not doing their own breeding and are, in most cases, relying on industrial breeders to provide their animals.

4. I realize that the documents that I'm using may not, in their rank exhibitionism, reflect the DIY slaughterer mentality as a whole. There's almost certainly a self-selection bias at work. But there is no reason to think they are exceptional cases, aside from their availability on the Web. In the public nature of these accounts—they were posted for anyone to see—and in there being quite a lot of them, and in their shameless honesty and eerie narrative sameness, they seem to capture something endemic to backyard slaughter. Those who post

this violence on the Web, making their butchery public, may be feeling more of a need to validate their act
than others. That need for validation, though, does not
suggest that the nature of what's being reported is ma-
terially different from what's not.

5. For more information on moral disengagement and
killing animals, see Scott Vellum et al., "Moral Disengagement and Attitudes About Violence Toward Animals," *Society and Animals* 12, no. 3 (2004).

6. James McWilliams, james-mcwilliams.com, accessed
April 17, 2013, http://james-mcwilliams.com/wp-content
/uploads/2013/02/chicken-boxing-mcd2.jpg. Photo credit:
mancavedaily.com.

7. Amy McCoy, "Not for the Faint: Killing It in 2010,"
poorgirlgourmet.com, January 9, 2010, accessed February 21. 2013, http://www.poorgirlgourmet.com/2010/01
/not-for-faint-killing-it-in-2010.html.

8. "Chicken died while I was holding her upside down," 2,
backyardchickens.com, July 14, 2011, accessed March
6, 2013, http://www.backyardchickens.com/t/540806/
chicken-died-while-i-was-holding-her-upside-down/10.

9. Jordan Eshay, "The Conscience of an Urban Farmer,"
jordaneshay.wordpress.com, May 10, 2010, accessed
March 22, 2013, http://jordaneshay.wordpress.com/2010
/05/10/the-conscience-of-an-urban-farmer/.

10. Here's a description of why pigs are shot with a .22,
recounting the expertise of Gabe, an experienced pig
slaughterer: "'First Gabe is going to shoot the pig in the
forehead,' he explained calmly, as the boy watched Hector snuffling. 'That will stun it, but it's not going to kill
the pig because they need his heart to still be pumping to

get out all the blood. Then they're going to be hoisting the pig up, and the butcher is going to slit his throat. He's going to be thrashing some, and all the blood is going to drain out of his throat. That's what will kill him.'" See Jonathan Kauffman, "What I Saw, and Ate, at the Pig Sacrifice," *Seattle Weekly*, January 22, 2008, accessed July 14, 2013, http://www.seattleweekly.com/2008-01-23/news/what-i-saw-and-ate-at-the-pig-sacrifice/.

11. "The Goat and I," *Danny in Mombasa's Blog*, July 19, 2009, accessed April 4, 2013, http://dannyinmombasa.wordpress.com/2009/07/19/the-goat-and-i/.

12. "Behavior: Goat Handbook, United States, 1992," goat world.com, accessed April 4, 2013, http://www.goat world.com/articles/behavior/behavior.shtml.

13. Patty Khuky, "The REAL 'omnivore's dilemma' (notes on my first slaughter)," *Fully Vetted Blog*, petmd.com, May 23, 2009, accessed April 7, 2013, http://www.petmd.com/blogs/fullyvetted/2009/may/real-omnivores-dilemma%C2%9D-notes-my-first-slaughter.

14. "Out of Sight, out of Mind: Behind the Curtain," suburbansustainability.com, April 26, 2011, accessed April 7, 2013, http://suburbansustainability.wordpress.com/2011/04/26/out-of-sight-out-of-mind-behind-the-curtain/.

15. accessed April 8, 2013, http://www.tysonfoods.com/Search%20Results.aspx?q=welfare.

CHAPTER FIVE: HUMANE CHICKEN

1. Mulegirl, March 26, 2013, 6:59 a.m., comment on "Rough Learning Week," Livestock Forums—Poultry,

Homesteading Today, accessed April 9, 2013, http://www
.homesteadingtoday.com/livestock-forums/poultry
/479998-rough-learning-week.html.

2. Ibid.
3. Ibid. The writer added, "It was likely a weasel."
4. Annie Potts, *Chicken* (London: Reaktion Books, 2012), 159–60.
5. N. E. Collias and E. C. Collias, "A Field Study of the Red Jungle Fowl in North-Central India," *Condor* 69, no. 4 (1967): 360–86.
6. Robert A. Johnson, "Habitat Preference and Behavior of Breeding Jungle Fowl in Central Western Thailand," *Wilson Bulletin* 75, no. 3 (September 1963): 270–72; Potts, *Chicken*, 37–43.
7. An exception is the Cornish X, which is a breed of bird used on factory farms. They do not do well in true free-range farms because they are bred to become top-heavy and develop terrible leg problems when they walk too much.
8. G. Vallortigara, "The Cognitive Chicken: Higher Mental Processing in a Humble Brain," accessed April 23, 2013, http://www.cimec.unitn.it/Images/CimecCollo quium_Vallortigara.pdf; Jennifer Viegas, "Study: Chickens Think About Future," *Discovery News,* July 14, 2005.
9. Lynn, August 11, 2007, 8:26 a.m., comment on "Can You Truly Freerange with Hawks Around," backyard chickens.com, accessed April 30, 2013, http://backyard chickens.yuku.com/reply/24741/Can-you-truly-Free range-with-Hawks-around#reply-24741.
10. Ibid.

11. Tammye, February 11, 2011, 6:40 a.m., comment on "Please Stop Your Chickens from Freezing to Death," backyardchickens.com, accessed April 9, 2013. http://www.backyardchickens.com/t/450534/please-stop-your-chickens-from-freezing-to-death.

12. October 28, 2009, 7:37 a.m., various comments and poll chart "The Worst Predator—Page 2," backyard chickens.com, accessed April 23, 2013, http://www.backyardchickens.com/t/261440/the-worst-predator /10.

13. Sara Shields and Ian J. H. Duncan, "An HSUS Report: A Comparison of the Welfare of Hens in Battery Cages and Alternative Systems," Humane Society of the United States, accessed April 13, 2013, http://www.fao.org/fileadmin/user_upload/animalwelfare/HSUS—A%20Comparison%20of%20the%20Welfare%20of%20Hens%20in%20Battery%20Cages%20and%20Alternative%20Systems.pdf.

14. Fire Pirate, March 1, 2013, 11:23 a.m., comment on "Shooting an Animal Guilt," backyardchickens.com, accessed April 13, 2013, http://www.backyardchickens.com/t/749646/shooting-an-animal-guilt.

15. ShowMe31, October 17, 2011, 6:30 p.m., comment on "What Are We . . . Boys or Girls . . . Devastating Update," backyardchickens.com, accessed April 15, 2013, http://backyardchickens.yuku.com/reply/102218/what-are-weboys-or-girlsdevasting-update#reply-102218.

16. Tweetypie62, July 24, 2011, 10:13 a.m., comment on "Coon Attack," backyardchickens.com, accessed April

15, 2013, http://backyardchickens.yuku.com/topic/15228
/Coon-attack.

17. Riceinhall14, April 16, 2008, 7:01 a.m., comment on
"Blind Rooster?," backyardchickens.com, accessed April
14, 2013, http://backyardchickens.yuku.com/reply/73154
/Blind-Rooster#reply-73154.

18. Jminnie0922, June 13, 2009, 9:09 a.m., comment on
country4ever's thread starter, "Hens Attacked by
Coon . . . Large Gashes," backyardchickens.com, accessed April 14, 2013, http://backyardchickens.yuku
.com/reply/85300/Hens-attacked-by-coonlarge-gashes
#reply-85300.

19. Darin367, November 30, 2011, 8:54 a.m., thread starter
on backyardchickens.com, accessed April 24, 2013,
http://www.backyardchickens.com/t/603850/flock
-massacred.

20. Momagain1, March 12, 2012, 8:14 a.m., thread starter,
"Chicken Massacre Overnight Last Night," backyard
chickens.com, accessed April 24, 2013, http://www.back
yardchickens.com/t/638198/chicken-massacre-over
night-last-night.

21. Debilorrah, March 12, 2012, 8:34 p.m., comment on
Momagain1's "Chicken Massacre Overnight Last
Night," backyardchickens.com, accessed April 14, 2013,
http://www.backyardchickens.com/t/638198/chicken
-massacre-overnight-last-night.

22. Telehillco, April 14, 2012, 4:08 p.m., thread starter,
"Chicken Massacre . . . We Are Very Sad," backyard
chickens.com, accessed April 25, 2013, http://www
.backyardchickens.com/t/651486/chicken-massacre-we
-are-very-sad.

23. F. Bailey Norwood and Jayson L. Lusk, *Compassion by the Pound: The Economics of Farm Animal Welfare* (New York: Cambridge University Press, 2011), 120.

24. Mary Rothschild. "Backyard Chicks Make More Kids Sick," *Food Safety News,* June 30, 2011, accessed April 25, 2013, http://www.foodsafetynews.com/2011/06/back yard-chicks-make-more-kids-sick/.

25. Ibid.

26. Calen Hellerman, "Egg Farming: Industrial vs. Organic," *CNN Health,* cnn.com, August 24, 2010, accessed April 25, 2013, http://www.cnn.com/2010/HEALTH /08/24/egg.safety.debate/index.html.

27. Kara_leigh, June 23, 2011, 12:27 p.m., thread starter and various comments on "Salmonella," backyardchickens. com, accessed April 25, 2013, http://www.backyard chickens.com/t/528905/salmonella/20; sealcovechickens, August 21, 2010, 6:23 a.m., thread starter and various comments on "Salmonella Risks," backyardchickens .com, accessed April 25, 2013, http://www.backyard chickens.com/t/389118/salmonella-risks.

28. Funky Feathers, June 4, 2012, 6:11 p.m., thread starter and various comments on "Salmonella Outbreak Warning—Please Read!," backyardchickens.com, accessed April 26, 2013, http://www.backyardchickens .com/t/673529/salmonella-outbreak-warning-please -read.

29. Mac in Wisco, August 22, 2010, 9:31 a.m., comments on sealcovechickens' "Salmonella Risks?," backyard chickens.com, accessed April 25, 2013, http://www.back yardchickens.com/t/389118/salmonella-risks/10; it can also be spread when hens lay eggs outside nests on

pasture where feces have fallen—this happens about 2–10 percent of the time. See Norword and Lusk, *Compassion by the Pound*, 121.

30. Newbie Donna, August 26, 2010, 1:29 p.m., thread starter "Re: Feed Causing Salmonella in Chickens and Their Eggs," backyardchickens.com, accessed April 25, 2013, http://www.backyardchickens.com/t/391432/re-feed -causing-salmonella-in-chickens-and-their-eggs.

31. Elizabeth Weise, "Egg Farmers: Good Managing Can Help Control Salmonella," *USA Today*, September 8, 2010, accessed April 26, 2013, http://usatoday30.usato-day.com/yourlife/food/safety/2010-09-03-egg-farms -salmonella_N.htm.

32. J. S. Bailey and D. E. Cosby, "Salmonella Prevalence in Free-Range and Certified Organic Chickens," *Journal of Food Protection* 68, no. 11 (November 2005): 245–43, as seen on US National Library of Medicine, National Institutes of Health, accessed April 26, 2013, pubmed .gov, http://www.ncbi.nlm.nih.gov/pubmed/16300088.

33. D. R. Jones, K. E. Anderson, and J. Y. Guard, "Prevalence of Coliforms, Salmonella, Listeria, and Campylobacter Associated with Eggs and the Environment of Conventional Cage and Free-Range Egg Production," *Poultry Science* 91, no. 5 (May 2012): 1195–202, doi:10.3382 /ps.2011-01795, as seen on US National Library of Medicine, National Institutes of Health, pubmed.gov, accessed April 26, 2013, http://www.ncbi.nlm.nih.gov /pubmed/22499879.

34. Norwood and Lusk, *Compassion by the Pound*, 121.

35. Silkiechicken, December 2, 2010, 3:47 p.m., comment on Jarsheart's thread "Coccidia Is Killing My Flock

One by One—Tried Everything," backyardchickens.
com, accessed April 26, 2013, http://www.backyard
chickens.com/t/425870/coccidia-is-killing-my-flock
-one-by-one-tried-everything.

36. Aly M. Fadly, "Marek's Disease in Poultry" (last full
review/revision), *Merck Veterinary Manual*, March 2012,
accessed April 28, 2013, http://www.merckmanuals.com
/vet/poultry/neoplasms/mareks_disease_in_poultry
.html?qt=&sc=&alt=.

37. W. F. Rooney and A. A. Brickford, "Marek's Disease in
Backyard Chicken Flocks," Suburban Rancher, n.d., accessed April 26, 2013, http://animalscience.ucdavis.edu
/avian/mareks2.pdf.

38. DWilkins, December 6, 2012, 8:07 a.m., thread starter
"Help!!!!! Is Is [*sic*] Marek's Disease??," backyardchick
ens.com, accessed April 26, 2013, http://www.backyard
chickens.com/t/728032/help-is-is-mareks-disease.

39. BetsyB0101, March 5, 2012, 8:18 a.m., thread starter
"Marek's Disease: Need Advice," backyardchickens
.com, accessed April 26, 2013, http://www.backyard
chickens.com/t/635466/mareks-disease-need-advice.

40. Livi, February 27, 2013, 10:50 a.m., thread starter
"Marek's, Will It Help to Cull My Hens?," backyard
chickens.com, accessed April 26, 2013, http://www
.backyardchickens.com/t/749016/mareks-will-it-help
-to-cull-my-hens.

41. Sandee123, March 18, 2011, 7:09 p.m., comment on
Dolphin.biddingfortravel's "Moving On After Marek's—
Advice Needed," accessed April 28, 2013, http://back
yardchickens.yuku.com/topic/15063/Moving-on-after
-Mareks-advice-needed.

42. ChicKat, September 20, 2012, 11:14 a.m., comment on CTGirls's thread starter "Marek's Disease," backyard chickens.com, accessed April 26, 2013, http://www .backyardchickens.com/t/709840/mareks-disease.

43. Dr. Maurice E. White, Cornell University College of Veterinary Medicine, Consultant, "A Diagnostic Support System for Veterinary Medicine," http://www.vet .cornell.edu/consultant/Consult.asp?Fun=Home& spc=Avian&dxkw=&sxkw=EYE&signs=1-R601-E22; "Common Chicken Diseases," avianweb.com, accessed April 26, 2013, http://www.avianweb.com/chickendis eases.html.

44. Coopncottage, July 5, 2012, 7:31 a.m., thread starter "Hen Died Unexpectedly," backyardchickens.com, accessed April 28, 2013, http://www.backyardchickens .com/t/685288/hen-died-unexpectedly.

45. Kcvalentine, October 21, 2012, 8:29 a.m., thread starter "One Chicken Has Died Unexpectedly, and the Others (3) Will Not Lay Eggs," backyardchickens.com, accessed April 28, 2013, http://www.backyardchickens .com/t/717635/one-chicken-has-died-unexpectedly-and -the-others-3-will-not-lay-eggs.

46. Hennyetta, March 9, 2013, 7:25 a.m., thread starter "Sudden Death—Is There Ever an Answer?," backyard chickens.com, accessed April 28, 2013, http://www .backyardchickens.com/t/752195/sudden-death-is -there-ever-an-answer.

47. Tburley, October 18, 2010, 8:38 a.m., thread starter "Broiler Chicks Dying???," backyardchickens.com, accessed April 28, 2013, http://backyardchickens.yuku .com/topic/14836/Broiler-chicks-dying#.UX18faU1ZlI.

48. Smoky73, April 5, 2008, 3:52 p.m., thread starter "Aye, I Am Fed Up with the Weather Causing Sickness," backyardchickens.com, accessed April 28, 2013, http://backyardchickens.yuku.com/topic/10764/Aye-I-am-fed-up-with-the-weather-causing-sickness.

49. "Marek's Disease Vaccine (Chicken and Turkey)," drugs.com, accessed April 28, 2013, http://www.drugs.com/vet/marek-s-disease-vaccine-chicken-and-turkey.html.

50. Seminolewind, February 8, 2012, 1:57 p.m., comment on Summer98's thread starter "How Important Is Marek's Vaccination?," accessed April 28, 2013, http://www.backyardchickens.com/t/620047/how-important-is-mareks-vaccination.

51. F. Davison and V. Nair, "Use of Marek's Disease Vaccines: Could They Be Driving the Virus to Increasing Virulence?," *Expert Review of Vaccines* 4, no. 1 (February 2005): 77–88, as seen on US National Library of Medicine, National Institutes of Health, pubmed.gov, accessed April 28, 2013, http://www.ncbi.nlm.nih.gov/pubmed/15757475.

52. Ahmed Din Anjum, November 9, 2011, "Re Forum: Cause of Vaccination Failure Against Marek's Disease," comment on Wozniakowski's forum "Cause of Vaccination Failure Against Marek's Disease," Poultry Industry, hosted by Engormix, November 4, 2011, accessed April 28, 2013, http://en.engormix.com/MA-poultry-industry/health/forums/the-possible-cause-vaccination-t5136/165-p0.htm.

53. "Marek's Disease: Important Lessons Learnt," the poultrysite.com, July 29, 2008, accessed April 28, 2013,

http://www.thepoultrysite.com/articles/1105/mareks
-disease-important-lessons-learnt.

54. Kimberley Willis, "How to Prevent Losses from
    Marek's Disease in Michigan Small Chicken Flocks,"
    examiner.com, February 13, 2012, accessed April 28,
    2013, http://www.examiner.com/article/how-to-prevent
    -losses-from-mareks-disease-michigans-small-chicken
    -flocks.

55. Ozexpat, April 20, 2013, 9:30 a.m., thread starter "Vac-
    cinations—My Research and How to Go About Vacci-
    nating a Backyard Flock," backyardchickens.com,
    accessed April 30, 2013, http://www.backyardchickens
    .com/t/770972/vaccinations-my-research-and-how-to
    -go-about-vaccinating-a-backyard-flock.

56. "Poultry Diseases Up Close—Marek's Disease," the
    naturalpoultryfarmingguide.org, April 16, 2013, accessed
    April 29, 2013, http://thenaturalpoultryfarmingguide
    .org/2013/04/16/poultry-diseases-up-close-mareks
    -disease/.

57. O. Ohe and A. Aradawa, "Effect of Feed Additive Anti-
    biotics on Chickens Infected with *Eimeria tenella*,"
    Poultry Science 54, no. 4 (July 1975): 1008–18, as seen on
    US National Library of Medicine, National Institutes
    of Health, pubmed.gov, accessed April 29, 2013, http://
    www.ncbi.nlm.nih.gov/pubmed/1161694.

58. Markallen, March 19, 2012, 3:34 p.m., comment on Olda
    Bat's thread starter "Vaccinated vs. Medicated Feed . . .
    Organic Eggs?," backyardchickens.com, accessed April
    29, 2013, http://www.backyardchickens.com/t/640596
    /vaccinated-vs-medicated-feed-organic-eggs.

59. "Chicken Help," mypetchicken.com, accessed April 29, 2013, http://www.mypetchicken.com/backyard-chickens/chicken-help/What-is-medicated-feed-all-about-do-I-need-it-H74.aspx.

60. ChinaChicks1, September 3, 2010, 5:36 a.m., comment on tweeteypie62's thread starter "Safe-Guard Dewormer for Goats for Chickens," backyardchickens.com, accessed April 30, 2013, http://backyardchickens.yuku.com/reply/98698/Safeguard-Dewormer-for-goats-for-chickens#reply-98698.

61. "Eprinex Questions," various backyardchickens.com threads started on April 19, 2007, 9:07 a.m., accessed April 29, 2013, http://backyardchickens.yuku.com/reply/28271/Eprinex-Questions#reply-28271; dlhunicorn, November 3, 2006, 3:41 p.m., comment on halo826's thread starter "I Have a Very Sick Hen Too . . . Please Help Me Again," accessed April 29, 2013, http://backyardchickens.yuku.com/reply/30124/I-have-a-very-sick-hen-tooplease-help-me-again#reply-30124.

62. Extoxnet, Extension Toxicology Network, Pesticide Information Profiles, "Carbaryl," extoxnet.orst.edu, June 1996, accessed April 29, 2013. http://extoxnet.orst.edu/pips/carbaryl.htm.

63. Henrysue, August 7, 2008, 7:17 a.m., thread starter, "Just Want to Share My Sevin Dust Experience with You . . . ," accessed April 29, 2013, http://www.backyardchickens.com/t/78926/just-want-to-share-my-sevin-dust-experience-with-you.

64. Accessed April 30, 2013, http://eatocracy.cnn.com/2010/08/20/egg-splained-free-range-cage-free-and-organic/.

65. Groverguy574, March 2, 2009, 10:37 a.m., comment on featheredpig's thread starter "The Yuku Battle," accessed April 30, 2013, http://backyardchickens.yuku.com/reply /83786/the-Yuku-battle#reply-83786.

66. ODINSWORN, March 31, 2013, 11:37 a.m., thread starter "Wounded Goose," homesteadingtoday.com, accessed on April 9, 2013, http://www.homesteadingto day.com/livestock-forums/poultry/480994-wounded -goose.html.

67. Mailmam71, December 9, 2008, 9:15 a.m., comment on jimnjay's thread starter "Pretty Interesting," accessed April 30, 2013. http://backyardchickens.yuku.com/reply /82167/Pretty-Interesting#reply-82167.

68. ODINSWORN, March 31, 2013.

69. Mamapeeps, March 24, 2008, 9:28 a.m., comment on jimnjay's "Dog Attack," backyardchickens.com, accessed April 30, 2013, http://backyardchickens.yuku.com/reply /71472/Dog-Attack#reply-71472.

70. Mailmam71, March 2, 2009, 10:13 a.m., comment on featheredpig's thread starter "The Yuku Battle," ac- cessed May 6, 2013, http://backyardchickens.yuku.com /topic/12620/the-Yuku-battle.

71. Lovin my birds, June 28, 2011, 8:45 a.m., comment on jennifersmith326's thread starter "Dog Killed My Chickens, I Killed the Dog," backyardchickens.com, accessed May 1, 2013, http://www.backyardchickens.com /t/531652/dog-killed-my-chickens-i-killed-the-dog.

72. Dustin Biery, July 24, 2011, 2:56 p.m., comment on Beckt's "Coon Attack," backyardchickens.com, accessed May 1, 2013, http://backyardchickens.yuku.com/reply /101820/Coon-attack#reply-101820.

73. Mthrclckr, November 30, 2008, 2:39 p.m., comment on jimnjay's thread starter "Pretty Interesting," backyard chickens.com, accessed May 4, 2013, http://backyard chickens.yuku.com/reply/81986/Pretty-Interesting #reply-81986.

74. Eggchel, December 1, 2008, 5:57 p.m., comment on jimnjay's thread starter "Pretty Interesting," backyard chickens.com, accessed May 6, 2013, http://backyard chickens.yuku.com/reply/81986/Pretty-Interesting #reply-81986.

75. Mailmam71, September 6, 2010, 7:44 a.m., comment on Sharisr32's thread starter "Egg Mess," backyardchick ents.com, accessed April 30, 2013, http://backyardchick ens.yuku.com/reply/98721/Egg-Mess#reply-98721.

76. Wabbit, November 11, 2005, 4:02 a.m., comment on SOAD's thread starter "Slaughtered lamb on Jamie Oliver tv show," Rabbits United, accessed on July 15, 2014, http://forums.rabbitrehome.org.uk/archive/index .php/t-57843.html.

CHAPTER SIX: UTOPIAN BEEF

1. James McWilliams, "All Sizzle and No Steak: Why Allan Savory's TED Talk About How Cattle Can Reverse Global Warming Is Dead Wrong," slate.com, April 22, 2013, accessed May 15, 2013, http://www.slate.com/arti cles/life/food/2013/04/allan_savory_s_ted_talk_is_wrong _and_the_benefits_of_holistic_grazing_have.html.

2. James E. McWilliams, "The Myth of Sustainable Meat," *New York Times* Opinion page, April 12, 2012, accessed May 15, 2013, http://www.nytimes.com/2012

/04/13/opinion/the-myth-of-sustainable-meat.html? _r=0; Salatin's admission: Joel Salatin, "Joel Salatin Responds to *New York Times*' 'Myth of Sustainable Meat,'" grist.org, April 17, 2013, accessed November 10, 2013, http://grist.org/sustainable-farming/farmer-responds-to -the-new-york-times-re-sustainable-meat/.

3. McWilliams, "All Sizzle and No Steak."

4. James McWilliams, "Beware the Myth of Grass-Fed Beef: Cows Raised at Pasture Are Not Immune to Deadly *E. coli* Bacteria," slate.com, January 22, 2010, accessed May 15, 2013, http://www.slate.com/articles/health_and_science/ green_room/2010/01/beware_the_myth_of_grassfed_ beef.html.

5. They should have retracted the entire article, as it was squarely premised on this claim. What makes Planck's error so dangerous is that purveyors of grass-fed beef, including ground beef, suggest cooking the meat to rare, thus preserving the *E. coli* O157.

6. "I do not consider myself a cattleman," writes one rancher. "I am a grass farmer."

7. Agmantoo, February 9, 2009, 5:20 p.m., comment on godsgapeach's "Any Ideas for Converting to Rotational Grazing," homesteadingtoday.com, accessed May 28, 2013, http://www.homesteadingtoday.com/cattle/286704 -any-ideas-converting-rotational-grazing-5.html.

8. Bossroo, May 18, 2011, 1:00 p.m., "Announcement," back yardherds.com, accessed May 28, 2013, http://www.back yardherds.com/forum/viewtopic.php?id=10206.

9. backyardherds.com, accessed May 29, 2013, http://www .backyardherds.com/forum/viewtopic.php?id=21872.

10. Herfrds, May 19, 2011, 12:11 p.m., "Announcement," backyardherds.com, accessed May 29, 2013, http://www .backyardherds.com/forum/viewtopic.php?id=10206.

11. WildRoseBeef, October 26, 2012, 9:45 p.m., "Announcement," backyardherds.com, accessed May 30, 2013, http:// www.backyardherds.com/forum/viewtopic.php ?id=22463.

12. Bossroo, June 15, 2010, 11:32 a.m., "Announcement," backyardherds.com, accessed May 30, 2013, http:// www.backyardherds.com/forum/viewtopic.php?id =22463.

13. Francismilker, March 23, 2009, 9:34 a.m., comment on "Any Ideas for Converting to Rotational Grazing," homesteadingtoday.com, accessed May 30, 2013, http:// www.homesteadingtoday.com/cattle/286704-any-ideas -converting-rotational-grazing-12.html.

14. All Cattle & Calves . . . Map of Cattle Distribution, "January 1, 2013, Inventory vs. 2012 Inventory . . . ," cattlerange.com, n.d., accessed May 20, 2013, http:// www.cattlerange.com/cattle-graphs/all-cattle-numbers .html.

15. R. N. Lubowski, M. Vesterby, S. Bucholtz, A. Baez, and M. Roberts, "Major Uses of Land in the United States, 2002," *Economic Information Bulletin*, no. EIB-14, May 2006, as seen on USDA Economic Research Service, ers.usda.gov, accessed May 30, 2013, http://www.ers .usda.gov/publications/eib-economic-information-bul letin/eib14.aspx#.UadowaWTORs.

16. US Environmental Protection Agency, "Major Crops Grown in the United States," epa.gov, 2013, accessed

May 30, 2013, http://www.epa.gov/agriculture/ag101 /cropmajor.html; USDA Economic Research Service, "Corn," ers.usda/gov, last updated June 18, 2013, accessed June 30, 2013, http://www.ers.usda.gov/topics /crops/corn/background.aspx.

17. WildRoseBeef, October 26, 2012, 9:45 p.m., "Announcement," backyardherds.com, accessed May 30, 2013, http:// www.backyardherds.com/forum/viewtopic.php?id =22463.

18. Herfrds, May 19, 2011.

19. Greybeard, November 14, 2012, 12:31 a.m., "Announcement," backyardherds.com, accessed May 30, 2013, http://www.backyardherds.com/forum/viewtopic.php ?id=22767.

20. Trisha in WA, January 14, 2009, 9:47 p.m., comment on homesteadingtoday.com, accessed May 30, 2013, http://www.homesteadingtoday.com/cattle/286704 -any-ideas-converting-rotational-grazing-3.html.

21. J. Schneekloth and A. Andales, "Seasonal Water Needs and Opportunities for Limited Irrigation for Colorado Crops," September 2009, Colorado State University Extension, ext.colostate.edu, accessed May 30, 2013, http://www.ext.colostate.edu/pubs/crops/04718.html; "Lower Colorado River Culture Water Demand— Agricultural Demand," ADWR, Arizona Department of Water Resources, az.gov, n.d., accessed May 30, 2013, http://www.azwater.gov/AzDWR/StatewidePlanning /WaterAtlas/LowerColoradoRiver/PlanningAreaOver view/WaterSupply-AgriculturalDemand.htm.

22. Accessed May 30, 2013, http://www.backyardherds .com/forum/viewtopic.php?id=22767.

23. Terry Mader, Bruce Anderson, and Dave Sanson, "Management to Minimize Hay Waste," *Beef Cattle Handbook*, iowabeefcenter.org, n.d., accessed May 30, 2013, http://www.iowabeefcenter.org/Beef%20Cattle%20Handbook/Management_Minimize_Hay_Waste.pdf.

24. Ibid.

25. DTP, May 30, 2008, 6:12 UTC, comment on decomom's "Grass-Fed Beef in Michigan," localharvest.org, January 18, 2008, accessed, May 30, 2013, http://www.localharvest.org/forum/thread.jsp?thread=872&forum=6.

26. Angela, November 20, 2011, 12:25 UTC, comment on angel5starr's "Topic: Raising a Beef Cow," localharvest.org, accessed May 30, 2013, http://www.localharvest.org/forum/thread.jsp?forum=6&thread=3733.

27. http://www.backyardherds.com/threads/now-that-winter-is-upon-us.22126/; accessed July 17, 2014.

28. Donald M. Ball, Garry Lacefield, and Carl S. Hoverland, "The Tall Fescue Endophyte Story," as seen on West Virginia University Extension Service, www.caf.wvu.edu/~forage/, n.d., accessed May 20, 2013, http://www.caf.wvu.edu/~forage/fescue_endophtye/story.htm.

29. Ibid.

30. Christopher D. Penrose, Henry M. Bartholomew, and R. Mark Sulc, "Stockpiling Tall Fescue for Winter Grazing," in Ohio State University Extension, Department of Horticulture and Crop Sciences, *Agronomy Facts*, n.d., accessed June 3, 2013, http://ohioline.osu.edu/agf-fact/0023.html.

31. Richard Browning, "Tall Fescue Endophyte Toxicosis in Beef Cattle: Clinical Mode of Action and Potential

Mitigation Through Cattle Genetics," as seen on Beef Improvement Federation, beefimprovement.org, n.d., accessed June 3, 2013, http://www.beefimprovement.org /proceedings/03proceedings/Browning.pdf.

32. Aggieterpkatie, July 23, 2010, 11:59 a.m., comment on "Announcement," backyardherds.com, accessed June 3, 2013, http://www.backyardherds.com/forum/viewtopic .php?id=5572.

33. Browning, "Tall Fescue Endophyte Toxicosis."

34. Glenn Selk and Kent Barnes, "Fescue Foot: Identifying and Minimizing the Problem," Oklahoma Cooperative Extension Service, Oklahoma State University, osuf acts.okstate.edu, n.d., accessed June 3, 2013, http://pods .dasnr.okstate.edu/docushare/dsweb/Get/Document -1982/ANSI-3357.pdf.

35. Tall Fescue Online Monograph, "Fat Necrosis," Oregon State University, n.d., accessed June 3, 2013, http://forages .oregonstate.edu/tallfescuemonograph/endophyte_cattle /fat_necrosis; Peter D. Constable, "Overview of Abdominal Fat Necrosis," in *The Merck Veterinary Manual*, March 2012, accessed June 3, 2013, http://www.merckmanuals .com/vet/digestive_system/abdominal_fat_necrosis_lipo matosis/overview_of_abdominal_fat_necrosis.html.

36. Craig Roberts and John Andrae, "Tall Fescue Toxicosis and Management," Plant Management Network, April 27, 2004, accessed June 3, 2013, http://www.plantmanage-mentnetwork.org/pub/cm/management/2004/toxicosis/.

37. http://www.homesteadingtoday.com/cattle/286704-any -ideas-converting-rotational-grazing-3.html; accessed July 15, 2014.

38. http://www.homesteadingtoday.com/cattle/286704-any

-ideas-converting-rotational-grazing-7.html; accessed July 15, 2014.

39. http://www.backyardherds.com/threads/new-to-cattle.21832/page-2, accessed July 15, 2014.

40. http://www.homesteadingtoday.com/livestock-forums/cattle/286704-any-ideas-converting-rotational-grazing.html. Accessed July 15, 2014.

41. http://www.homesteadingtoday.com/cattle/286704-any-ideas-converting-rotational-grazing-5.html; http://www.homesteadingtoday.com/cattle/286704-any-ideas-converting-rotational-grazing-7.html. Accessed July 15, 2014.

42. Rick Rasby, UNL Beef, July 18, 2012, accessed June 21, 2013, http://beef.unl.edu/amountwatercowsdrink.

43. John Robbins, "2,500 Gallons All Wet?," earthsave.org, n.d., accessed June 29, 2013, http://www.earthsave.org/environment/water.htm.

44. Cassandra Profita, "Which Is Greener: Grass-Fed or Grain-Fed Beef?," *Ecotrope*, October 26, 2006, updated February 19, 2013, accessed June 19, 2013, http://www.opb.org/news/blog/ecotrope/which-is-greener-grass-fed-or-grain-fed-beef/.

45. http://www.homesteadingtoday.com/cattle/286704-any-ideas-converting-rotational-grazing-6.html. Accessed July 15, 2014.

46. Christopher Weber, "Upping the Steaks: How Grass-Fed Beef Is Reshaping Ag and Helping the Planet," grist.org, February 1, 2013, http://grist.org/food/upping-the-steaks-how-grass-fed-beef-is-reshaping-ag-and-helping-the-planet/.

47. "Fredericksburg Grassfed Beef," no last modified date, http://www.fredericksburg-grassfed-beef.com.

48. Carrrie Oliver, "Grass-Fed Beef & Droughts Don't Mix," Discover the World of Artisan Beef website, November 9, 2008, http://discoverbeef.blogspot.com /2008/11/grass-fed-beef-droughts-dont-mix.html.
49. Otago Regional Council, "Why Is Pugging a Problem," n.d., http://www.orc.govt.nz/Documents/Publications /Farming%20and%20Land%20Management/Pugging %20near%20waterways.pdf.
50. http://www.localharvest.org/forum/thread.jsp?forum=6 &thread=3733. Accessed July 15, 2014.
51. "Pugging and Compaction," Ballance Agri-Nutrients Limited, n.d., http://www.dairynz.co.nz/file/fileid/37481.
52. http://agronwww.agron.iastate.edu/Courses/ agron515/Historical%20vs%20modern%20footprint .pdf.
53. Judith L Capper, "Is the Grass Always Greener?: Comparing the Environmental Impact of Conventional, Natural and Grass-Fed Beef Production Systems," *Animals* 2, no. 2 (2012): 127–43, doi:10.3390/ani2020127.
54. Nathan Pelletier, Rich Pirog, and Rebecca Rasmussen, "Comparative Life Cycle Environmental Impacts of Three Beef Production Strategies in the Upper Midwestern United States," *Agricultural Systems*, elsevier.com/ locate/agsy, April 22, 2010, http://www.leopold.iastate .edu/sites/default/files/pubs-and-papers/2010-04-com parative-life-cycle-environmental-impacts-three-beef -production-strategies-upper-midwestern-unite.pdf.
55. https://www.facebook.com/Polyfacefarm/posts /10150655771121105. Accessed on July 15, 2014.
56. Richard Oppenlander, *Global Depletion and Food Responsibility* (Hillcrest, 2011), 128–129.

CHAPTER SEVEN: PAINFUL PORK

1. Natalie Angier, "Pigs Prove to Be Smart, If Not Vain," *New York Times* Science, November 9, 2009, accessed June 25, 2013, http://www.nytimes.com/2009/11/10 /science/10angier.html?_r=0.

2. "The 10 Smartest Animals, How Do Humans Compare to Other Intelligent Creatures," NBCNews.com, Science, n.d., accessed June 25, 2013, http://www.nbc news.com/id/24628983/ns/technology_and_science -science/t/smartest-animals/#.Ucm1xaWTORs.

3. Angier, "Pigs Prove to Be Smart." Interestingly, on the day I wrote this paragraph, a friend of mine—a doctor who teaches emergency-room tactics—had just ordered "forty pig tracheas."

4. Wind Ridge Farm, George and Elaine Kohram, "Pot Belly Pigs," 2004–13, accessed June 25, 2013, http:// www.windridgefarm.us/potbellypigs.htm.

5. Ibid.

6. "Joy of Pigs, Pigs as Pets," PBS, *Nature*, pbs.org, premiered November 17, 1996, accessed June 25, 2013, http://www.pbs.org/wnet/nature/episodes/the-joy-of -pigs/pigs-as-pets/2124/.

7. Gloria Riviera, "They're Clean, They're Cute and They Cuddle," ABC News, January 11, 2010, accessed June 25, 2013, http://abcnews.go.com/Nightline/micro -pigs-latest-tiny-trendy-pets/story?id=9502599#.Uc nrI6WTORs.

8. Associated Press, "Some New Yorkers Keep Pigs as Pets Despite the City's Ban," *Daily News*, March 22, 2013, accessed June 25, 2013, http://www.nydailynews .com/new-york/new-yorkers-pet-pigs-ban-article-1

.1296276; Jen Doll. "If Loving Pigs Is Wrong, New Yorkers Don't Want to Be Right," *Atlantic Wire*, March 22, 2013, accessed July 15, 2013, http://www.theatlan ticwire.com/national/2013/03/if-loving-pigs-wrong -new-yorkers-dont-want-be-right/63428/.

9. "Lil'Orphan Hammies," n.d., accessed June 27, 2013, http://lilorphanhammies.org/adopt.

10. http://www.theguardian.com/commentisfree/2009 /may/18/food-and-drink. Accessed May 22, 2014.

11. Aaron R. Jex, Shiping Liu, Bo Li, Neil D. Young et al., *"Ascaris suum* Draft Genome," *Nature* 479 (November 24, 2011): 529–33, doi:10.1038/nature10553, accessed June 26, 2013, http://www.nature.com/nature/journal /v479/n7374/full/nature10553.html.

12. I. A. J. M. Eijck and F. H. M. Borgsteede, "A Survey of Gastrointestinal Pig Parasites on Free-Range, Organic and Conventional Pig Farms in the Netherlands," *Veterinary Research Communications* 29, no. 5 (July 2005): 407–41, as seen on link.springer.com, accessed June 26, 2013, http://link.springer.com/article/10.1007/ s11259-005-1201-z.

13. Annette Nygaard Jensen, Anders Dalsgaard, Anders Stockmarr, Eva Møller Nielsen, and Dorte Lau Baggesen, "Survival and Transmission of *Salmonella enterica* Serovar Typhimurium in an Outdoor Organic Pig Farming Environment," *Applied and Environmental Microbiology* 72, no. 3 (March 2006): 1833–42, doi:10.1128 /AEM.72.3.1833–1842.2006, http://aem.asm.org/content /72/3/1833.full.pdf.

14. Bill Chameides, "Is a Free-Range Pig a Good Pig," *The Green Grok* (blog), Duke, Nicholas School of the Envi-

ronment, April 23, 2009, accessed June 27, 2013, http://
blogs.nicholas.duke.edu/thegreengrok/porkop-edreac
tion/.

15. Siddhartha Thakur and Wondwossen A. Gebreyes,
"Prevalence and Antimicrobial Resistance of Campylobacter in Antimicrobial-Free and Conventional Pig
Production Systems," *Journal of Food Protection* 68, no.
11 (November 2005): 2402–10(9), as seen on ingenta
connect.com, accessed June 27, 2013, http://www.in
gentaconnect.com/content/iafp/jfp/2005/00000068
/00000011/art00021.

16. W. A. Gebreyes, S. Thakur, and W. E. Morrow,
"Comparison of Prevalence, Antimicrobial Resistance,
and Occurrence of Multidrug-Resistant Salmonella in
Antimicrobial-Free and Conventional Pig Production," *Journal of Food Protection* 69, no. 4 (April 2006):
743–48, as seen on US National Library of Medicine,
National Institute of Health, pubmed.gov, accessed
June 26, 2013, http://www.ncbi.nlm.nih.gov/pubmed
/16629014.

17. PETA, "The Organic and Free-Range Myth," peta
.org, n.d., accessed July 2, 2013, http://www.peta.org
/issues/animals-used-for-food/free-range-organic
-meat-myth.aspx.

18. The Pig Site, "*Toxoplasma gondii* Infection and Outdoor
Swine Production," thepigsite.com, February 24, 2011,
accessed June 27, 2013, http://www.thepigsite.com/ar
ticles/3372/emtoxoplasma-gondii-em-infection-and
-outdoor-swine-production.

19. http://www.ncbi.nlm.nih.gov/pubmed/21117987. Accessed July 15, 2014.

20. Steve G, October 28, 2010, 13:01, comment on "Rooting . . . ," thepigsite.com, accessed June 27, 2013, http:// www.thepigsite.com/forums/showthread.php?p=27647.

21. Rhodie, November 5, 2010, 18:45, comment on "Rooting . . . ," thepigsite.com, accessed June 27, 2013, http:// www.thepigsite.com/forums/showthread.php?p=27647.

22. http://www.thepigsite.com/forums/showthread.php ?t=11126. Accessed May 22, 2014.

23. A. John F. Webster and John Webster, eds., *Animal Husbandry Regained: The Place of Farm Animals in Sustainable Agriculture* (New York: Routledge, 2013), 144, as seen on Google Books, http://books.google.com /books?id=D6v-Tdhm5SgC&pg=PA144&lpg=PA144 &dq=nose+rings+free-range+farms&source=bl& ots=9w04g_vyo1&sig=jLdXzA_OLzflaIFTJupQ2s 7iNVs&hl=en&sa=X&ei=h2fRUY-NJJHe4APOvo HYDQ&ved=0CFwQ6AEwAzgK#v=onepage&q=nose %20rings%20free-range%20farms&f=false.

24. Gemma Gadd, "Graser's Free Range Pigs," *Weekly Times Now*, July 6, 2011, accessed July 1, 2013, http://www .weeklytimesnow.com.au/article/2011/07/06/353631 _on-farm.html.

25. James McWilliams. "Hog Heaven? Life Is No Picnic for Free-Range Pigs," slate.com, June 29, 2009, accessed July 1, 2013. http://www.slate.com/articles/life /food/2009/06/hog_heaven.html.

26. "How to Grow Free Range Pork in Iowa," *Heart to Heart* (blog), October 24, 2009, accessed July 1, 2013, http://hearttoheart.wordpress.com/2009/10/24/how-to -grow-free-range-pork-in-iowa/.

27. DM, December 14, 2009, 1:49 p.m., comment on Free Range Pork Farmers Association's "How to Butcher a Free Range Pig," accessed July 1, 2013, http://ialsoli veonafarm.wordpress.com/2009/12/10/how-to-butcher -a-free-range-pig/.

28. Piper Hoffman, "World Farm Animals Day: Top Five Questions About Veganism," piperhoffman.com, October 2, 2011, accessed July 1, 2013, http://piperhoff man.com/2011/10/02/world-farm-animals-day-top -five-questions-about-veganism/.

29. Rosery Farm, "The Importance of Free Range Pork," roseryfarm.com, n.d., accessed July 1, 2013, http://ros eryfarm.com/free-range_rare-breed/.

30. R. I. Horrell, P. J. A'Ness, S. A. Edwards, and J. C. Eddison, "The Use of Nose-Rings in Pigs: Consequences for Rooting, Other Functional Activities, and Welfare," *Animal Welfare* 10, no. 1 (February 2001): 3–22, as seen on ingentaconnect.com, accessed July 1, 2013, http:// www.ingentaconnect.com/content/ufaw/aw/2001 /00000010/00000001/art00002.

31. RSPCA Farm Animals Department, "The Welfare of Pigs," information sheet, January 2013, accessed July 1, 2013, http://www.rspca.org.uk/ImageLocator/Locate- Asset?asset=document&assetId=1232712122111& mode=prd.

32. Brent, June 10, 2009, 22:44, comment on tchappetta's "Ring a Pig's Nose," The GardenWeb, forums2.gar denweb.com, May 22, 2006, accessed July 1, 2013, http:// forums2.gardenweb.com/forums/load/farmlife /msg0517332926865.html.

33. Anna Bassett, "Nose Ringing Pigs," *Animal Welfare Approved*, April 2011, accessed July 1, 2013, http://www.animalwelfareapproved.org/wp-content/uploads/2012/01/TAFS-16-Nose-ringing-pigs.pdf.

34. McWilliams, "Hog Heaven?"

35. Beau Ramsburg, "An Open Letter to James McWilliams, Texas State University," *The Gatepost: News, Muse, and Views from Rettland Farm* (blog), rettlandfarm.blogspot.com, July 9, 2009, accessed July 1, 2013, http://rettlandfarm.blogspot.com/2009/07/open-letter-to-james-mcwilliams-texas.html.

36. Daniel Maurer, "Is *Slate*'s Takedown of Free-Range Pork Just a Bunch of Hogwash?," *Grub Street* (blog), grubstret.com, July 1, 2009, accessed July 1, 2013, http://www.grubstreet.com/2009/07/is_slates_takedown_of_free-ran.html.

37. Suzanne McMinn, "The Pig Man Cometh," *Chickens in the Road: Life in Ordinary Splendor* (blog), September 22, 2009, accessed July 2, 2013, http://chickensintheroad.com/barn/the-pig-man-cometh/.

38. Ann Widdifield, *Passing Through Shady Side* (Bloomington, IN: AuthorHouse, 2013), 220.

39. This assessment is borne out by comprehensive overviews of the industry. "In the USA," writes a Texas Tech guide to pig castration, "virtually all males are physically castrated without anesthesia or analgesia (pain relief)": Laboratory of Animal Behavior, Physiology and Welfare, "The Pig Castration Site," Texas Tech University, depts.ttu.edu, 2012, accessed July 2, 2013, http://www.depts.ttu.edu/animalwelfare/Research/PigCastration/.

40. "Welfare Implications of Swine Castration," thepigsite
.com, June 7, 2013, accessed July 2, 2013, http://www
.thepigsite.com/articles/4371/welfare-implications-of
-swine-castration. The AVMA's opinion on pig castration without painkillers has been supported by the USDA
and even the pork industry itself. See "National Pork
Board: Stop Painful Piglet Castration," change.org, 2012,
accessed July 2, 2013, http://www.change.org/petitions/
national-pork-board-stop-painful-piglet-castration.

41. Galapas, February 17, 2011, 12:03, comment on Zuri-
el's "Castrating Newborn Pigs?," thepigsite.com, accessed July 2, 2013, http://www.thepigsite.com/forums
/showthread.php?t=11542

42. http://www.thepigsite.com/forums/showthread.php
?p=31633. Accessed July 2, 2013.

43. VetStudent, November 16, 2006, 16:14, comment on
Beth's "My 9 Month Old Boar Died After Being Castrated??," thepigsite.com, accessed July 2, 2013. http://
www.thepigsite.com/forums/showthread.php?t=1099.

44. Beth, November 18, 2006, 6:33, an update on Beth's
"My 9 Month Old Boar Died After Being Castrated??,"
thepigsite.com, accessed July 2, 2013, http://www
.thepigsite.com/forums/showthread.php?t=1099.

45. Compassion in World Farming, "Welfare Issues for Pigs,"
ciwf.org.uk, n.d., accessed July 3, 2013, http://www.ciwf
.org.uk/farm_animals/pigs/welfare_issues/default.aspx.

46. Ibid.

47. RSPCA Australia Knowledgebase, "What Are the Animal Welfare Issues Associated with Pig Farming,"
kb.rspca.org.au, September 9, 2011, accessed July 3, 2013,
http://kb.rspca.org.au/?View=entry&EntryID=109.

48. Frances Flower, "No Gestation Crates for Our Pigs," Whole Foods Market website, March 22, 2012, accessed July 3, 2013, http://www.wholefoodsmarket.com /blog/whole-story/no-gestation-crates-our-pigs.

49. Birdlove, September 23, 2008, 00:36, "Mother Pig Is Squashing Baby," thepigsite.com, September 23, 2008, accessed July 3, 2013, http://www.thepigsite.com/fo rums/showthread.php?t=7271.

50. Hywel2, August 17, 2009, 8:43, "Crushing," thepigsite .com, August 17, 2009, accessed July 3, 2013, http:// www.thepigsite.com/forums/showthread.php?t=7271.

51. Rhodie, February 22, 2009, 14:59, comment on vendel-boe's "Do You Want to Produce 31 Pig Pr Pr Year?," and comments made by blonde, February 22, 2009, thepitsite.com, accessed July 3, 2013, http://www.thepig site.com/forums/showthread.php?t=7975.

52. Bruce King, July 2, 2009, 4:00 p.m., "Piglets," *Meat: Raising Animals for Food in Western Washington* (blog), accessed July 2, 2013, http://ebeyfarm.blogspot.com /2009/07/piglets.html.

53. Heath Putnam, "Outdoor Farrowing," *Wooly Pigs: The Mangalitsa Blog*, July 5, 2009, accessed July 3. 2013, http://woolypigs.blogspot.com/2009/07/outdoor-far rowing.html.

54. Bonnie Taylor, "Ban Farrowing Crates in US Hog Pro-duction," forcechange.com, 2012, accessed July 14, 2013, http://forcechange.com/7767/ban-farrowing-crates-in -u-s-hog-production/#gf_1.

55. Kat Kinsman, "A Day Two Pigs Would Die: Ethical Slaughter," *Eatocracy* blog, CNN, July 12, 2010, ac-

cessed July 14, 2013, http://eatocracy.cnn.com/2010/07/12/a-day-two-pigs-would-die/.

56. Kate's Bookshelf in Books, Life, Writing, "My First Hand Experiences in Slaughtering Pigs," *Escaping the Inkwell: Voyages on Paper as Words Escape the Pen* . . . (blog), October 4, 2011, accessed July 14, 2013, http://inkwell splatters.wordpress.com/2011/10/04/my-first-hand-ex periences in slaughtering pigs/.

57. Lori Bell, "Responsible Meat: A Lesson from a Pig Called Eddie," *Missoula Independent*, May 16, 2013, accessed July 14, 2013. http://missoulanews.bigskypress .com/missoula/responsible-meat/Content?oid=1860313.

58. Josh and Brent, comments on "Hog Heaven," Beekman 1802, 2012, accessed July 14, 2013, http://beekman1802 .com/hog-heaven/.

59. Ibid.

60. Widdifield, *Passing Through Shady Side*, 220

61. Bell, "Responsible Meat."

62. Jonathan Kauffman "What I Saw, and Ate, at the Pig Sacrifice," *Seattle Weekly News*, January 22, 2008, accessed July 14, 2013, http://www.seattleweekly.com/2008-01-23 /news/what-i-saw-and-ate-at-the-pig-sacrifice/.

63. John_lee, February 1, 2009, 1:00 p.m., comment on Zamboni's "Forum: Bacon," jamieoliver.com, February 1, 2009, accessed July 15, 2013, http://www.jamieoliver .com/forum/viewtopic.php?id=40640.

64. Mummza, February 1, 2009, 1:55 p.m., comment on Zamboni's "Forum: Bacon," jamieoliver.com, February 1, 2009, accessed July 15, 2013, http://www.jamieoliver .com/forum/viewtopic.php?id=40640.

CONCLUSION: OUR UNTHINKING DECISION

1. I came up with this term on my own, used it in a talk I
   gave at the Colorado Veg Fest in July 2013, and then, a
   week later, came across the phrase in Berlin's *Crooked
   Timber of Humanity*. So he got the glory, until a philosopher at McGill informed me, alas, the quote is, in fact,
   Kant's.

INDEX

abstract reasoning, 29, 232*n*20
Agmantoo, 180
agriculture
  animal, 70–21
  ecstasy, 115
  industrial, 5, 8–21, 43, 183
  mythology of, 159
  nonindustrial, 39, 68, 78–22
  pasture-based alternatives in,
    54–26
  pornography of, 72, 238*n*3
  production of, 4–2
  radical alternatives in, 34–29
  reform of, 17–29
ambiguity, 25–28, 231*nn*16–28
American diet, 14–25
American Veterinary Medical
  Association (AVMA), 210
amprolium, 155, 156
Anderson, Chris, 167
anesthesia, 208
anger, 5
Angier, Natalie, 196
animal consumption
  abolishing, 48–21, 63–24,
    66–27
  animal suffering and, 17, 27

consumers reducing, 61,
  226–28, 236*n*22
contradictions in, 42, 51,
  56–27, 60–22
emotion and rethinking,
  34–29
ethical aspects of, 58–29,
  236*n*17
happy meat and, 41–22, 81,
  164
industrial agriculture and, 8
moral exoneration and, 62
morality and consumption of,
  6–2, 9–20, 25, 52–26, 62
nonindustrial agriculture and,
  68
online resource and evasion
  of, 63
pleasure and acceptance in, 66
questioning health without, 30
real change by stopping, 68
reasons for less, 38, 45
sidestepping awareness of, 59
unnecessary killings and,
  50–21
Animal Husbandry Regained
  (Webster), 206

Animal Liberation (Singer, P.), 40, 63
Animal Minds (Griffin), 20
animal suffering, 4–2, 16, 18–29
  acknowledging, 35–26, 47–28, 82
  animal consumption and, 17, 27
  in commercial pig trade, 215
  despair and, 36–27
  factory farms overlooking, 42, 47, 49, 52
  food movement and, 118
  human like emotions and, 34
  mother cows and, 4
  reduction of, 59–20
  rigors of science and, 28
  slaughter resulting in, 99
  small-scale farms and, 98–29
  vegans' morality of, 58
  willful causing of, 47–28, 82
animal welfare, 45–28, 53, 68–29, 204–2
animals, 1–2, 13–24, 178, 229n1.
    See also human-animal relationship; *specific animals*
  agriculture, 70–21
  anthropomorphization and, 16, 34
  awareness of emotions in, 20–21, 36–27, 116–27
  backyard butchery and, 110–21
  bleeding out of, 89
  cheaper products and, 67–28
  chickens threatened by, 160–22
  cognition and, 20, 33
  cognitive space shared with, 4
  diet and domesticated, 10–21
  ̲nity in treatment of, 5
  ̲nal lives of, 46
  ̲ responses of, 27–28,

emotional space shared with, 3–2
endemic exploitation of, 35–28, 45
ethology, 19–20
exploitation of, 71, 108
factory farm abusing, 5–2, 54, 65–26
factory farm facts on, 45
false virtue in slaughter of, 57–28
farmers sensitive to, 8–2
in food system, 116–27
horrific treatment of, 43–24
human characteristics placed on, 164–25
human compassion and, 118, 129–20
human consciousness and, 20–22
humans and emotions of, 38
human's connecting with, 37–28
humans projecting happiness on, 126
land sanctuary for, 80
learning behavior of, 21
loving and killing of, 75–20
minds of, 23
moral status granted to, 224–25
MSU's and blood of, 96–27
naming, 71, 238n1
neglecting emotions of, 18, 230n3
nonindustrial farms loving, 82–23
objectifying of, 118–29, 246n55
observational thought and, 29, 34, 232n21, 233n30
oxytocin and domestication of, 23–24
quality of life of, 130–21

rethinking consumption of, 34–29

rights of, 6, 9

science and, 26–27, 33, 232*n*17

scientific ambiguity on emotions of, 25–28, 231*nn*16–28

scientific perspective on emotions of, 19–22

semiveganism and, 59–20, 236*n*20

slaughtered for food, 120–21

slaughterhouse pleas of, 37

speaking without language, 21

specie and personality traits of, 124–25

squeeze pen entrance of, 85–26

10 billion killings of, 36–27

violence against, 17, 91–22, 229*n*2

water after processing of, 95–26

welfare of, 207

willpower of, 83–22, 240*n*24

wrongful slaughter and caring for, 73–23

Anjum, Ahmed, 153

anthropomorphization, 27–28

agricultural reform and, 17–29

animal welfare with, 45–28

domestication and, 24–25

emotional connections in, 16, 34

failure to nurture, 17–29

intuition and common sense for, 15–26

sentimentality and, 15–26

antibiotics, 151–23, 155–27

antimicrobial-free production system, 202

antisocial behaviors, 91

arid lands, 174

AVMA. *See* American Veterinary Medical Association

axe-and-stump method, 110

backyard butchery, 100, 247*n*3

animal sentiment and, 110–21

common excuses in, 130

cruelty numbed by, 101–2

denial repressed in, 102

distortion in, 106

factory farming countering, 129–20

marginalization in, 106

moral disengagement in, 105–2

moral justification in, 107

nerves and anxiety in, 112

object becomes gross in, 115

omnivores contradiction and, 113–25

pig slaughter in, 122–25

psychological tactics in, 129, 131

rationalization of, 104–2, 119

self-promotion in, 102–2

self-selecting bias in, 128–29

self-sufficiency notions in, 103

slaughter narrative in, 103–2, 122–25, 129–20, 247*n*4

vivid descriptions of, 104

women and, 103

YouTube video preparation for, 113

backyardherds.com, 181

bacon, 197–28, 219

bacteria, 145

battery farms, 134

Baytril, 156

behaviors, 1–2, 21, 91, 225–26, 232*n*17

Bekoff, Marc, 32, 34, 71, 23⁹

Biery, Dustin, 150

biology, evolutionary

biophilia, 23–24
bird flu, 149
Bittman, Mark, 45–29, 57, 59–22
bleeding out, 89, 196–27, 248n10
blood, 96–27
boar taint, 209
bonding, 22–25
bottom line, of small-scale
    farms, 159–20, 184–25
bovine behavior, 1–2
bovine fat necrosis, 182
Brown, Harold, 80–21

CAFOs. *See* concentrated
    animal feeding operations
cage-free farms
    chickens on, 142–23
    diseases on, 144–21
    Salmonella on, 146–27
    sanitation of, 145
calves, 1–2, 4, 183–25
Capper, Judith L., 191
Carbaryl, 157
carbon dioxide, 210
carnism, 14, 229n1
carnivores, 70, 81
carotid arteries, 88
Carpenter, Novella, 120–21,
    247n2
castration, of pigs, 208–21
cattle, 45
    economic exploitation of, 71,
        108
    fescue-related conditions of,
        182
    grass eaten by, 170
    grass farmers affection for, 184
    industrial agriculture
        enhancing, 183
    killed per day, 243n41
    knocking box killing, 86–27
    metio with, 173–24
    methat grass, 181–22
    ed by, 173–24

native grass pasturing of,
    172–23
rotational grazing of, 166–28
slaughter weight for, 175–26
trampling of soil by, 188–29
water for processing of, 95–26
water usage for, 186–27
Chameides, Bill, 201–2
Cheever, Holly, 32–23, 34
chemicals, 151–22, 157–28
chickens, 45
    animals threatening, 160–22
    botched killing of, 121–22
    bottom line and, 159–20
    cage compared to cage-free,
        142–23
    cage-free farms and diseases
        of, 144–21
    coccidiosis contracted by,
        147–28, 155
    culling of, 120
    difficulties raising, 133
    dying, 133–24
    freeranging, 139
    humane products from,
        163–24
    humane slaughter of, 112–23,
        134, 163–24
    industrial feed for, 168
    jungle fowl and, 137–29
    justification for killing, 112
    litany of despair raising, 150
    Marek's disease and, 148–20,
        152–24
    medicated feed for, 155
    moral disengagement and,
        113–25
    natural conditions for, 136–28
    natural protection of, 141–22
    nonindustrial farms and,
        134–25
    Poor Girl Gourmet and, 107–2
    predators killing, 140–22
    recognition abilities of, 138
    slaughter horrors of, 63, 89

sudden death of, 150–21
welfare of, 47
women's empowerment and,
109–20
children, 81
chimps, 231*n*16
China, 236*n*22
chronic respiratory disease, 149
coccidiosis disease, 147–28, 155,
190, 199–200
Coe, Sue, 235*n*6
cognition, 4, 20, 33, 239*n*9
Colorado, 174
Comfortably Unaware
(Oppenlander), 194
Comis, Bob, 75, 80, 238*n*6
commercial pig trade, 215
commercial slaughterhouses, 83,
84, 240*n*17
brutality of, 134
consumer complicity and, 92
dangerous environment of,
91–22
electric rod prodding in, 86
gruesome reality of, 86–27
human suffering at, 90–21
killing cattle at, 86–27
local communities and, 92
MSU's compared to, 93–24
problems accompanying,
242*n*39
small-scale farmers and,
241*n*27
squeeze pen in, 85–26
sticker and pre-sticker at,
88–29
tail ripper at, 89
compassion, 118
concentrated animal feeding
operations (CAFOs), 44
confinement, 44, 51, 212
conscientious carnivores, 84–25,
168, 222–24, 227–28
consciousness, human and
animal, 20–22

"Consider the Lobster," 64–25
consumers, 92, 163
animal consumption and, 61,
226–28, 236*n*22
animal rights and, 6, 9
better choices needed by,
225–26
farrowing crates and, 215
free range conditions and, 147
happy meat wanted by, 41–22,
81, 164
pig mutilation surprising, 204
small farm concerns of, 135
coop cleaning, 146
Cornish cross, 133
Cornish X, 112, 117, 250*n*7
cost issues, 95, 168–29
cow-per-acre ratio, 174–26,
179
cows, mother, 2–2, 32–23, 43
cruelty, 1–2, 101–2, 127
culling, of calves, 183–24
cycle-of-life principles, 167

Daiya, 80
dangerous environment,
91–22
Danny (goat owner), 125–28
Darwin, Charles, 2–2, 19, 22,
231*n*9
Daston, Lorraine, 27–28
data of experience, 226
Davies, Peter, 203
Davis Farm, 184
Dawkins, Marian Stamp, 21–22
death, 43–24
chicken's sudden, 150–21
collective endorsement of,
119–20
factory farm horror and, 5–2,
54, 65–26
MSUs and intimacy of, 97–28
depression, 44, 51
The Descent of Man (Darwin), 4

diet, 10–21, 14–25, 49–20
dignity, of animals, 5
diseases
  cage-free farms and, 144–21
  chickens with Marek's,
    148–20, 152–24
  chronic respiratory, 149
  coccidiosis, 147–28, 155, 190,
    199–200
  ease of transmitting, 145
  Newcastle, 149
  Salmonella and, 144–27
  on small-scale farms, 149–20
disposal, of blood, 96
distortion, 106
diversity, biological, 3
do-it-yourself slaughter, 101–2,
    106, 126–27
domestication, 23–24
droughts, 187–29
dry matter ration, 176
Dust Bowl conditions, 188

E. coli 0157:H7, 170, 262n5
earwigs, 157
Eating Animals (Foer), 40, 46–27
Ebner, Paul, 170
ecological benefits, 171
economics, 67–28, 71, 94–25, 108
egg industry, 47, 134–25, 143–25,
    152, 162
Eisnitz, Gail, 87
electric rod prodding, 86
electrified water, 89
elephants, 31–22
emotional choreography, 113
emotional complexity, 104
emotional responses
  animals' spectrum of, 27–28,
    232n18
  to farm animals, 224–25
  observational thought and, 29,
    232n21
  to pig slaughter, 217–21

scientific perspective on,
    19–22
emotions, 81
  animal consumption and,
    34–29
  animal enjoyment and, 46
  animals and humans sharing,
    3–2
  animal's awareness of, 20–21,
    36–27, 116–27
  animals communicating with,
    38
  anthropomorphization and,
    16, 34
  diet reform and, 14–25
  elephants circling and, 31–22
  neglecting animal's, 18, 230n3
  observational thought to, 29,
    232n21
  scientific ambiguity on, 25–28,
    231nn16–28
  scientific perspective on,
    19–22
  suffering and human like, 34
empathy, 42–28
employees, 91–22, 241n32
endophyte fungus, 180–22
energy usage, 168–29, 177–28
entrepreneur-in-residence, 80
environmental mimicry, 136–29
ethics, 18, 55–26, 58–29, 236n17
Every Twelve Seconds (Pachirat),
    97
evolution, 2–2, 21–23, 231n9
exploitation, 35–28, 45, 71, 108,
    160, 216
Ezell-Vandersluis, Cheri, 79–20

factory farms. *See also*
    commercial slaughterhouses
  alternative farms not ending,
    65–28
  alternatives to products of, 7–2
  animal abuse on, 5–2, 54, 65–26

animal suffering and, 42, 47, 49, 52
backyard butchery counter to, 129–20
challenging dominance of, 8–2
cheaper products provided by, 163
empathy and, 42–28
facts about animals on, 45
free range pigs compared to, 199–203, 221
grass-fed beef and, 191–24
human psyche damaged by, 46, 235n6
humane chicken slaughter in, 134
mortality rates on, 140–21
outrage of exposed, 39
protests of, 6
Salmonella found in, 146–27
small farms compared to, 136, 223–24
strengthening of, 67
falcons, 33–24
false moral justification, 107
farm animals, 44–29, 171, 216, 223–25
Farm City (Carpenter), 120
Farm Sanctuary, 208
farmers, 8–2, 78–21, 229n2
farming industries, 55–26, 61
farms, 98–29, 134
alternative, 10–21, 65–28
dairy, 1–2, 71–22, 238nn2–2
farms, nonindustrial, 77–28
agriculture business and, 78–21
alternatives reality and, 10
animals truly loved on, 82–23
better but not right, 68–29
chicken parts and eggs from, 134–25
happy pigs and intact tails at, 44
hidden flaws of, 132–24
medications needed at, 151–22

moral considerations and, 52–23, 235n13
pasture-based alternatives in, 54–26
psychological torment of, 74 21
slaughter as tormenting in, 73–21
vaccinations reliance of, 153
veganism and, 75, 78–20
farrowing crates, 212–26
Fast Food Nation (Schlosser), 40
feed, 155, 168, 174, 178
fescue turf, 179–22
Fickle, Barbara, 75
Field Roast, 80
Flying Pigs Farm, 209
Foer, Jonathan Safran, 40, 46–29, 57, 62–24, 68, 225–26
food movement
animal suffering and, 118
eating plants and, 228
human's sustainable, 41–22, 101, 222
omnivores contradiction and, 225
Food Safety and Inspection Service (FSIS), 95
food system
animals in, 116–27
dysfunctional, 10–21
global resources for, 178
industrial, 10–21, 116, 131
know your, 128
omnivores and restructuring of, 51
questioning reform of broken, 42, 48–29
slaughtering animals for, 120–21
tastemakers' influencing, 48–20, 57
tastemakers' reform evasion of, 57–25
food-borne illness, 202–2
forage, 183

4-H Clubs, 81
fowl, 149, 232n17
Fredericksburg Grassfed Beef,
    188
free-lunch claim, 168, 169
freeranging, 139
    factory farm pigs compared to,
        199–203, 221
    Marek's disease influencing,
        153–24
    mutilation and humane, 208
    pigs, 196–29
    pigs inserted with septum
        rings, 204–2
    predatory mishaps in, 142–23
Friedrich, Bruce, 208
Front Yard Farmer (blog), 122
FSIS. *See* Food Safety and
    Inspection Service
fungicides, 151
Fungizone, 152

Gallimycin, 152
gastrointestinal parasites,
    199–200
Gebreyes, Wondwossen, 201–2
genetic heritage, 138
Ghetto Dunn (blogger), 151
GHG intensities, 191
global resources, 178
global warming, 167, 187–28
goats, 79–20, 125–28
Goddess Kristie (blogger), 184
Godsgapeach (blogger), 184
Goodall, Jane, 231n16
Gourmet, 64–25
grain, 178–29
grain-fed beef, 170
Graser, Jordan, 206
grass, cattle eating, 181–22
grass farmers
    arid lands and, 174
    calves and bottom line of,
        184–25

calves culled by, 183–24
cattle affection of, 184
conditions required for,
    172–23
despair and frustration of, 190
dry matter ration and, 176
endemic problems of, 171–22,
    186
fescue turf used by, 179–22
hay supplies required by,
    176–27
industrial agriculture and, 183
inherent volatility faced by,
    189–20
land required for, 173–25
poor management by, 192–23
as water-intensive business,
    186–27
grass-fed beef
    conscientious carnivores and,
        168
    conventional production and,
        191–24
    critical costs in, 168–29
    droughts influencing, 187–29
    E coli prevalence in, 170
    no ecological benefits of, 171
    grieving capacity, 31, 33–24
Griffin, Donald, 19–20
ground beef, 262n5

hand-washing, 146
happy meat, 41–22, 81, 164
hay, 176–29
health, 30, 199–203, 221
Held, Suzanne, 195–27
herd circling, 31–22
historic opportunity, 34–29
Hoffman, Piper, 206
hogs. *See* pigs
holistic grazing, 169
homesteading, 108, 133
hoof action, 169–20
Houle, Marcy Cottrell, 33–24

HSUS. *See* Humane Society of the United States
human-animal relationship, 10–21, 14, 15, 27
humane slaughter
  animal consumption and, 42, 51, 56–27, 60–22
  of chickens, 112–23, 134, 163–24
  factory farmed chickens and, 134
  questioning, 16, 73–23
  slaughterhouses and, 83
Humane Society, 46, 80
Humane Society of the United States (HSUS), 164
humans, 3–2
  animal consciousness and, 20–22
  animals and characteristics of, 164–25
  animals and companion of, 118, 129–20
  animals' emotions and, 38
  behavioral changes required by, 225–26
  connecting capacity of, 37–28
  factory farms influencing, 46, 235n6
  mother cow compared to, 2–2
  natural environment concept of, 139
  pig genome compared to, 195–26
  pigs appreciated by, 197–28
  projecting happiness on animals by, 126
  slaughterhouses and nature of, 83
  suffering and emotions like, 34
  suffering of, 90–21
  sustainable food movement of, 41–22, 101, 222
  tandem evolution of animal and, 23

ILT. *See* infectious laryngotracheitis
"In Praise of Bacon," 198
industrial food systems, 10–21, 116, 131
infectious laryngotracheitis (ILT), 149
instinct, animal, 1–2
Iowa Beef Center, 178

"Jamie [Oliver] Saves Our Bacon," 220
Jenna (blogger), 115–20
Jones, Maren Bell, 156
Jordan, 122–23
journalism, foodie, 58–20, 62–23
"The Joy of Pigs," 195, 197
Jugular veins, 88
jungle fowl, 137–29

kale, 191, 194
Kant, Immanuel, 226
Kerr, Chris, 80–21
killing, 36–27, 64, 65, 121–24
  justification for, 112
  knocking box, 86–27
  loving of animals and, 75–20
  predators, 140–22
  unnecessary, 50–21
Kimm, Frankie, 100
King, Bruce, 214
Kingsolver, Barbara, 120
Kinsman, Kat, 217
Kirschenmann, Fred, 193–24
knocking box, 86–27
Kristof, Nicholas, 70–24, 98

Lacy, Michael, 144
land use, 173–25, 193–24
language, 21
livestock, 77–28, 186–27
lobsters, 64, 65

local communities, 92, 96
locavores, 8
logical liberation, 29, 232n20
Lusk, Jayson L., 142
Lyman, Harold F., 78

Made for Each Other (Olmert), 23–24
management, 192–23
Marek's disease, 148–20, 152–24
marginalization, 106
marketing, 62
MaxQ, 181
McMinn, Suzanne, 209
MDV (herpesvirus), 153
meat industry, 94–25
meat markets, 185, 236n22
medicated feed, 155
medications, 151–22
Meet Your Meat (documentary), 99
methane, cattle emitting, 173–24
Mitman, Gregg, 27–28
mobile slaughterhouse unit (MSU), 243n41, 244n48
    animal blood at, 96–27
    commercial slaughterhouses and, 93–24
    economic feasibility of, 94–25
    intimacy of death at, 97–28
    offal disposal of, 94
    small-scale farmers using, 92–23
    USDA-certified-and-inspected, 93
    water use at, 94
moral disengagement, 105–2, 114, 117–28
moral status, 224–25
morality, 34, 233n30
    animal consumption and, 6–2, 9–20, 25, 52–26, 62
    animal suffering and vegan, 58
    humane systems and, 55–26

lobster killing and, 64, 65
nonindustrial farms and, 52–23, 235n13
worthiness and, 5–2
mortality rates, 140–21
Moss, Cynthia, 31
MSU. *See* mobile slaughterhouse unit
mutilation, 204, 208
mythology, of agriculture, 159

narcissism, 230n4
native grass, 172–23
natural conditions, 136–28
natural defense mechanisms, 140
natural environment, 139
The Natural Poultry Farming Guide, 154
natural protection strategies, 141–22
natural psychologists, 20
neanderthal management, 192–23
Neighbors Opposed to Backyard Slaughter, 100
nervous system, 20, 33
neurobiology, 23–24
neurological substrates, 232n18
Newcastle disease, 149
Niman Ranch, 206
nitrous oxide, 210
North Carolina State University, 202
Northern California, 174
Norwood, F. Bailey, 142
nose rings. *See* septum rings
"Not for the Faint: Killing it in 2010," 107

objectifying, of animals, 118–29, 246n55

observational thought, 28–24
  animal treatment and, 34,
    233n30
  emotional response and, 29,
    232n21
offal disposal, 94
offspring, 3, 32–23
O'Hagan, Maureen, 240n17
Old Post Farm, 112
Olmert, Meg Daley, 23–24
omnivores, 40–22, 48–29, 51
omnivores contradiction, 56–27,
    67, 71–22, 172
  backyard butchery and, 113–25
  children and, 81
  dodging, 60–22
  emotional manifestation of, 81
  farm animals and, 224–25
  food movement and, 225
  nonindustrial agriculture and,
    82
  understanding, 42, 51
The Omnivore's Dilemma
    (Pollan), 40, 166–27
omnivores wanting reform, of
    factory farms, 40–22, 48–29
online resources, 63
Oppenlander, Richard, 194
overlays, 212–24
oxytocin, 23–24

Pachirat, Timothy, 87, 97
pasture-based alternatives,
    54–26
pathogens, 201
Pelletier, Nathan, 191
personality traits, 124–25
pesticides, 151, 245n52
pets, pigs as, 197
philosophy, 232n20
piglets, pigs crushing, 212–26
pigs, 204, 206, 215
  bleeding out of, 196–27,
    248n10

  boar taint and, 209
  castration of, 208–21
  consumers surprised at
    mutilation of, 204
  depression of confined, 44, 51
  emotional responses to
    slaughter of, 217–21
  endangered species and,
    75–26
  factory-farming, 199
  farmer eaten by, 229n2
  female, 212
  food-borne illness of, 202–2
  free-range farms' happy, 44
  freeranging, 196–29
  gastrointestinal parasites in,
    199–200
  health and safety of, 199–203,
    221
  human genome compared to,
    195–26
  humans appreciating, 197–28
  intelligence of, 195–26
  killing, 123–24
  pathogens in, 201
  as pets, 197
  rendered unconscious, 88
  Salmonella found in, 202–2
  screaming, 209–20
  septum rings inserted in,
    204–2
  slaughter of, 122–25, 216–27
  Smithfield's chilling abuse of,
    46
Planck, Nina, 170, 262n5
plant-based products, 80
plants
  animal feed conversion of,
    178
  diet appeal limited of, 49–20
  food movement and eating,
    228
  resource demand growing, 171
  vegetarians' and tough issue
    of, 58–29

Pollan, Michael, 51, 53, 57–21,
    120
  farm animal plight and, 44–29
  marketing slogan by, 62
  The Omnivore's Dilemma by,
    40, 166–27
Polyface farm, 186
Poor Girl Gourmet (blog),
    107–2
pornography, agricultural, 72,
    238n3
possum, 161
Postville, IA, 242n39
predators
  chickens killed by, 140–22
  freeranging mishaps by,
    142–23
  prey's relationship with, 169
  property protection from,
    160–22
  on small-scale farms, 140–21
pre-sticker, 88–29
prodding, 86
production methods, 222–23
property, protection of, 160–22
protein source, 101
protests, 6
psychological fallout, 90
psychology, 20, 46, 74–21, 235n6
pugging, 188–29
Putnam, Heath, 215–26

quality of life, animals, 130–21
quinoa, 194

rabbits, 89–20
raccoons, 161–22
radical alternatives, 34–29
rams, 77–28
Ramsburg, Beau, 208
rationalization, 104–2, 116, 119
recognition abilities, 138
Red Wattle, 75–26

reform, 40–22, 48–29, 57–25
  of agriculture, 17–29
  diet, 14–25
rescue, whale, 30–21, 233n23
Rhode Island Reds, 150
Rock Cornish hens, 116–27
Rollin, Bernard, 20–21
rooting, of pigs, 204, 206
Rosery Farm, 207
rotational grazing
  available forage in, 183
  of cattle, 166–28
  energy-saving promise of,
    168–29
  global warming ended by, 167
  hoof action in, 169–20
  Savory's claim about, 169–20
roundworms, 200
Rowlands, Mark, 232n20
RSPCA, 207, 212

safety, 199–203, 221
Salatin, Joel, 166–27, 173, 228
  cow-per-acre ratio of, 174–26,
    179
  neanderthal management
    comment of, 192–23
Salmonella, 144–27, 200–203
sanctuary, animal, 80
sanitation, 145, 146
Savory, Allan, 167, 169–20
Schlosser, Eric, 40
science, 25, 231nn16–28
  animals and scholarly
    skepticism of, 26–27, 33,
    232n17
  suffering obscured by, 28
scientific perspective, 19–22
screaming pigs, 209–20
self-promotion, 102–2
self-selecting bias, 128–29
self-sufficiency notions, 103,
    108, 247n2
semiveganism, 59–20, 62, 236n20

septum rings, 204–2
Serpell, James, 23–24
Sevin dust, 157–28
sexual manipulation, 43
shelter-seeking tendencies, 126
Shook, Lawrence, 195
Sierra Nevada, 174
Sinclair, Upton, 59
Singer, Isaac Bashevis, 18
Singer, Peter, 40, 63
skepticism, 26–27, 33, 232n17
slaughter. *See also* commercial
    slaughterhouses; death;
    killing; mobile
    slaughterhouse unit
animal pleas before, 37
animal suffering from, 99
animals for food and, 120–21
backyard butchery and, 103–2,
    122–25, 129–20, 247n4
cage-free chickens and,
    142–23
caring for animals and, 73–23
cattle's weight for, 175–26
cruelty of, 9, 127
dairy farms and, 1–2, 71–22,
    238nn2–2
decentralization of, 101
dismissed as insignificant,
    53–24
do-it-yourself, 101–2, 106,
    126–27
emotional choreography of,
    113
emotional complexity in, 104
emotional responses to pig,
    217–21
employee's impacted by,
    91–22
ethical implications of, 18,
    55–26
evasion on issue of, 59, 65, 80
factory farm horrors and, 5–2,
    54, 65–26
false virtue in animal, 57–28

in farming industries, 55–26,
    61
of goats, 125–28
horror of chicken, 63, 89
increased consolidation for,
    83–24
nonindustrial farmers and,
    73–21
of pigs, 122–25, 216–27
Poor Girl Gourmet's first,
    108–2
questioning of "humane," 16,
    73–23
raising animals for, 57–28
sanitized depiction of, 117
unnecessary, 82
whitewashing of, 72–24
Slaughterhouse (Eisnitz), 87
Small, Jennifer, 209
small-scale farms, 228. *See also*
    cage-free farms; farms,
    nonindustrial; grass farmers
agricultural mythology of, 159
animal suffering and, 98–29
antibiotics used on, 151–23,
    156–27
bottom line and chickens on,
    159–20
chicken's sudden death on,
    150–21
commercial slaughterhouses
    and, 241n27
conscientious carnivores and,
    84–25, 223–24, 227–28
consumer concerns of, 135
cost-effectiveness of, 95
disease hit list of, 149–20
downside of, 164–25
factory farms compared to,
    136, 223–24
humane chicken products and,
    163–24
Marek's disease on, 152–24
mobile slaughterhouses used
    by, 92–23

small-scale farms (*continued*)
   mortality rates on, 140–21
   predators influence on,
     140–21
   sanitation measures on, 146
   Sevin dust used on, 157–28
   slaughterhouses and, 241*n*27
Smithfield Foods, 46
snakes, 162
society, 18–29, 230*n*4
species, 20
   barrier, 21–22, 231*n*9
   traits, 124–25
squeeze pens, 85–26
steel bolt shot, 87
sticker, 88–29
stillborns, 214
Stony Brook Farm, 74
supplemental feed, 174
sustainable food movement,
   41–22, 101, 222
Swoope, VA, 166–27, 173, 186
system of movement, 137–28
systematic violence, 91–22

tail ripper, 89
tastemakers, 48–20, 57–25
Terramycin, 152, 156
Texas Panhandle, 174
toxoplasma, 201
Toxoplasma gondii, 203
trichinosis, 201
Tyson Foods, 131

United States
   cattle industry water usage in,
     186–27
   cattle killed per day in, 243*n*41
   land use in, 193–24
   total land available in, 175–26
USDA recall, 143–24, 145

USDA-certified slaughterhouses,
   84, 239*n*14
USDA-certified-and-inspected,
   93

vaccines, 151, 153
VB6: Eat Vegan Before 6:00
   (Bittman), 60
veganism, 58, 66, 75, 78–21
vegetarians, 58–29
VetRx, 152
Vickery, 156
video, 46, 113
violence, 17–29, 43, 91–22,
   229*n*2, 230*n*4

Wallace, David Foster, 64–25
wastewater, 96
water, 89, 96
   animal processing using, 95–26
   cattle industry use of, 186–27
   grass farmer's use of, 186–27
   hay's requirements of, 177–28
   livestock consuming, 186–27
   MSU's use of, 94
Wazine, 157
Weber, Christopher, 187–28,
   193
Webster, John F., 206
Welch, Bryan, 77–28
whales, 30–21, 233*n*23
willpower, 83–22, 240*n*24
Wilson, F. O., 23
Wind Ridge Farm, 196
Winfrey, Oprah, 58
women, 103, 109–20
Wooly Pigs Farm, 215–26
Working on Me (blog), 120

YouTube video preparation, 113

ABOUT THE AUTHOR

Margaret Menninger

James McWilliams, who currently serves as the Ingram Professor of History at Texas State University, is a historian and writer living in Austin, Texas. He is the author of five previous books on food, animals, and agriculture, including *Just Food* and *A Revolution in Eating*. His work has appeared in *The New York Times*, *Harper's*, *Slate*, *The Atlantic*, *The Paris Review Daily*, and a wide variety of other publications.